H-BOMBS &
HULA GIRLS

H-BOMBS & HULA GIRLS

Operation Grapple 1957 and the Last
Royal Navy Gunroom at Sea

Written and compiled by Michael Johnston

UNIFORM

Published by Uniform
An imprint of Unicorn Publishing Group
101 Wardour Street, London W1F 0UG

www.unicornpublishing.org

A catalogue record for this book is available from
the British Library

5 4 3 2 1

ISBN 978-1-910500-68-2

Cover design Unicorn Publishing Group
Typeset by Vivian@Bookscribe
Printed and bound in Spain

CONTENTS

Albatross following Warrior through the Magellan Straits (John Hutchinson)

Epic events seem to disappear into history with remarkable ease. 2014 saw the centenary of the start of the First World War, and there have been major international events to mark various anniversaries of significant dates during the Second World War.

I happened to be serving in the British Pacific Fleet when the first nuclear bombs were dropped on Japan in 1945. As it brought 6 years of total and brutal war to an end, I think we were all more relieved than anxious about the dawning of the nuclear age. But then the major powers started testing ever more efficient nuclear weapons and it was quite impossible not to feel anxiety about the future.

That ominous event in Japan ushered in the nuclear age and after the war, the major powers started a whole series of tests of nuclear weapons. In 1957 Great Britain tested its own weapons near the Pacific atoll of Christmas Island. Among the fleet of ships attending those tests was the aircraft carrier HMS Warrior and serving in that ship at the time was a group of National Service Royal Naval Volunteer Reserve Midshipmen. They have remained in touch with each other ever since, and to mark the 60th anniversary of those nuclear weapons tests, they have put together their accounts of those days from their Midshipman's Journals and their letters home. It makes fascinating reading, and I hope that many will read it, because all the proceeds will be donated to Royal Naval Charities.

15 MAY 1957

....

'Bomb gone!'

In the cloudless sky nine miles above Malden Island, around 300 miles south of the equator, the bomb started its fifty-two second parabolic descent. No ordinary bomb. This was a live hydrogen bomb. The RAF Valiant bomber went into a tight turn to port, the bomb aimer placed the light-tight cover over his sights. The telemetry sender switch was pressed on HMS *Narvik* and the recording instruments on the island responded.

Within less than a minute, history would be written, and a memory of the moment would be permanently etched in the mind's eye of all those present – not least the ten young men who made up the National Service members of the Gunroom in HMS *Warrior* twenty-six miles from Ground Zero. *Warrior*, a Colossus Class light fleet aircraft carrier, was the lead ship of the Royal Navy squadron forming part of Operation Grapple, Britain's first ever nuclear fusion test programme. At that same moment a bond would be fused between the ten that has not been broken in nearly sixty years.

On *Warrior*'s flight deck, and at their watch stations in the several ships of the Grapple Squadron, the crews were already turning their backs on the coming explosion, pulling the white hoods on their anti-flash overalls up and their dark goggles down, closing their eyes, and finally covering the goggles with their gloved hands. From the starboard wing of *Warrior*'s compass platform, standing beside the Commodore and the Commander, Midshipman Cooper relayed the countdown over the ship's Tannoy.

'Thirty seconds … twenty seconds … ten seconds … five seconds, four, three, two, one.'

In every listening radio in the central Pacific came a loud click, caused by the electro-magnetic radiation from the nuclear reaction, and the bomb's trace on HMS *Narvik*'s telemetry receiver vanished, leaving only the straight base line. The weapon exploded at 8,000 feet. On the backs of all spectators on *Warrior*, *Narvik*, *Messina* and the other ships of the squadron, came a sudden flash of heat, as though the fire door of a great furnace had momentarily been opened behind them; and despite tightly shut eyes and hands over them, there was a sensation of brilliant light. There are many, indeed, in telling of it afterwards, who can recall seeing an image of the bones in their fingers.

Ten seconds later, permission was given to turn round and gaze with awe at what man had wrought. At this stage, there was still a large orange and red fireball, churning in the sky to the south and steadily rising. A thin pancake of cloud formed above the rapidly greying fireball. Steam and water vapour from ground zero were drawn upwards in a slender cone towards the underside of the vast cloud, creating the iconic mushroom image that twelve years of nuclear fission and fusion explosions had made so very recognisable.

Recognisable or not, surely none of those spectators had actually witnessed such an awesome sight before. Some say they didn't hear anything, but Sub-Lieutenant Johnston on the flight deck remembers instinctively ducking as the sound wave from the explosion, travelling much slower than the flash of light, caught him unawares. From the compass platform, Cooper, an experienced sailor, saw the air pressure wave radiating out across the surface of the Pacific. Midshipman Riches on the flight deck felt the wind, saw the sea ruffling and heard the sound wave – like prolonged but distant gunfire.

On board *Messina*, when the ban on private camera use was lifted after two minutes, Midshipman Anson began to shoot what is thought to be the only private ciné film made of the explosion. On all the ships, crews were passing each other their cameras to be photographed standing in front of the cloud pillar and dome. In *Warrior*'s Ops Room, where the tension during the drop had been palpable, Midshipmen Reed and Hume joined the rush outside to stare and take photographs. Hume recalls the looks of amazement on the faces of everyone. Midshipman Hutchinson, on watch on the compass platform in protective clothing, turned to gaze at the fireball when the all clear was given and felt a deep sense of awe.

Within thirty minutes, a helicopter took off from *Warrior*, flew to *Narvik* to pick up the Health Physics team, and made the first, post-nuclear approach to Malden Island, checking the levels of radiation as it approached and descended. Fires were burning on the island and a low dark cloud stretched out some two or three miles down wind. But there was no radiation detected: the instruments had all survived and made their vital measurements.

Britain was now a megaton thermonuclear power and here was the evidence to prove it – or was there?

1956

. . . .

It would be no exaggeration to say that 1956 was a busy year at any and every level. One year before, in February 1955, the British Government had announced its decision to build the country's own hydrogen bomb, immensely more powerful than the atom bombs that had ended World War II. At the end of that year, the Pope, in his Christmas broadcast, had spoken of the need to suspend nuclear tests. If Britain had ambitions to possess a fully operational H-bomb, the Government would need to move swiftly so that this could be achieved before world opinion, in the form of a test ban treaty, brought testing, especially atmospheric testing, to an end.

At a geopolitical level, April 1956 saw the much anticipated visit to the UK of the Soviet leaders Bulganin and Khrushchev on board the Soviet's latest warship, the *Ordzhonikidze*, which docked at Portsmouth, the Royal Navy's most important base. At that same moment, several of the future 'Warriors' were RNVR Ordinary Seamen doing their fortnight's training and finding time to exchange their RN cigarettes, known as 'blue liners' for the blue line down each cigarette, with their Russian opposite numbers who gladly traded their strange cardboard-and-black-tobacco Russian ones. While on the surface the diplomats, politicians and sailors were all smiles, beneath the surface, literally, less diplomatic events were taking place. A botched CIA/MI6 undersea operation, aiming to explore the then state-of-the-art *Ordzhonikidze*, ended in the disappearance of MI6 diver Commander Lionel 'Buster' Crabb. The body of Crabb, one of several MI6 agents involved in the operation, was never recovered. In 2007, Eduard Koltsov, a retired Russian military diver, said he killed a man he thinks was Crabb, as he was 'trying to place a mine' on the Soviet ship.

1956 was also the year of Suez and Hungary, often bracketed together since the British/French/Israeli actions in Egypt were then, and are still now, perceived as a very convenient public relations excuse for the Soviet invasion of Hungary. In Cold War terms, the USA was already a thermonuclear power and had carried out an aerial H-bomb test at Bikini Atoll on 21 May; with the aircraft missing the target site by around four miles, resulting in the loss of all the scientific data that instruments at the target site were set up to collect. In the UK, the DIDO heavy-water enriched uranium nuclear reactor began operation at the British Atomic Weapon Research

Establishment (AWRE) at Aldermaston. In October, the Queen opened the world's first commercial nuclear power station at Calder Hall, a by-product of which was weapons grade plutonium, while the Campaign for Nuclear Disarmament (CND) was in the process of formation, being launched the following year.

Meanwhile, at a national level, Tesco opened its first self-service stores in St Albans and Maldon, while double yellow lines were painted on the road to forbid parking in certain parts of Slough. The Queen Mother's racehorse Devon Loch was within sight of the winning post in the Grand National, ridden by the so far unpublished author Dick Francis, when it collapsed inexplicably, only fifty yards from the finish. Chancellor of the Exchequer Harold Macmillan introduced Premium Bonds in his Budget speech in April, with the winners to be chosen by ERNIE (the electronic random number indicator equipment). The Minister of Health, R H Turton, rejected a call for a government-led anti-smoking campaign, stating that no ill-effects had yet been proven. Espresso bars were beginning to be opened, mainly in the London area, but the availability at that time of 'frothy coffee' at least as far north as the Scottish Borders has been verified. John Osborne's play *Look Back in Anger* opened on 8 May at the Royal Court Theatre to a combination of bafflement, disapproval and critical acclaim. Dodie Smith's book *101 Dalmatians* was published and Third Class railway travel was abolished by the simple expedient of rebranding it as Second Class. Manchester United won the Football League First Division title in April and then went on to win the FA Cup in May.

In December, the Irish Republican Army (IRA) launched its Border Campaign in Northern Ireland leading to the use of the Special Powers Act by the Government of Northern Ireland to intern several hundred republican suspects and sympathisers.

What the public certainly did not know at the time was that in early September, even as early negotiations were under way to establish the European Common Market, Guy Mollet, then Socialist Prime Minister of France, visited London and proposed to Sir Anthony Eden, his British opposite number, that their two countries should merge. Eden rejected that idea; just as, later that month, he would reject the alternative proposal of allowing France to join the Commonwealth of Nations. However, it did demonstrate a certain cordial entente between the two countries that would be further exemplified by the Protocol of Sèvres, concluded in October (its existence subsequently denied by Eden) between Britain, France and Israel, aimed at covertly engineering sufficient justification for an Anglo-French invasion of Egypt in order to seize back control of Suez from Colonel Nasser who had nationalised the Canal Company in July. Even more significant in the longer term, as revealed almost half a century later in Michael Karpin's 2001 documentary 'A Bomb in the Basement', Abel Thomas, chief of political staff for France's Defence Minister at the time, claimed that François Perrin, head of the French Atomic Energy Commission, had advised Guy Mollet that Israel should be provided with a nuclear bomb. According to the documentary, France provided Israel with a nuclear reactor and staff to set it up in Israel together with enriched uranium and the means to produce plutonium in exchange for support in the Suez War.[1]

For Air Commodore Wilfred Oulton, 1956 really got under way on a chilly Monday morning in February when he was summoned to an unexpected meeting with ACAS(Ops), otherwise known as Air Vice Marshall Lees. Oulton recalls that meeting in his attractively 'Biggles'-like memoir.

Air Vice Marshal Wilfred Oulton (www.alamy.com)

Two quick knocks on the inner door and he went in to the large, quiet office, but with no eyes at this moment for the lovely view of the Embankment Gardens and the river.

'Good afternoon, sir. You wanted me?'

The piercing blue eyes looked up and the rugged pugnacious face behind the desk took on a cheery welcoming smile.

'Hello, Wilf. Come and sit down. I've got a new job for you.' Just a trace left of that Australian accent.

Air Vice Marshall Lees got up and moved over to a couple of armchairs fronted by a low, glass-topped coffee table. Broad, stocky, aggressive, he was every inch a fighter ace and leader. A first-class operator – direct, uncompromising and knowing his job inside out.

They sat down and Lees proffered a cigarette, which was refused with a smile and a shake of the head.

'A new job, sir?'

'Yes,' with a wide grin. 'I want you to go out and drop a bomb somewhere in the Pacific and take a picture of it with a Brownie camera.'

'Well, that doesn't sound too difficult at first sight and might be fun.' Then, more cautiously, 'What kind of a bomb?'

A pause for a pull on the cigarette.

'A megaton thermo-nuclear device.'

'Good God!'[2]

Lees went on to explain both the extent and the urgency of the project. With pressure mounting on the major powers to agree a test-ban treaty outlawing above ground testing of nuclear weapons, if Britain wanted to be in the nuclear club then the capability to design, build, deliver and explode an H-bomb that could be perceived as a credible deterrent in the Cold War stand-off, had to be demonstrated before the middle of 1957, lest the much-mooted treaty came into force and prevented it. Britain had been conducting atomic weapons research at the Monte Bello Islands off Western Australia and the Americans' H-bomb tests were ongoing at Bikini Atoll. *With hindsight*, the precautions against radiation injury from the 'fall-out' had been seen, in both cases, to be less than wholly adequate. Thus the stipulation, according to Lees, that 'the one immutable condition was […] there should be no injury to non-

British personnel and property. We can't have another 'Dagon-sha' incident like the American trouble at Bikini.'[3]

According to Oulton, that 'somewhere in the Pacific' mentioned by Lees just might have been the very remote French Kerguelen Islands, 49°S in the southern Indian Ocean with a climate similar to the Falklands, and known on some charts as the Desolation Islands, which are almost equidistant from South Africa, Australia and the Antarctic continent. Fortunately for those who might have been sent for many months to these rocky, snow-covered islands in the Roaring Forties, the choice fell instead on Christmas Island, part of the Line Islands District of the Gilbert and Ellice Islands, lying almost on the equator, due south of Hawaii. However, in letters exchanged between Sir Anthony Eden, UK Prime Minister, and his New Zealand opposite number Sidney Holland in 1955, in the National Archives of New Zealand, Eden asks about using the *Kermadec* Islands in the South Pacific, some 800 miles north-east of Auckland.[4] After careful consideration, New Zealand turned the request down. In addition, it would seem unlikely that France would have consented to the use of *their* territory for British tests when France had not yet tested an atomic weapon, despite having an unlimited supply of uranium from a mine near Limoges. So it seems probable that Oulton's recollection, on this particular point, is incorrect.

Christmas Island was, like many landfalls in the Pacific, 'discovered' by Captain (then Lieutenant) James Cook RN on Christmas Eve 1777: hence the chosen name which it has kept to this day, but now in Gilbertese, Karitimati (the 't's are sounded like an 's'), the principal island of the Republic of Kiribati, independent since 1979 and a member of the Commonwealth.

It seems somehow typical of a very British attitude to forward planning, that Oulton was supposed to pull everything together from all three services and a handful of separate ministries, including building *from scratch* an airfield capable of receiving Valiants, the newest in the RAF's range of jet bombers; aeroplanes so new, in fact, that the intended aircraft were not yet in service. The logistics were daunting; especially for the 1950s when almost everything electronic was in its infancy and AWRE had not yet given birth to a workable megaton nuclear weapon that could be dropped on target with pinpoint accuracy. Such accuracy was required not only for the purpose of accurately measuring the weapon's output but, even more politically important, for the safety of the thousands of service and scientific personnel who would be involved, never mind any visiting Japanese fishermen or

Grapple map of Christmas Island (Rowsell)

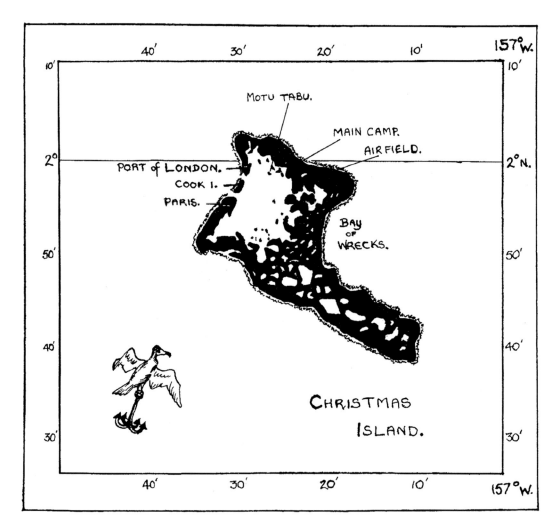

inquisitive Russian submarines. It seems, however, just as typical of that period that, despite some hair-raising moments and *ad hoc* solutions to problems on the move, Oulton and those he led were able to deliver *everything* asked of them by the middle of May 1957. The whole enterprise was to be called 'Operation Grapple', a name of no particular significance when chosen as a code word by the Ministry of Supply, but Oulton would later tell those taking part that the four hooks of the grapnel held by the cormorant represented the three armed services and the civilian scientists. He did not, however, anthropomorphise the cormorant.[5]

Initially, it was all supposed to be 'co-ordinated' by the Grapple Committee. Since, like many experienced managers, Oulton believed nothing good was ever created by a committee, he knew from the outset that he would have to be a ruthless leader in order to deliver the required result within the narrow time frame laid down. Attending Sunday Service just two days after his appointment and consequent promotion to Air Vice Marshal, Oulton's mind was not on the sermon but he did like the text; 1 Corinthians 14 vv 8 & 9. 'And if the bugle gives an indistinct sound, who will get ready for battle? So with yourselves, if with your tongue you utter speech that is not intelligible, how will anyone know what is said? For you will be speaking into the air.' Sitting in the pew of his parish church, he resolved to act decisively.[6]

Oulton was not only put in command of the Services, but out at Christmas Island he had authority over the scientists as well, so that, in any crisis, he had no need to refer any decision upwards or argue the toss with civilians as the fuse burned lower. Decisions ranged across life or death issues such as what to prepare for should the megaton weapon malfunction, fail to drop, or, in the worst possible scenario, explode at ground level resulting in considerable radioactive pollution. Thanks to the combined efforts of all those taking part, none of these things happened. However, one lesser decision was to approve the adoption of an Operation Grapple tie. It was suggested by Captain Guy Western RN that since many at the HQ staff in London worked in plain clothes and could be strangers to one another, it might help to have a Grapple tie. Oulton suggested that choosing the emblem of the Joint Services Staff College would reflect the multidisciplinary nature of the task force and that a grappling iron with four hooks could be added. So it was agreed, and the Jermyn Street outfitters T M Lewin were tasked with its production, a silver cormorant and grapnel with a diagonal silver line on a black background.[7]

Grapple tie fabric

Perhaps the only problem with the tie was unavoidable in 1957. The narrowness which was the fashion then for tie wearers and small boys holding up cricket shorts became almost unwearable in the 21st century.

However, when contacted by the *Warrior* Gunroom several decades later, Lewin's rose to the occasion again and produced for them the wider, longer version that all those Gunroom officers now own, but so far have not needed in order to be able to recognise each other.

Apart from a six inch thick concrete airstrip built to the highest specifications, plus dispersal areas and repair facilities protected from the Trade Winds, a tented camp for sleeping accommodation for 3,000 men and huts for offices and messing, the very basic 'harbour' at Port of London would need the channel dredged plus an anchorage and buoys for the larger ships. There would also have to be a reliable and efficient ship-to-shore unloading set-up that could safely move the heavy equipment needed for building the airfield. All of this, plus the personnel to carry out the tasks, had to be shipped by sea and air and deployed with speed and purpose. Decca Navigation signal stations had to be established with their necessary logistic support on the outlying islands of Palmyra, Starbuck, Fanning, Jarvis and Penrhyn to allow their radio beams to generate an accurate fix for the ships and aircraft. Weather forecasting data, at heights of up to 100,000 feet, needed to be compiled over a long enough period in advance of the tests to allow the day-to-day information coming in from ships and radiosonde balloons in the upper atmosphere to be used to forecast the conditions ahead of each test. If there was going to be radioactive fallout, the scientists and the Task Force Commander needed to know where it was drifting and where it might land. At the outset, detailed weather, wind and forecasting knowledge such as this was, for the extensive test area, simply non-existent.

Over and above the four Valiant Bombers required for dropping the weapons, there had to be a small armada of different aircraft each chosen for its specific capabilities. Shackletons would have to deliver the initial staging post party to Christmas, and would also be needed for low and medium level photography, from about February 1957 onwards, and later for low-level radiation measurements. Hastings would operate the shuttle service to Honolulu and, on occasions, to Australia. Dakotas would operate between Christmas, Malden and the other islands to airlift stores and equipment that could not wait for 'surface delivery'. PR7 Canberras with periscope sextants, 'Green Satin' doppler radar, and Loran would carry out the vital high level wind finding, photography and, after each test, the ultra-rapid delivery of the cloud samples back to the UK; but it would be the B6 Canberras that would carry out the actual post-test, cloud sample gathering.

It would be *Warrior*'s Whirlwind helicopters and fixed wing Avengers that would ferry instrumentation records back from the test site on Malden and, using *Warrior* as a staging post, deliver these to the Canberras for despatch with the cloud samples back to AWRE in England. And, apart from the Avengers, every aircraft would need some mission-specific modifications; modifications which totalled over two thousand for the Valiants alone. A sobering thought in the minds of all senior officers was that, for most of these aircraft, there would be no easily-accessible diversionary airfield in the event of any emergency.[8]

In total, seven warships would have roles to play in Grapple. They included the light fleet carrier HMS *Warrior*, which started the year in reserve in Devonport, together with the survey ship HMS *Cook*, named after the Navy's revered explorer who had charted much of the area chosen, the Bay class frigate HMS *Alert* borrowed from C-in-C Far East to act as a spectators' viewing platform during the second test, HMS *Messina*, an LST (Landing Ship Tanks), located in Malta and brought back to Chatham for a refit and extensive modification, a second LST, HMS *Narvik*, at that time out at the test site off the Monte Bello Islands in Australia, HMS *Salvictor*, an ocean-going salvage ship brought in to lay mooring buoys off the steeply shelving coasts of the Pacific islands, together with the New Zealand Navy Loch class frigates, HMNZS *Pukaki* and *Rotoiti* to provide essential high altitude meteorological data. In addition seven Royal Fleet Auxiliaries, the Navy's own merchant shipping line, were deployed: *Fort Beauharnois*, *Fort Constantine*, *Fort Rosalie*, *Wave Chief*, *Wave Prince*, *Wave Ruler* and *Gold Ranger*. And, of course, the Navy was only one of the armed services involved, together with the scientists and other civil servants.

By early November 1956, the new runway was complete and, almost literally, the last steamroller moved off the end of it as the first aircraft was touching down. No slippages in the timetable were needed at this late stage. Nor did the Foreign Office need the protest from the French, who raised concerns expressed by a scientist friend of the territory's Governor about the possible effects of radioactive fallout on Tahiti from the planned weapon tests. Diplomats smoothed relations between the FO and the Quai d'Orsay but the scientist was not mollified by being overruled.

Unaware of much of these high political, military and scientific events, there was, for many in the UK in 1956, a feeling that 'things' were finally improving. However, for many young men there was still the prospect, viewed with mixed feelings, of being called up for National Service. Eligible men already had their Certificate of

Registration from their local office of the Ministry of Labour and National Service. Ten young men who would later serve together in the Gunroom in HMS *Warrior*, sailing via the Panama Canal to the Pacific and then all round South America and the Falkland Islands, were called up during the first half of the year and at various times progressed to become Temporary Acting Midshipmen in the RNVR by the end of 1956.

First to be called up was Michael Anson who received the standard letter from the Ministry. 'In accordance with the National Service Acts you are called up to serve in the Royal Navy and are required to present yourself at Victoria Barracks, Portsmouth and Southsea.' In earlier centuries he might well have been snatched by the Press Gang off the London street where he lived. But this was 1956 and, instead of the King's shilling, those called up were given a travel warrant to be exchanged for a Third Class railway ticket from their nearest station to Southsea and the generous advance of *four* shillings pay. Anson came from a family with a long connection with the Navy, being an indirect descendant of the famous 18th century circumnavigator of the globe, Admiral George Anson, the first and last Lord Anson who died without issue. As our *Warrior* story begins to unfold, in January 1957, Anson had already been serving for several months as a Midshipman in HMS *Messina*, sailing round the Pacific Islands delivering supplies and essential equipment as Operation Grapple built up, and had enjoyed a month in New Zealand while his ship underwent repairs there.

Anson was followed in early 1956 by Jeremy Riches, the son of a Royal Marines senior officer but called up into the Navy as a Writer in the Supply & Secretariat Division. These are the ship's Pursers (pronounced 'Pussers') who have the crucial job of keeping warships fed, watered, paid and supplied with all their manifold logistic requirements. After training at HMS *Ceres* near Wetherby, one of the Royal Navy's 'stone frigates', Riches joined *Warrior*'s sister ship, HMS *Theseus*, as a Midshipman and took an active part in the Suez invasion before returning for ten days leave and then joining *Warrior* as assistant to the Captain's Secretary.

There were eight others who were enrolled as Ordinary Seamen; starting, in alphabetical order, with Rupert Cooper, a doctor's son from Dorset, already an experienced and enthusiastic sailor, also keen on hunting, shooting and fishing, and an avid reader of *The Field*. He spent some time at sea on the lower deck but had demonstrated his seamanship and 'officer-like qualities' by captaining a storm-stricken yacht and navigating it from the open sea out of sight of land safely back to port, leading to his Captain's 'red recommendation' that he become an Upper-Yardman.

Richard Dennis had salt in his blood. His great-grandfather was a Master Mariner and his grandfather had been born at sea in the Indian Ocean. He was taught to sail at the age of six by his uncle, a national dinghy sailing champion. At fourteen he had to join the school CCF and opted for the Naval section. Then, at seventeen, he enlisted in the RNVR and spent two glorious weeks sea training in HMS *Theseus* listening enthralled to Captain (later Rear Admiral Sir Anthony) Miers VC as he recounted his exploits in command of a submarine during the raid on Taranto where he earned his decoration.

Ian Maitland Hume joined the RNVR early in 1955, doing a fortnight's training on HMS *Vanguard*. He left school in July 1955 and went to Paris to further his French language studies, staying there seven months. Returning to the UK, he spent the next three months as a hospital porter at Atkinson Morleys Hospital, before being called up at the end of May 1956.

John Hutchinson, whose experiences of torrential downpours at a Combined Cadet Force camp in Wales had convinced him that the Army was no place to spend two years, joined the RNVR and during a fortnight's sea training met one of his future Midshipman colleagues who encouraged him to keep trying to go for something he had already targeted, namely the Joint Services School of Languages in Bodmin. Next thing he knew was his call-up and arrival at Victoria Barracks where he was very soon selected to be an Upper Yardman. Despite continuing to enquire, his expressed wish to be sent to JSSL remained unfulfilled.

Michael Kirchem would distinguish himself as a euphonium player in the ship's band and have mixed fortunes as a coxswain of small boats. After National Service, Michael would go on to read law at Oxford, qualify as a solicitor, and work for the Inland Revenue. Sadly, he died in 2011, in his 74th year.

Michael Johnston, the oldest of the group, was already a qualified textile designer, destined for the family weaving business in the Scottish Borders, but had also pursued a hobby of freelance broadcasting for the Younger Generation programmes of the BBC. Although pretty much of a landlubber, National Service in the Navy seemed to him the most attractive of the three options and he joined the RNVR just in time to do two weeks training in April before being called up in July. He too went from Victoria Barracks directly to his Upper Yardman course.

Before doing National Service, Laurance Reed worked in the Display Department of the family business, Austin Reed, where he was taught the art of window dressing by a certain John Inman, later to become famous for his part in the television sitcom *Are you being served?* His first lesson, however, was about the law window dressers were required to observe. To display naked mannequins was not only immodest but illegal. Unless they were clothed or draped, the window blinds had to be drawn. Later, Reed spent six months working for Liberty's, employed in several departments and ending up in Exports, despatching Liberty silks to exotic places. The department was in a separate building in the rather dull and uninteresting Carnaby Street, before its swinging sixties transformation.

Gillespie – inevitably nicknamed 'Dizzy' – Robertson joined straight from school, in his case Eton, where he had been Head Boy. That might have influenced the Navy's decision to send him off straight away for officer training. He observed in his Journal that, in those rather more 'class'-conscious days, the National Service officers were predominantly from 'public' (i.e. private) secondary schools. That was certainly true of *Warrior*'s Gunroom. However, Robertson and most of the others welcomed the experience of being 'taken down several pegs' serving on the lower deck before promotion. This observation is confirmed in Richard Vinen's 2014 book, *National Service*:

> 'National service naval officers were almost always drawn from relatively privileged backgrounds, but they often commented that social class counted for less in the navy than in the army. This was in part because many regular naval officers had been educated at Dartmouth and were thus less preoccupied by the hierarchy of public schools that so interested army officers. It was also because naval officers generally lived in ships and were not required to indulge in the expensive entertainments that were sometimes expected of officers in smart regiments. Most importantly, officers who might be required to guide a destroyer into Valetta harbour, for example, placed a higher value on technical competence than social polish.'[9]

All having opted to do their two-years of National Service in the Royal Navy, they had carried out at least two weeks basic training, at sea, sleeping in hammocks which they had to learn how to lash tightly and stow away every morning. This was usually on board HMS *Theseus* or HMS *Ocean*, two of the Royal Navy's *six* aircraft carriers in service at that time. In *Theseus*, several of the group gazed with awe and respect at the carrier's second-in-command, Commander (later Rear Admiral) Godfrey Place VC CB CVO DSC RN, who had captained the midget submarine X7 in the attack up a Norwegian fjord on the German battleship *Tirpitz*. Indeed, most of the officers they met of the rank of Lieutenant Commander and above were veterans of active service in World War II; in no sense a distant memory for anyone in 1956.

The Upper Yardman training was usually carried out in various vessels of the Training Squadron and 'stone frigates', but some disruption to the usual courses resulted from ships like *Ocean* and *Theseus* being detached and sent to take part in the Suez operations. Experienced, and some of them recently Suez-hardened, NCOs were both the principal instructors and occasional tormentors of the Upper Yardmen, as well as regaling them with tales of 'the one shot which blew the Egyptian destroyer out of the water' and similar stories of how many of those on the front line felt Suez could and should have been 'won.' For a while stationed in the battleship HMS *Vanguard*, in the reserve fleet, the group finished up at HMS *Raleigh*, a training barracks at Torpoint in Cornwall across the Saltash from Devonport. On the whole, as Hutchinson recalls, 'we liked to demonise the Chiefs and Petty Officers but we actually liked them. It was they who taught us seamanship. They affected to despise us but were quite intrigued by what we had to say and think.' He noted too that, 'There were a lot of intelligent, able and athletic people among us, several from interesting family and cultural backgrounds.'

The Upper Yardmen eventually took their Appointment Board interviews and, duly commissioned, went on what amounted to 'embarkation leave'. As they packed up and returned their bell bottom trousers and sailors' round caps, and donned their brand new officers' uniforms that had been made for them 'on spec' by approved Naval Outfitters, they came to terms with not only an increase in pay but also the activation of a monthly allotment to their chosen tailors to pay off the balance not covered by the Admiralty's modest grant for these new clothes. Reed was the exception, as his uniforms were made for him by the family firm. However, since the Plymouth branch had been destroyed by enemy action during the war, he had to travel several times to the nearest branch in Exeter for fittings. As a member of the family, he was entitled to a thirty per cent discount!

The Midshipmen would travel home in their new glory. Because it was the immediate aftermath of Suez and petrol was now rationed, one newly promoted Midshipman wearing the white flashes of his lowly rank, and naturally *not* one of the future Warriors, was reported later to have stopped at almost every filling station he passed on the way home to Scotland, saying, 'My, but it's cold here after Suez. Could you just top her up please?'

1 http://en.wikipedia.org/wiki/Guy_Mollet#Suez accessed 6 November 2013

2 Oulton, *Christmas Island Cracker*, London: Thomas Harmsworth, 1987, p.7

3 Oulton, p. 8. Lees is referring to *Lucky Dragon 5*, a Japanese tuna fishing boat, which was exposed to and contaminated by nuclear fall-out from the United States' thermonuclear device tested on Bikini Atoll, on 1 March 1954, with fatal results.

4 Archives New Zealand [ABHS 950 W4627/3379 121/5/2 pt 1 (R20758368)], [ABHS 950 W4627/3379 121/5/2 pt 2 (R20758369)].

5 The name was recycled in 1992 for the Army operations in the Balkans

6 Oulton p.39

7 Oulton p.120

8 Oulton, pp.127/8

9 Richard Vinen, *National Service: Conscription in Britain, 1945–1963*, London: Allen Lane, 2014, p.199

JANUARY

Devonport to Portsmouth

For some, January 1957 began the day before. Officers appointed to ships of the Royal Navy receive a printed form letter telling them the name of their new ship, what their job would be, and where the ship would be lying on the date they had to join. During their training, towards the end of the course, when it is a reasonable assumption they are going to be promoted, Upper Yardmen aspiring to be Midshipmen, are taught the strict form of their reply to the Captain of their new ship.

CONFIDENTIAL.
516.
N.C.W. 504 (20/12/56)

By *Command of the Commissioners for Executing the Office of Lord High Admiral of the United Kingdom, &c.*

To Midshipman M.W. Johnston. RNVR.

THE Lords Commissioners of the Admiralty hereby appoint you Temporary Midshipman. RNVR. of Her Majesty's Ship PEMBROKE addl. (pending appointment) (not to join)

and direct you to repair on board that Ship at
_____ on _____

Your appointment is to take effect from that date*. 14.12.56. You are also appointed HMS WARRIOR addl. for Training 1.1.57. (To join at Plymouth)

You are to acknowledge the receipt of this Appointment *forthwith*, addressing your letter to the Commanding Officer. HMS WARRIOR. c/o GPO. London. taking care to furnish your address.

By *Command of their Lordships,*

Woodburn.
Morville Rd.
Galashiels.

(* "Appointments. Time of Joining.—Officers appointed to ships at home are to join by 0900 on the day of appointment, with the exception that officers appointed to shore courses are to join after noon on the previous day unless otherwise ordered."—Q.R. & A.I. Art. 0205.)

Admiralty, S.W.1. 19/12/56.

(1265) Wt. 52856/P6655 8M (I) 12/54 S.E.R. Ltd. Gp. 647

Johnston's appointment letter

25

'Sir, I have the honour to acknowledge receipt of my appointment to HMS *Warrior* under your command to take effect from 1 January 1957. I request permission to join the ship on the day before in plain clothes. I have the honour to be, Sir, Your obedient servant,' and the letter had to be signed with their name and lowly rank; Temporary Acting Midshipman, RNVR; *temporary* because they were on National Service and *acting* because, depending on their skill and their conduct, they would have to be confirmed in their rank. All their appointments were described as 'additional for training.'

HMS *Warrior* was a 'Colossus class light fleet carrier' built in 1944 by Harland & Wolff, 695 feet long, with a displacement of 18,300 tons, a fully operational complement of 1,300, and a maximum speed of 25 knots. After the war she had been loaned to the Canadian Navy and then came back to the UK where the Royal Navy used her to transport troops and aircraft to the Korean conflict. Before being selected for Grapple, *Warrior* had been in reserve and had to be sent for a refit in Devonport. The refit and trials having been completed to a very tight schedule, she awaited her new crew.

The log of HMS *Warrior*, lying at 5 and 6 Wharfs, RN Dockyard, Devonport, shows that four newly promoted Midshipmen; Robertson, Reed, Johnston and Hutchinson; struggled up the starboard after-gangway during the evening of 31 December, carrying their fully packed standard issue light green suitcases and receiving their first real salute. Each one faced aft and raised his hat to the quarterdeck before being shown the way aft and then down, down, down to the Chest Flat on 4 deck, their large metal dormitory, *just* above the waterline and almost immediately over the propellers. To begin with, until others joined later in the month, it seemed spacious with ample locker space; into which, in addition to his uniforms and other clothes, Johnston carefully stowed his prize possession, a Boosey & Hawkes reel-to-reel, clockwork driven, tape recorder.

For the officers of HMS *Warrior*, New Year celebrations began the night before. First of all there was the imminent start of a brand new year that needed to be suitably marked. Music was being provided on the harmonium by Lieutenant (SD) Calcutt, who was known affectionately by everyone as 'Harpic'; the Navy's regular nickname for anyone displaying more than mild eccentricity and considered, therefore, to be 'clean round the bend'. A fair number of wives and girlfriends had also been invited aboard, adding glamour to the party.

In the brand new uniforms they were all still paying for, the four 'Snotties' joined the party, but scarcely needed to buy their own drinks, such was the welcoming generosity of the Wardroom. It was distinctly rosy-cheeked, even flushed, Midshipmen who heard for the first time the naval tradition of marking midnight and the start of the first Middle Watch of the year by ringing out the Old Year with eight bells and ringing in the New Year with a further eight. This was done on the quarterdeck by the youngest Junior Seaman on board. Robertson used his 'going-away present', a new Rolex chronometer watch, to mark the time and change of date. Johnston used his tape recorder to capture the sixteen bells and the singing of *Auld Lang Syne*. (None of these recordings now exist but they did survive long enough for him to make a radio programme for the BBC of the music heard and played during the voyage of the Warriors.)

The Royal Navy custom was then that in their larger ships the most junior officers constituted the Gunroom as their own mess; separate from the Wardroom, the domain of more senior officers except the Captain. The Midshipmen were joined in *Warrior*'s Gunroom by five RN Sub-Lieutenants, both engineers and pilots, and by Lt Jeffrey Bagg RN who would be Gunroom President. By contrast with the somewhat spartan life of Upper-Yardmen which they had been putting up with for the previous several months, life as Midshipmen was one of significantly improved comfort, quality of food served by Officers' Stewards, and, above all, the respect of naval ratings, up to and including war-veteran Chief Petty Officers whose opposite numbers during training had bawled them out for the slightest misdemeanour. Even the fearsome Master-at-Arms, the ship's chief of police, would salute and address these young men, scarcely half his age and one-hundredth of his experience as 'Sir!!!'

That first night, the Midshipmen had blankets but no sheets. Hutchinson threw a chocolate over to Johnston who failed to catch it and, in the morning, thought at first he had been bleeding.

On New Year's Day, the four Midshipmen met formally the officer responsible for the training for which they had been appointed. Lieutenant-Commander Donald T Watts RN was also the ship's Navigating Officer who would be plotting *Warrior*'s passage and position for the next ten months and 40,000 miles. They were now going to have to put into practice one of the mnemonics they had been taught; this one as the check-list of points for the Officer of the Watch as he took over. It ran '*Sacks of wet medical beans*'. Probably C was for 'Captain's whereabouts' but none of the Midshipmen can now remember the rest.

Watts was blue-eyed and fair-haired and a seaman to his fingertips, and hailed from Hunstanton, near where Horatio Nelson was born. Then, and throughout their service in *Warrior*, the National Service Midshipmen held him in high esteem; and forty years later he would be their guest of honour at their 1997 reunion held at the Royal Yacht Squadron.

Watts (left) at 40th anniversary reunion at the Royal Yacht Squadron

Watts was to be their Divisional Officer and would supervise their practical experience in navigation; the use of the sextant to take the altitude of sun and stars and then how to transform these accurate timed measurements into a precise calculation of the ship's position by triangulation, plus the more modern but not yet more accurate electronic means of Radar, Loran and Decca Navigator.

They also met the very impressive ship's Executive Officer, Commander (later Captain) Robin A Begg RN, second in command to the Captain; a mountain of a man, tall and broad, with a voice like a foghorn, and every inch and ounce a seaman.

Commander Begg (Rowsell)

He had been in command of *Warrior* during the refit. His larger-than-life manner went with a broad smile and a wicked sense of humour. During the voyage, the Midshipmen would see this smile, enjoy his humour and get the occasional tongue-lashing for anything less than wholly satisfactory execution of their duties. This last started the same day for Johnston who was cheerfully whistling as he crossed the flight deck and the path of the Commander. He was smartly referred to the chapter on Naval Customs in his Manual of Seamanship Vol. I, where it makes clear that whistling is expressly forbidden in HM ships lest it be confused with the piping of orders: though perhaps in sailing days an exception had to be made when it was necessary to 'whistle for a wind'?

At lunchtime there was yet another high-fluid-content party in the Wardroom to celebrate the administrative promotion of every Commissioned Branch Officer in the Navy. These were men who, like the brand-new Midshipmen, had been promoted to officer rank from the lower deck; former Petty Officers and Chief Petty Officers all of whom, on the stroke of midnight, had become Lieutenants and Sub-Lieutenants SD (Special Duties).

Roles and responsibilities were allocated during the day. Robertson became an Assistant Divisional Officer for the Quarterdeck Division and Assistant Boats Officer under Lt Harland, a role in which he revelled. Johnston became Lt Bagg's deputy as Assistant Divisional Officer for the Junior Seamen on board. He wondered if, somewhere in his records, they had seen he had been a Boy Scout. And life became serious in other ways as the Gunroom officers drew lots to see who would be wine caterer. Naval Officers on board ship may drink alcohol, but their consumption is restricted on a 'per stripe' basis. A Lieutenant-Commander, for example, may buy two and a half times what is permitted for a Sub-Lieutenant, but Midshipmen only half of that. Officers sign chits for what they consume and the wine caterer has to tally up the chits and, harder still, reconcile the amount consumed with the stock remaining, which *never* tallies. Much to everyone else's relief, but to his own satisfaction, Hutchinson drew the black spot. He relished the opportunity to make important decisions such as whether to stock Mersault and/or Chablis – a decision he reached only after careful research.

Johnston's relief did not last long, however, as he became the mineral caterer, responsible for the mixers such as Canada Dry Ginger Ale which, with a tot of brandy, made the very tasty Horse's Neck, with a duty-free price outside British territorial waters of 4d; four old pence each, or less than 2p in today's decimal coinage, for the brandy and the ginger ale. Since a can of lager cost a colossal 9d, spirit drinking was made very tempting. However, some officers would drown their brandy in a whole small bottle of GA while others would make it do for two tots of brandy. Johnston was later to get into total confusion and need help (and counselling) to sort out who was due to pay what. Payment for drinks was made by the signing of a Mess Chit which was then recorded in the Messbook. Alcohol consumption was strictly monitored and one of the duties of purser Midshipman Riches was to take the Wardroom and Gunroom Messbooks each week to the Captain. These the Captain would peruse and call before him any officer he considered to be drinking excessively.

On 3 January, *Warrior*, with the assistance of a tug called, of all things, 'Grappler', moved down the Hamoaze to F buoy inside the breakwater in Plymouth Sound and,

Warrior *in the Channel*

early the following day, slipped her moorings and sailed for Spithead, the anchorage in the Solent off Gilkicker Point, made famous by the Fleet Reviews held there, most recently to celebrate the 1953 Coronation. Despite spanking along at 16 knots it took *Warrior* until the next day to reach Spithead; at which point the ship's complement of RN and RAF helicopters flew on board for exercises. In the first of many letters home, Johnston recalls that on the evening of the 4th, he relieved Hutchinson in the Operations Room from where, if asked, he was required to pass information to the bridge. He had found he'd had to hold on as he made his way up for his watch as the

Avenger landing on Warrior *(Rowsell)*

Avenger taking off (Rowsell)

31

ship was bashing along 'like a Jeep on a cart track'. Using radar, the Operations Room watched the movements of other ships in the vicinity and plotted their positions on a large Perspex-topped table. This was all completely new to him but fortunately the bridge did not ask for anything and the radar ratings said 'Sir' to him so much that he felt embarrassed. He tried to conceal this by drinking copious amounts of kai;[1] the ship's cocoa, rich, dark and strong; and smoking 'Senior Service'.

On the 6th, *Warrior* weighed anchor and carried out more exercises, testing out the ship, the helicopters and the crew after the refit. These included practice with one of the RAF Valiants which would be dropping the megaton weapon some four months later on, but the purpose here was to test the procedure for controlling the aircraft from the ship's radar. Johnston was there as the anchor broke the surface and then went up to the roof of the 'island', that off-centre tower block on the starboard side of the flight deck, and from the Gun Director Platform was able to watch the fixed wing Grumman Avengers doing landings and take-offs.

The Avengers were elderly, near-obsolete US Navy single-engine torpedo bombers with a normal crew of three, but rugged and reliable and judged useful during the Grapple operation for transport between *Warrior*, Christmas Island and Malden Island, designated as the test site.[2] They needed, of course, to be catapulted into the air off the angled flight deck, a very modern innovation, and Johnston saw that the wire strop that attached the plane to the catapult dropped into the sea as the plane became airborne. He wondered if Stores had enough strops to last out for the duration of the mission. He wrote home, 'The adrenalin rush I felt as the Avengers landed and came to an almost immediate halt as their hooks caught the arrester wires must have been nothing compared with that for the pilots; especially on their first carrier landing. It certainly beats an emergency stop during the driving test.' An aircraft carrier usually steams into the wind to increase the relative wind speed over the flight deck; however, the Commander would later regale the Gunroom with his story that, during earlier flying trials, he had had to steam slowly astern so as to *reduce* the wind speed across the flight deck. Conning a ship the size and peculiar shape (with the island off-centre creating a high wall to the wind) was never an easy task, as one of the RN Lieutenants found to his embarrassment, leading to his admonishment being recorded in the ship's log – not a career-enhancing event.

After her sea and flying trials, *Warrior* berthed at Pitch House Jetty and the work of provisioning and leave taking (in both senses of the words) got under way. There was a visit on the 23rd from Air Vice-Marshal Wilfred Oulton, Task Force Commander of Operation Grapple. The AVM records that Commodore Gretton, then in overall Naval command under Oulton, had previously been offered command of *Warrior*, but that had been cancelled as a defence cut saving. He was now going to have *Warrior* under his control but with Captain Roger Hicks as her commanding officer.[3]

Later he mentions approving an RAF liaison officer (who would turn out to be S/Ldr 'Roly' Duck) to join the ship and work alongside *Warrior*'s Commander (A) Whitfield who had been involved in the forward planning since 1956.[4] By this time HMS *Messina* was already out in the Pacific.

Captain Hicks (Rowsell)

Another 'snotty' joined the ship briefly, Midshipman Wedgwood; but his earnest wish to go into submarines instead was unexpectedly granted and he left within days for HMS *Dolphin*. However, on 20 January, *Warrior* welcomed not one replacement for him but four newly hatched, ten-day-old Midshipmen; Rupert Cooper, Ian Maitland Hume, Richard Dennis and Michael Kirchem, all seamen officers. Hutchinson reflected that, 'there was speculation about the choice of the Midshipmen on *Warrior*. No notable sportsmen were selected. Good rugby players were too valuable to lose from Navy Teams. [Robertson, conscious of his *three years* in his school's first XV disputes the accuracy of this assessment!] Nor did we have any notorious entrepreneurs and public bores. Whatever was the formula, random or deliberate, it worked very well.' Cooper had asked permission to bring his fishing rods and a pair of 12 bore shotguns on board which were duly secured in the ship's armoury. Cooper then learned that Fleet Air Arm pilots were encouraged to undertake shooting practice to instil in them the habit of firing at where the target *would be* at the moment of impact rather than where it *was* at the moment of firing. This meant he could be sure of regular practice and an endless supply of clay pigeons.

The new arrivals made the Chest Flat, Cabin 108, seem crowded until all settled down and got used to it. Life for the Gunroom mineral caterer, however, became much more complicated! Mind you, age also had its privileges and Johnston's letter home says that having eight seamen Midshipmen should make it easier for him to get a long weekend's leave before the ship sailed for the Pacific. He used that to go up to London and see a BBC boffin to get the okay for his tape recorder to make sure it was up to broadcast quality. He also met his parents there who had come down from Scotland to say their goodbyes.

All the while, vast quantities of stores were being loaded, not least 150,000 crates of beer, each crate holding twenty-four cans and all destined for the troops on Christmas Island. All the cans had printed on them 'Specially prepared for HM forces engaged on the Megaton trials, Christmas Island'.

Towards the end of the month, around 170 soldier and airmen passengers came on board. Then, on 29 January, Midshipman Jeremy Riches, from the Supply and Secretariat Division, brought the tally up to ten, if we include Anson who was, by this time, already out in the South Pacific. Riches was not long back from active service off Suez during that brief campaign, where he witnessed action and helped to ferry wounded back to Malta and the UK, having been granted only ten days leave before being posted to *Warrior* almost immediately before she sailed for the Pacific. He was thrown in at the deep end with a variety of duties ranging from assisting the Captain's secretary to assisting the pay officer and working with the Chief Petty Officer in charge of stores. This would have the unfortunate consequence for him of a lighter workload while at sea but rather less time off than the other Midshipmen when in port.

Shipboard routine for the deck officer Midshipmen in harbour included an 0700 session of PT on the quarterdeck and some practise in boat running at which some were more adept than others. Hume recalls Johnston heading full throttle for the jetty before his own urgent counsel prevailed. Boats Officer Lt Harland complained that during the month in Portsmouth the Midshipmen had holed every one of his boats. The trickiest moment would come, however, when the officer on deck in charge of lowering boats with a swell running shouted 'Slip!' and the crew member manning the 'Robinson's release gear' did his job.

The boat, engine already running, was supposed to drop neatly onto the crest of the next wave and set off steering away from the ship's side. If an inexperienced officer, such as most Midshipmen were, misjudged the timing of the wave it could

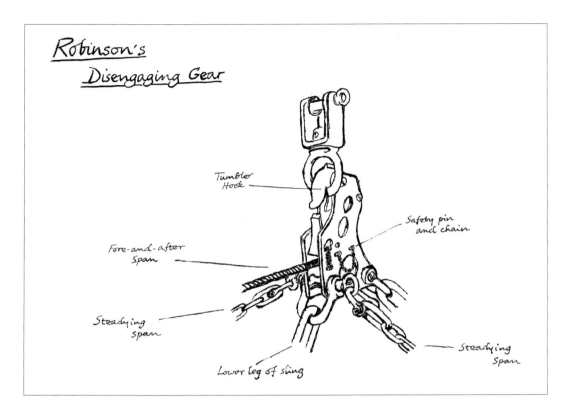

Diagram of Robinson's release gear (Robertson)

seem like a long drop. Other naval education included learning the Morse code and operating Aldis lamps and generally becoming familiar with the whole ship and its many routines and regulations. There was some diversion, however.

First there was the excursion by floating crane to pick up a piano from HMS *Theseus*, in which Riches had served in the Mediterranean and others knew from their RNVR training. The piano was piped over the side as it left *Theseus* and made the journey to *Warrior* suspended in a sling from the crane while Johnston (according to Robertson, although the alleged pianist cannot now recall this), 'his ravaged features creased in a wild grin', gave a very creditable rendition of *Rule Britannia* with the piano swaying perilously across the water. The instrument turned out to be a Bechstein, worth about £90 in 1957 money; the equivalent purchasing power of at least £2,000 in 2017 terms! Then, at the end of the month, the Gunroom was transformed into a grotto and a dinner party was held for the girlfriends or chosen female acquaintances. Robertson, given the responsibility of meeting them at the railway station, had some difficulty in recognising which young ladies to accost and then escort to the Queen's Hotel, Southsea.

Whether Officers' Steward Smith, who spilled soup down what one of Reed's shipmates still recalls as the 'delectable *décolletage*' of his girlfriend Angela, was 'under training' or maybe even 'under the influence' is now long forgotten, but the said Angela has recently confirmed that she still remembers the incident. Whether it was the same event differently recalled or yet another incident is not clear, but Hume says one young lady had sherry spilled down her back! Cooper had a new Rock'n'Roll record to which the Gunroom and guests all danced, the young officers resplendent for the first time in their mess jackets.

31 January was meant to be the last day before sailing. Hume went for a pint of scrumpy at the Lennox and then the front row of the stalls at the Empire, with a very good view of 'ladies in the nude'; only one of whom he thought was anything to write home about. [Although, there is no record of his *actually* writing home about this!]

But now the preparation was over and it was off to sea.

---

1 It came in large blocks of solid dark chocolate. It was broken down into the required amount and boiling water added. Optional additions were condensed milk, sugar and occasionally 'pusser's rum'.

2 Oulton, p.46

3 Oulton, p.84

4 Oulton, p.90

FEBRUARY

....

English Channel to the Pacific

Some families and friends came to wave goodbye but it wasn't the weather for spectators. Sailors, however, lined *Warrior*'s flight deck and were called to attention by bugle and boatswain's pipe to salute the various Admirals whose flags flew in Portsmouth; C-in-C Portsmouth whose flag flew in HMS *Victory*, the C-in-C Western Approaches, and the Admiral Superintendent of the Dockyard; and to return the salutes of lesser ships. It was the start of a month's passage from 51° N, 1° W to their new temporary base, Christmas Island, right in the middle of the Pacific, deliberately chosen for its remoteness, 1° N, 157° W; some 9,000 nautical miles from Portsmouth. But, depending on who was telling the story, there were lighter moments. Midshipman Kirchem, watch-keeping on the bridge, and fiddling with something, suddenly managed to broadcast the BBC Light Programme to the whole ship and was hung up by his shirt collar by the gigantic Commander, and characterised as 'my little thrush'! There was probably no direct connection but Kirchem, along with Reed, spent a storm-tossed February in the Engine Room.

Apart from an immense amount and variety of essential stores and scientific equipment secured in the hangars, there was also provision for recreation that included a number of surf boats, 15,000 rounds of 12 bore ammunition and some 400 lbs of plaster of Paris for making clay pigeons.

At the very civilised hour of 1315 on 2 February, a day later than planned due to the weather reports from the Channel, *Warrior* slipped from Pitch House Jetty and headed to St Helen's Roads, the anchorage off Bembridge on the Isle of Wight, to take on Avgas, fuel for the choppers and Avengers; a procedure carried out offshore for safety reasons. At that point too, eight helicopters, six Navy and two RAF, and three Avengers flew on board from HMS *Daedalus*. While the Royal Navy and RAF flying crews came aboard with their aircraft, the ground crew came off by lighter. Already a sea was running and the only *relatively* safe way they could come on board was by using scrambling nets. The knack of doing this safely is to jump for the net as the lighter is rising, otherwise one is likely to be knocked off the net by the boat on its next rise; a lesson some learned the hard way. Then, at 1745 during the First Dog Watch, *Warrior* weighed anchor and set course for Kingston, Jamaica. For the ship and her crew plus the ninety-seven RAF and seventy-one Army personnel, it would be a bumpy passage.

As *Warrior* reached her cruising speed of 16 knots, the weather was dull with drizzle and the wind was a light sou'westerly. A slight sea was running: all in all, English Channel weather for the time of year; but the forecast was it might get worse. Just how much worse, the levels of weather forecasting sophistication in 1957 were not able to say. All hands were deployed to doubly secure for sea, but as the crew would soon discover, this was never going to be enough. The last *Warrior* saw of the UK was a vague gleam whipping across the horizon on the starboard beam – the Lizard Light – during the morning watch on the 3rd. As instructed by the Officer of the Watch, Johnston took a bearing of it from the wings of the bridge and measured its distance from the ship on the radar plot, entering the details in the Ship's Log. The winds were already Force 6 from the south-west, the direction in which *Warrior* was sailing, towards the deepening depression. The sea was rough and those who had any were already taking Kwells with their tot. By the First Dog Watch, the wind speed had risen to Force 8, fresh gale according to the Beaufort scale description, and there was spray driving over the flight deck. The ship was already pitching heavily. Only nine of the Gunroom's fifteen officers sat down to dinner.

By 1000 on 4 February, some one hundred miles south-west of Ushant, *Warrior* steamed directly into a storm that would last for five days and at times reach hurricane Force 12, with winds gusting to 105 knots. Instead of 'running from the storm' as a more cautious ship might have done, *Warrior*, with a schedule to try and maintain, steered directly into it. The engine revolutions were set for about 15 knots but after twenty-four hours the Navigator calculated that the ship had gone *astern* sixteen sea miles. Looking out from the bridge, watch-keepers saw a scene of utter desolation; the sea at its cruellest. *Warrior* was not a small ship but a light fleet carrier with a length of 695 feet and beam of 80 feet. Her angled flight deck was over 700 feet long and was 60 feet above the ship's water line. The island bridge on her starboard side was a further 30–35 feet above the flight deck. And yet the ship rolled and pitched in the sea like a toy boat and the wave troughs were on some occasions 60–70 feet deep.

Movement round the ship was restricted and over half the ship's company was laid out, seasick and ill in their hammocks or on their bunks. Though a Monday, the

ship worked Sunday routine. The whole sea was a whirling white mass of spindrift, and visibility from the bridge was at times no further for'ard than the end of the flight deck, say 100–150 ft. Every thirty minutes, risking life and limb, a bridge messenger went out onto the walkway in front of the bridge windows and washed off the encrusted salt to restore visibility from a virtual nil to at least as far as the ship's bow. The ship was asking the engine room for the revolutions that, in a calm sea, would have made for 12 knots but in the prevailing conditions the Navigator estimated a speed made good of, at best, three!

Every third wave the whole ship plunged down into a trough and the gigantic crest broke over the flight deck and ran in all directions like water thrown from a barrel. Often, as the ship dipped into a trough, there would be a solid thud as the bow hit the oncoming wave head on and the ship seemed to stop in her tracks. 'Getting from stern to bridge was a dodgy ascent. You collided with every bulkhead and piece of equipment en route to stay upright, often caught by the whirling power and noise of the wind,' wrote Hutchinson. Looking aft to the stern one saw the flight deck whip up into the air and felt the enormous shudder as the propellers, which had risen close to or even above the surface, raced and then sank back into the sea. It was an awe-inspiring sight; not that those on board had time to engage in profound thoughts. It was 'one hand for the ship and one hand for yourself' in order to avoid personal injury. This was especially true when, every hour, the Midshipman of the Watch and the Coxswain or a Bosun's Mate went on rounds throughout the ship. They would report back to the Officer of the Watch the considerable damage they had seen. Twenty life rafts, some of which were seen to inflate perfectly, were washed overboard together with a whaler and two dinghies. There was water in the cable locker which had to be continuously pumped out and the for'ard trim tanks had so much water in them that the tanks in the stern had to be filled to compensate and try to keep the bows from digging so deeply into the waves. It was clear, as later external inspection would confirm, that there was a massive dent in the starboard bow, as if some mighty fist had punched it. The ship's carpenter's stores and workshop were wrecked and the bulkheads needed shoring up with massive balks of timber and wedges hammered in.

Shoring up with timber balks (Rowsell)

*Ship's boat going
0745 (Rowsell)*

*Ship's boat gone
0800 (Rowsell)*

*Storm damage
to starboard
bow (Rowsell)*

*Chaos in
bosun's locker
(Rowsell)*

The Midshipmen could see that whatever they had to put up with in the stern, those in messes near the bow had it much worse. Amidships, where the Army and RAF passengers were living, most of them were violently sick and more than a few did not expect to survive. As the waves broke over the ship, all the fan trunking began to spurt dirty, salty water and had to be turned off, making the atmosphere below decks into a real fug. Life, as even the ever-cheerful Cooper noted, became sordid. On a darker note, watch-keepers picked up one or two Mayday calls but too distant for *Warrior* to do anything about.

In the aircraft hangars, there were generally two or three inches of sea water which slopped from side to side and back and forth, as the ship rolled and pitched. The Avengers were lashed down with very strong steel lashings but as the ship pitched their hydraulic undercarriages compressed, only to try to expand again as the motion was reversed. This was sufficient on several occasions to rupture the lashings which had to be swiftly replaced.

Mess trays of food, often stacked three or four high, had to be collected from the ship's galley and carried up to the seamen's messes, through hatches in watertight doors that had to be opened and closed as the trays ascended. Too often, the meat and potatoes became intimately mixed with the 'figgy duff' and custard.

In the Midshipmen's chest flat, as the stern rose and the propeller shafts began to whine as their blades broke surface, the Snotties would take firm hold of stanchions waiting for the crash as the stern hit the water again; if one was in bed it was like going down too fast in a lift and hitting the ground. A chest of drawers managed to walk six feet and two bunks were dislodged and had to be lashed back into position. Johnston's tape recorder had a miraculous escape, leaping off his desk, where he thought he had firmly wedged it, and sailing across the chest flat to land, completely undamaged, on a pile of sheets and blankets, but the HT batteries disappeared, never to be found. He had managed not to be sick so far but, on the fourth day, after losing his grip coming down a ladder as he was doing his rounds, he fell on his arm, the one that had had his tropical injections, and was confined below decks with his arm in a sling; which was enough to make him very sick for the next couple of days. When he couldn't sleep, he found himself reciting the instructions for watch-keepers that had been dinned into him and his colleagues during training. '*Green to green, red to red, perfect safety, go ahead; but if to starboard red appear, 'tis your duty to keep clear.*'

Access to the carrier's flight deck and sponsons was forbidden and watertight hatches were all shut. The Damage Control state was raised as a precaution which meant that movement along a deck from one flat to another was an awkward question of opening and shutting DC doors and locks. Moving along the passageways and through the mess decks of the ship became an exercise fraught with danger, needing a great sense of balance and two hands to hold on in the more severe moments. Tremendous care was needed opening and closing the watertight doors, but on occasion the ship would lurch and the heavy door would slip from one's grasp and slam shut, or worse, come lurching back towards one. Some of the rolls seemed as if the ship were canting over almost 45 degrees to port or starboard. Below decks there was scarcely a handful of men left standing, although there was, as always, that hard core of stalwarts with good sea-legs who were quietly going about their business as usual. Cooks that still could, were on duty, meals were produced, and those off watch would try to eat them, sleep if possible, read, or do their minor chores. Mess decks were generally kept clean and orderly, but it took very little to turn them into a pig's breakfast. The Engine Room, mostly below the waterline, was the steadiest part of the ship, and seamen watched Engineer Officers and ratings going down to the engine room with a mild twinge of envy. At least there one could be warm, dry and have plenty to hang onto. Robertson recalls at one point hearing the weather forecast and heaving a sigh of relief when it said that the winds would be *moderating* to 'strong gale', Force 9.

On 5 February, in the forenoon, the wind actually eased to Force 5, what Beaufort calls a fresh breeze, relatively speaking a pleasant day; but it became clear by the second Dog Watch that *Warrior* was heading into a second gale. By this time, several radar and wireless aerials had been snapped off, and guard rails and pre-wetting pipes were twisted out of shape, where they had not been torn completely off. Two plates for'ard had sprung. The ship was still taking water into the for'ard trim tanks.

The officers had a cook who was one of those who, completely unperturbed by the movement, carried on as usual and swore at his own galley crew for being weedy and, as far as he was concerned, useless. The yellow-white faces of the cooks, matching the bulkhead paint, seemed to confirm this as he urged them to fry eggs, sausages and bacon for breakfast, make tea, cook steaks and everything that would be acceptable and consumable in a flat calm. The Wardroom and Gunroom stewards were in an enfeebled state too and some were completely incapable. Sea sickness, from which anyone can suffer, is a great leveller of men; some men at least. However, experienced seaman and sea-lover Midshipman Cooper was bright and full of go throughout the whole storm, doing extra watch-keeping for smitten colleagues and eating great quantities of food at the Gunroom table every mealtime; which others could admire but, feeling as they were, not envy. At 1000 on 6 February the Navigator estimated *Warrior* had travelled 1,187 nautical miles and that there should be a sighting of the Azores that evening. However, it began to blow another gale, Force 9–10, and around 1800 a watertight door burst open on the port side. Shoring with heavy timbers was tried but the timbers snapped and there was further flooding.

Most of the Midshipmen felt awful for at least twenty-four hours and were sick or very squeamish all the way to the Azores. This contrasted with the ship's captain who remained calmly on the bridge throughout, using the navigator's 'cuddy' just aft of the chart house for the odd quarter of an hour of shut-eye. Experienced sea-dog Captain Hicks remarked with a smile to one land-lubberly Midshipman, that it was probably the worst weather he had ever experienced. Somehow, that information was not as reassuring to all of them as he may have intended it to be. Cdr Begg noted in his unpublished autobiography that *Warrior* had to try and press on through the storm as it had a slot booked for passage through the Panama Canal. Begg also mentions that at the height of the storm he was taking a bath in his cabin right astern when the waves lifted the stern like a whip and tossed him and his bathwater out of the tub.[1]

Midshipman Hutchinson records that during the worst of the hurricane 'We heard Mayday calls, but we could do nothing.' Yet overall he had 'not felt too worried, naively confident in the quality of British ship-building, yet awestruck by the weather.'

By the time the storm abated and *Warrior* was approaching the Azores, most of the Midshipmen had managed to get back to normal; eating, watch-keeping and sleeping, and feeling thankful that their baptism, or more like drenching, had been endured and had now become something to write home about. Suddenly, everyone had an appetite and the obliging cook, and the now recovered Gunroom stewards, organised a 'traditional' breakfast of fried bacon, egg and sausage followed by toast and marmalade, washed down with great mugs of tea. They were on the mend but the starboard bow looked as if it had received a direct hit and, after four days of shipping seawater, *Warrior* was not riding the waves like she should and there were even doubts about the remaining quantity of fuel and whether it would be sufficient to take her to Jamaica. The ship was running on only two of her four boilers.

Once the ship approached the Azores on the 7th and got close under their lee the storm had passed and the other two boilers were flashed up, allowing *Warrior* to make 14 knots despite the headwinds. These strange mountains in the middle of the Atlantic looked beautiful with splinters of sunlight falling on them across a dark sea. *Warrior* sailed right through the middle of the islands, within a mile of St Jorge and in sight of Terceira. With glasses, one could see the orange groves. The steep cliffs were a ruddy brown and fields an emerald green with, dotted about here and there, white cottages with bright red roofs. However remote and windswept, it was land, terra firma, which had been out of stock for several days! The sea calmed and the ship's motion eased dramatically. At 1600 hrs on that afternoon there was a 'pipe' for 'All hands to clear lower decks' and the whole ship's company, excluding those actually on watch, was made to walk round the flight deck for a good hour to get exercise and breathe some fresh air again.

Positions at noon from Johnston's letter home

Since leaving Portsmouth on the 2nd our noon positions have been –

3rd	1200 (ZN)	49° 11'N	07° 41'W	Decca fix.
4th	1200 (N)	47° 30'N	13° 35'W	Consol fix
5th	1200 (NO)	44° 47'N	20° 18'W	☉ OBS
6th	1200 (O)	41° 31'N	24° 45'W	☉ OBS
7th	1200 (O)	39° 30'N	26° 50'W	☉ OBS
8th	1200 (OP)	36° 24'N	32° 20'W	☉ OBS
9th	1200 (P)	34° 07'N	39° 21'W	E.P

The pounding of the waves did some physical damage in the bows and there is probably a hole in the bows letting water into the cable locker, since the pumps have to be kept going. The Bosun's store has been dented in several places. All the ships boats have been damaged in some way. Two inflatable rafts were lost overside

The ship's time changed as *Warrior* sailed westwards, each time zone designated with a letter. GMT was always Z (Zulu) and, from the daily positions at noon local time recorded in the log, it seems that in that first week *Warrior* had sailed 15 degrees of latitude south and 32 degrees of longitude west. Still the winds did not abate and on the 8th even increased to Force 9 once again. However, Saturday came with a significant rise in temperature and a much calmer sea. The Gunroom had its first Mess Dinner in relative calm but there was still the need to use damp towels and tablecloths to stop the cutlery, plates and glasses sliding about. The Commander came to dinner and regaled the Gunroom with stories of the ship's time being refitted in Devonport. Apparently, the officers used the Gunroom and everything, including the toilet paper, was kept in the fridge. 'I've always felt that cool toilet paper was an unnecessary refinement, except perhaps after a particularly hot curry.'

Then came a wonderful Sunday. It seemed like a perfect day. The maximum temperature was 69°F and the sea temperature was recorded as 70°. Weary sailors sunbathed on the flight deck and sponsons for the first time and found time to catch their breath and, in a very British way, talk about the weather, exchanging storm stories. On the Monday, before the flight deck was stable enough for fixed wing aircraft, one of *Warrior*'s Whirlwind helicopters took off to allow officers to inspect the damage to the starboard bow. The Commander, accompanied by Robertson and Riches on their first ever helicopter flight, made rather more nerve-wracking since the Midshipmen were hauled off the flight deck strapped in a stretcher as part of the chopper crew's training, stood off the bows and assessed the extent of the damage as the chopper hovered. It looked a sorry, indeed depressing, sight, given that the damage had not been sustained in action but through the sheer strength and force of the elements. They also managed to get a close look at the enormous patches of seaweed, floating past in large clumps with an endless tail trailing behind each clump like a comet's tail. Later that day, Johnston too was 'rescued' by a Whirlwind and did not enjoy dangling on a wire and remembers with mild panic that when the crew pulled his feet in first and unhooked the stretcher more than half his body was still outside the safety of the cabin. Once up there, he wished he had brought his camera and had to remind himself, not for the last time since joining *Warrior*, that he was not on a holiday cruise, however much it might seem like one. Then, instead of the chopper landing on the flight deck and his stepping out, they lowered him on a wire strop under his armpits. He hung onto that strop like he was clinging on to life itself.

Lift Certificate

That Monday was the first really hot day, with a maximum of 74°, and the swimming pool was rigged on the flight deck; a popular attraction but Riches did note in his diary that, after the Commander had been in, there was rather less water than there had been before. The following day, the crew changed from blues to whites which was just as well as the temperature climbed further. Their working rig consisted of a white shirt and shorts plus long white stockings and sandals, with white buckskin shoes for formal occasions; very smart, but much of it had to be bought rather than issued from 'slops'. In the evening, it was 'Red Sea rig' when the shorts were exchanged for black trousers and a cummerbund. Riches and many others took an early morning dip in the pool and resolved to make it a daily practice. There were even plans to find camp beds and sleep on the starboard after sponson. Meanwhile, Johnston took his two blues jackets to the ship's tailor to have gold braid sewn on and collected a pair of epaulettes for his white short-sleeved shirt before sending out an RPC (Request Pleasure of your Company) to the Gunroom and a fair number of other officers – all this because, on the following day, he would turn twenty-one and be promoted to Temporary Acting Sub-Lieutenant RNVR and, not to be sneezed at, gain a fifty per cent increase in his daily pay. Plus, as it turned out, Local Overseas Allowance; a generous top-up for all sailors sent to serve in foreign parts; but not every foreign part as would be revealed later. By now, the ship was making 18 knots through the Sargasso Sea.

Despite the many old sailors' myths, there appears to be no sort of death trap for ships in the slowly circulating, enormous gyre of floating sargassum seaweed, although the calms encountered in the 'horse latitudes', 30 to 35 degrees north (and south), could have led thirsty, becalmed sailors, such as those that sailed with Columbus in 1492, to fear they might never escape its clutches. These regions, under a ridge of high pressure called the subtropical highs, receive little precipitation and have variable winds mixed with calm. Myths apart, sailing through large patches of seaweed, extending to the horizon in every direction, has a mystical, even an hypnotic effect. Cooper, the keen fisherman, managed to hook some weed aboard and sent a piece home to his parents. The vast Sargasso Sea; as large as Western Europe and bounded on every side by ocean currents, and where, mysteriously, eels from both Europe's and North America's freshwater rivers migrate several thousands of miles to breed and die; has tended nowadays also to become a repository for non-biodegradable plastics and other detritus but this was not in evidence in February 1957 to the *Warrior*'s Midshipmen and one Sub-Lieutenant.

That newly-minted Sub-Lieutenant turned up for the forenoon watch on Wednesday 13th, self-consciously resplendent in his shiny new epaulettes, saluting the Officer of the Watch smartly. At this point, however, the Captain came onto the compass platform, spotted from across the width of the bridge that Johnston had put on his new badges of rank 'back-to-front,' and sent him below, red-faced, to get himself 'properly dressed'. It was a still rather subdued Sub who went off watch at noon to receive his birthday guests for drinks in the Gunroom. His letter home posted from Jamaica revealed that the whole drinks bill for nearly thirty thirsty well-wishers had cost him only eleven shillings and sixpence at duty-free prices – less than 57p in today's money. However, he had rather overspent on his pay and already drawn an advance, so he knew he would have to economise when he went ashore in Jamaica.

In the evening of that day, *Warrior* sailed through the Turks & Caicos Islands and came within five miles of the lighthouse on Turks Island. In the early morning of the 14th, *Warrior* passed through the Windward Passage between Haiti to the east and Cuba to the west, both countries clearly delineated on the radar screens but only

Haiti visible from the bridge. The forenoon was taken up with deck launching and landing exercises by the Avengers. Hume noted in his Journal the use of the mirror landing aid which shines a light that is reflected back in a gyro-stabilised mirror to the approaching pilot who can immediately tell from this if his approach is too high, too low or just right. His Journal sketch of this was commended.

Mirror landing aid diagram (Hume)

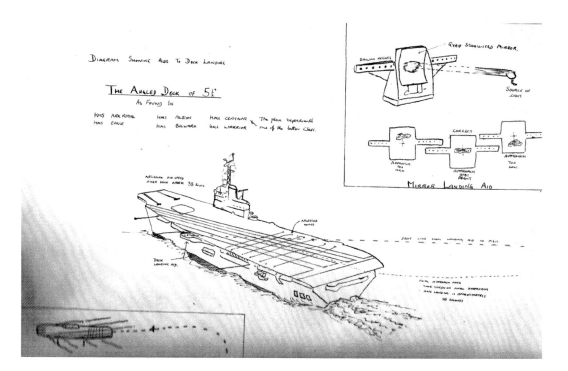

Then there was sudden drama as, around noon, it was decided that the ship's Padre, who had developed acute appendicitis, would have to be flown in one of the Avengers to Palisadoes (now Norman Manley) Airport, Kingston for an urgent operation, with a second Avenger as escort. For those left on board, it was the hottest day so far, touching 83°.

Later in the day, *Warrior* despatched a helicopter with bags of outgoing mail which must have included many grim accounts of the ship's battering by the elements. The Avengers returned two hours later bringing very welcome sacks of mail from home. There was no censorship of their outgoing mail but the Midshipmen had been advised to confine their comments to 'descriptions of daily life, friends, etc.' and not to discuss 'operational matters'. It was also the day the first flying fish were spotted, but so distant as to look more like a sudden shower of rain falling on the sea.

The following morning at around 0600 the ship passed Port Royal at the mouth of Kingston Harbour. Four hundred years earlier, that might have been the destination since it was a harbour much used by privateers waiting to pick off the treasure-laden ships returning from the Spanish colonies. As a port city, it was notorious for its gaudy displays of wealth and loose morals. Moralists might say that was why, in 1880, Port Royal was battered, shaken and more or less washed away by a hurricane, an earthquake and a vast tidal wave. By 1957, it had long been eclipsed by Kingston where *Warrior* berthed first at the Shell Oil jetty to replenish its near exhausted supplies of fuel before moving out to anchor in the harbour.

Jamaica was, to young European eyes, unforgettably beautiful with the dark green mass of the Blue Mountains rising against a deep blue sky. Later, as *Warrior* sailed away, the blueness of the Blue Mountains became more obvious but, right then, in the middle of February 1957 everyone was wanting to get ashore and stand on dry land. The ship's boat landing stage was the jetty of the luxurious Myrtle Bank Hotel. Robertson wrote his next two letters home on the hotel's notepaper. He walked into Kingston looking at the shops and bargaining with the hordes of street traders for shirts, hats and other knick-knacks. Not a few traders had already managed to get on board *Warrior* and it was noticeable that they were asking more for their goods than their colleagues ashore. Alas, his shopping complete, Robertson stepped into a bar for some refreshment and walked off later leaving all his purchases behind. Although he rushed back as soon as he realised his loss, it was too late.

Fortunately, Robertson had not yielded to the temptation to buy a stuffed crocodile from a truly ancient old woman who complained to him bitterly about life. 'I'm tellin' ya, we're in a hard times, man. Busta an' Manley are cousins, an' that's no good for us. I'm tellin' ya, man, we need a *white* guvhament. Buy a crocodile, sir. Think of the fatherless children. The little ones must eat.' Looking around, Robertson saw lots of little ones running around barefoot but looking suspiciously well-fed, so he put his wallet away.

That evening, he went into the bar of the Myrtle Bank and joined several other Warriors including Hutchinson who were chatting with the popular American singer of the time, Johnnie 'Mr Emotion' Ray. This early example of pop music stardom turned out to be surprisingly pleasant company while somehow appearing lonely, due in part, or so it seemed, to his increasing deafness. *He* didn't sing but the bar crowd were entertained all evening by calypso music. Some of the words were 'very coarse' but others were quite beautiful, reminding the *Warrior* visitors of African-American spirituals. Others were songs about West Indian heroes, such as *Cricket, lovely cricket* with the line '*And de bowling was superfine / Ramadin and Valentine.*'

The next morning, Robertson had to put in a hectic spell on the ship's gangway trying to welcome official visitors and fight off eager traders and, critically, knowing which were which. Distinguished guests who came on board for a cocktail party included not only the Governor, Sir Hugh Foot, who avoided the crush by arriving in one of *Warrior*'s helicopters, but also the Duke of Norfolk and Lord Cobham, the Governor-General Designate of New Zealand; these latter on the island to play in a cricket tournament.

Sir Hugh Foot arriving on board (Rowsell)

This meant being in full No 10 uniform of long white trousers and a high-collared jacket with little gold buttons and 'Midshipman's squiggles' at the neck. It was really much too hot for such formal wear and Robertson envied the Duke who, once on board, took off his jacket to display his bright purple braces. Perhaps the shore-going young officers themselves looked different from the general crowd; but talking over their recollections later, several of the Gunroom had noted the 'uniform' of rich American tourists; knee-length 'Bermuda' shorts, gaudy socks, flowery shirts and hats sometimes rather strange to British eyes. However, it was these tourists who contributed a large proportion of Jamaica's foreign earnings. Hume did his bit for Jamaica by buying a spectacular black shirt decorated profusely with yellow bananas, which attracted considerable, mostly favourable, comment from the Gunroom. Hutchinson didn't meet the Governor, father of his victorious rival for the Latin verse competition at school, but did meet an old friend and talented leg-spin bowler, Alan Duff, on the island for a cricket tour and a namesake, another Hutchinson, now on the staff of the Botanic Gardens.

Anson, already out in the Pacific in *Messina*, had also passed through Kingston on his way out to Christmas Island – intriguingly for him since he had been born on the island. He had written home about one incident and its aftermath.

'We pulled out of Jamaica in a terrible hurry, intent on reaching our destination as soon as possible with our stores that they needed so badly. Together with three other officers, I had ordered from a local man, who came on board in Kingston, a pair of lightweight black trousers to wear in the Mess in the evenings. We had each paid a £2 deposit on them and ten minutes before we sailed he had still not turned up. Just as the last wire was cast off we saw him in the crowd at the far end of the jetty frantically struggling with a large parcel. There was a shout to the Captain on the bridge: "Stop! He's got our trousers." It wasn't very much approved of, but at least we delayed long enough for him to throw the parcel up onto the fo'csle. The only slight drawback was that he had made all the trousers in pale blue material – with turn-ups!'

His story continued:

'The day after we left Panama was a Sunday, and we spent most of the day dyeing our pale-blue trousers black. It was a very messy business, done in the galley in a bucket that had to be kept on the boil. We managed to get nearly everything black except the trouser material which seemed almost impervious to the dye and needed boiling for a long time. Mine went in first and so came out the blackest – but oh! The fun and games I had trying to iron them. They had shrunk in different places and had to be stretched before they were pressed. Now that the turn-ups have been fixed and they have been pressed several times they look quite good.'

Riches recalls several events; such as the very satisfying discovery of Special Amber Rum and Coke, and the purchase after successful haggling of a light-weight tropical suit for 'only' £4/10/-; but cannot now recall what happened to have him make a diary entry saying that he got a ducking. Meanwhile Hume, who had the good fortune to know a family who had lived on the island for some time, was able to see more of the contrasts of wealth and poverty. American limousines shared the road with elderly Austins and both had to make room for the ubiquitous mule carts. Many streets were narrow and the houses on them shabby. The majority of the population seemed to be poor and throngs of little boys ran around trying to sell visitors anything from a newspaper or a postage stamp to a camera. Not from a little boy but from a small shop, Hume managed to buy a superb Leica camera for half what he would have paid in the UK. He was later driven by his friends to visit Port Royal and see Nelson's old fort and then, more poignantly, past the airport where Jamaicans, in thin suits and dresses, were queueing for flights to the UK, many encouraged to leave the island because of the ongoing sugar strikes and very high unemployment.

Cooper was on watch the first day at Kingston but contacted an old school friend who was stationed on the island with his regiment. He came by the following day in his elderly Austin 10 and took Cooper off for a jaunt up into the Blue Mountains and over to Ocho Rios. The car managed the climb well but they paused at the summit to give it a rest and persuaded some local boys to climb the palm trees and knock down some green coconuts. The milk was cool, sweet and very refreshing. They reached the Jamaica Inn with its own private beach of silvery sand fringed with palm trees, fanned by an onshore breeze coming in off a deep blue sea that broke gently on the beach. After a swim, they hired a couple of glass-bottomed canoes and paddled out to the reef to gaze at the vivid shoals of fish, the baby octopi and the colourful coral. Cooper became so excited at seeing one fish three feet long that he fell out of his canoe and was stung by a 'wasp' fish. In the way one measures these things in one's youth, he reckoned the pain was worth it for the fact that a beautiful American woman doctor staying at the hotel was there to anoint his arm. The two young men dined magnificently and then went on to a night club, recommended by the hotel manager, where they danced until nearly dawn. Cooper even managed to demonstrate the business acumen that would be developed during his later civilian career by getting the nightclub to cash a sterling cheque and sell him twenty US dollars at a very favourable rate; dollars he would later spend in Hawaii. This made all the rest of the Gunroom envious as they had been told (wrongly, as it turned out) that they would only be allowed six dollars each which, even back in 1957, wasn't going to buy very much. With his friend too tired (and emotional), Cooper drove the seventy-eight miles back to Kingston, managing the unfamiliar winding road and the hazard of unlit cars and bicycles, to catch a boat back on board in time to climb into his uniform in order to greet and entertain guests at the morning cocktail party. Then every guest was shipped ashore, the boats were hoisted and the anchor weighed as *Warrior* set sail for Cristobál at the northern end of the Panama Canal.

Although some of the ship's company were suspected of having started a day or two earlier, *Warrior*'s departure was also the official start of the ship's beard-growing competition – with prizes for the biggest, smallest, straggliest, scrubbiest, blackest, reddest, and so on – that would be judged just before arrival in Honolulu, still some three more weeks distant.

The Isthmus of Panama showed up on *Warrior*'s radar at 0225 on 19 February and at 0630 she approached the very busy harbour of Cristobál, the port at the Atlantic end of the Canal. It is located on the western edge of Manzanillo Island and is part of the city and province of Colón; Cristobál Colón being the Spanish version of Christopher Columbus after whom so many places in Central and South America are named. *Warrior* was making this transit since the timetable of the Grapple operation could not allow for the longer time it would take to go round the Horn, where, as had been seen in an Atlantic hurricane, there would be risk of still more damage, if not worse, in sailing round the tip of South America and into the Roaring Forties. The alternative of going via Suez was, for perhaps obvious reasons, not an option. So Panama it was: a younger canal than Suez, but with a 'back story'.

President Theodore Roosevelt had been ready to sign a treaty with Colombia until he was told that Panamanian rebels would offer the United States a much better deal if they could be supported against their Colombian rulers. In consequence, on 2 November 1903, US warships blocked sea lanes for possible Colombian troop movements en route to put down the rebellion. Panama declared independence the next day, 3 November 1903. The United States quickly recognised the new nation. On 6 November 1903, Panama's new ambassador to the United States signed a treaty granting rights to the United States to build and indefinitely administer the Panama Canal Zone and its defences.

Two long moles extend from both sides of one of the busiest entrances and exits in the shipping world. Very soon, Commander Begg's measurements and calculations would be put to the test. *Warrior* was going to be the ship with the widest beam ever to traverse the Canal, or so everyone believed at the time. However, research by Reed into the post-war history of *Warrior* reveals that when she was lent to the Royal Canadian Navy for a couple of years (1945–1947) she was sent from Halifax,

Canal pilot on temporary bridge (Riches)

Nova Scotia to winter on the Canadian west coast at Esquimalt near Vancouver and came back to Halifax the following Spring. So, in point of fact, this was *Warrior*'s *third* passage through the Panama Canal, but she remains the ship with the widest beam to have done so. On the passage from Jamaica, the Royal Engineer contingent on board had demonstrated their skills by erecting a temporary extension to the bridge out from the compass platform to just past the centre line of the flight deck, directly over the keel.

This was for the use of the Chief Pilot who needed to stand there equidistant from both sides of the locks. For a ship of *Warrior*'s size, there were, in fact, five pilots who came aboard via the starboard after gangway, each coming on deck announcing 'Hi, I'm Captain A, the pilot' and so on through B, C, D and E. The senior pilot, Captain Duncan, took station on the temporary bridge and B to E went two aft and two for'ard on the gun sponsons. As *Warrior* approached the entrance to Gatun locks, to be raised in stages the 85 feet to the level of Gatun Lake, she took lines on board from ten electric mules that ran on tracks alongside the waterway. The

Nine inches to spare (Rowsell)

Through the first locks (Rowsell)

*Into the narrows
(Rowsell)*

*And round the
bend (Rowsell)*

for'ard mules would pull the ship while the aft mules were there to apply a brake to forward progress if it was too rapid. The mules in the middle had the additional task of keeping *Warrior* on the centreline of the lock; just as well as there seemed to be little more than nine inches to spare on either side, if that.

Oulton remarks[2] that Commander Begg's 'careful calculations were vindicated'. Everything outboard of the sponsons had been removed during the refit in Devonport. However, Johnston, in the second sponson on the starboard side with one of the pilots, discovered that the supposedly detachable plate, for a navigation light, had been welded to the outside at one point. Sailors managed to get it half off, but within moments of entering the first lock the whole thing was scraped right off to the bare metal.

The pilots controlled the mules through their walkie-talkies, so the conversation went along the lines of 'Hold her Bill; I got about six inches, say four inches. Hold her, Bill. Fine! I'm towing on 1 and 2. Cut 3s. Let's send the 1s up the incline. Hey, Benny, how much you lack to get her in? Hold her, Bill. I can always stop her if you go too far.' Then the Chief Pilot yelled from his centreline perch, 'Pete! 50 feet lacking.' And so on. Once *Warrior* was at the level of Gatun Lake, a tug pulled her carefully out of the lock, the cable cars casting off at the very last moment, so tight was the clearance. As the ship was raised in each lock, the clearance widened; but the test would come on the way down. Were *Warrior* to be too far to one side she might tilt and get stuck; not something the Navy, never mind the pilots, could afford to let happen.

With only one pilot in control at this point, the ship was navigated from one set of leading marks to the next. The lake was dotted with little islands. It was possible to speed up slightly. It so happened that one Supply and Secretariat Sub-Lieutenant was doing his obligatory spell of deck duty, and he was on the compass platform relaying the pilot's instruction by microphone to the Quartermaster closed up on the wheel and engine telegraphs on the deck below. He had translated, 'Left 10' as 'Port 10' only to be told by the pilot he had meant come round to a course ten degrees to port, but when the Chief Pilot suddenly said to him, 'Right then, we're out into the Lake. Full ahead!' no one was fast enough to stop the unfortunate man before he issued what, in the Royal Navy, is an order to push the propellers up to maximum revolutions and never mind what it does to the boilers. The Navy's usual way of making greater speed is to order 'Half ahead both; revolutions One-eight-oh [for example].' It was the Captain himself who stepped over to the microphone and bellowed, 'Belay that,' then telephoned the Commander (E) in the engine room to apologise. Smug RNVR deck officers in the vicinity who had themselves only recently been taught the right way of doing things said nothing and looked away. Fortunately, by the time it came to 'cross the line' for the first time, King Neptune had either not been told or had forgotten and the Sub-Lieutenant's blushes were spared; perhaps because everyone was rushing to take a look at the alligator that had been seen on a raft passing by on the starboard side. Also passing by was luxuriant tropical forest on the islands and the shores of Lake Gatun; 'like sailing through the Palm House at Kew', remarked Riches in his diary. It did seem somewhat out of place to be sailing in an aircraft carrier through the jungle.

The next tight squeeze was the Gaillard Cut, not a lock but a narrow channel that twists and turns through a rocky, man-made gorge, past Gold Hill and Contractor's Hill and through which the ship was towed by yet another tug. This part of the Canal is a one-way system as there certainly was not room for two large ships to pass each other. The narrow channel also made it feel oppressively hot with the thermometer touching 90°F. The pilot still stood out on the centreline, calling out 'Stop Starboard' to someone standing in Flyco (Flying Control Position) who relayed the instruction to the Midshipman of the Watch, who would call to the Officer of the Watch standing by the pelorus (the ship's compass on its pillar) who repeated it into the microphone to the wheelhouse where the Quartermaster would repeat the order in acknowledgement and the Telegraphsman would ring 'Stop Starboard' to the engine room where the Chief of the Watch would ring the reply gong and turn his repeater to Stop. The Quartermaster would then announce, 'Stop starboard repeated, Sir!' With hindsight, this might seem just a trifle over manned, but this was 1957.

Warrior passed in similar fashion through Pedro Miguel and Miraflores Locks, without getting stuck, but at the point where the final lock gates opened to let in the salt water of the Pacific to mix with the fresh water brought down from the Lake, this caused a disturbance that created a current of up to six knots and *Warrior* had to wait for thirty minutes for this to subside before sailing out to Balboa to berth alongside the oiling jetty. The British Ambassador to Panama who had come aboard at Gatun Locks took his leave. The ship's passage had taken twelve hours compared to the average seven to eight for merchant vessels. While *Warrior* was oiling, Johnston managed to slip ashore just to say he had set foot in Panama, although it might possibly still have been in US territory. As he strolled there, he met up with an American and his family who had come to look at the ship and to gaze wide-eyed at the extent of the damage the force of the waves had done to the bow on the starboard side just below the flight deck. Then the American told Johnston he was a US Army Colonel and that he had spent some time on Christmas Island during the war – so the only person Johnston met ashore had already been to *Warrior*'s remote destination. At 2245 the ship cast off and sailed out into the Gulf of Bilbao and the start of the ocean passage to Christmas Island. However, to remind everyone this was an operational deployment and not a cruise, flying trials started in the early morning, only to be interrupted by the need to fly a medical case back to hospital in Bilbao. The chopper pilots reported sighting sharks following the ship! The next day, however, they spotted something else.

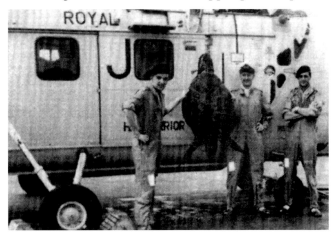

The turtle awaiting execution (Rowsell)

The safety helicopter was airborne during flying with a large net suspended below, large enough to scoop up a man in the event that there were to be a flying accident and an aircraft had to ditch. The immediate intention had been to retrieve Robertson who, for this exercise, was floating in a rubber dinghy. However, the CO of the ship's flight, Lt. Cdr Bricker, spotted and netted instead a large turtle. The unfortunate creature was landed on the flight deck and strung up by its back legs.

Then someone remembered Robertson, who had been left some *miles* back and was beginning to be concerned he had been cast adrift in the vast Pacific and would never see home again. He was picked up and landed just in time to witness the ship's M.O., Surgeon-Commander Pugh, a very tall and saturnine man with, already, a substantial black beard like a pirate's, administer the *coup de grâce* with a carving knife as big as a cutlass. Then it was *real* turtle soup in the Wardroom and Gunroom which was held to be a great treat. The Chief Officers' Cook announced, however, that such had been the smell in his kitchen that the Wardroom would have to cook the next one themselves.

There were regular sightings now of sharks, dolphins and flying fish as *Warrior* steamed majestically into the sunset, only some eighty to ninety miles north of the equator. As she sailed more or less due west, the sun rose astern, reached its zenith overhead, and set, very swiftly, dead ahead. The sunsets were spectacular. For ten days, no other ship was sighted. The night sky was wonderful; full of stars but not where the Midshipmen were used to seeing them. The Pole Star was just above the horizon with the Plough circling it and dipping below the horizon for part of the time. Orion's belt was overhead while the Southern Cross, which many were seeing for the first time, was visible above the south-east horizon. Sirius was brilliant and they could see Jupiter and Mars. Hutchinson recalls practising with his sextant and making full use of the wealth of available stars, 'A wonderful display.' Officers turned one of the sponsons into a shaded terrace with awnings and a few seats. To make up for lack of other excitement, there being no Japanese protesters or Russian submarines within sight, attention focused on the beard growers. Some had given up as a result of feeling too hot and prickly but the Gunroom reckoned Midshipman Dennis, with a jet black growth on a pale skin, was well-placed to win a prize. Others were *told* to desist. On watch one forenoon Johnston was examined by the Captain who shook his head and told him to go below and 'take an India-rubber to your chin'. Lt Bagg rather unkindly said of the youthful-looking and smooth-skinned Midshipman Reed 'Laurance has been cheating! He hasn't shaved for nineteen years!'

Some 500 miles from Christmas, an RAF Hastings flew low over *Warrior* and dropped a package into the sea which, despite lowering the ship's duty boat to retrieve it, sank without trace. Commander Begg sent an anxious signal ahead asking what was in the package; after all, it might have been something precious like mail from home. The signal came back quickly; 'Crustacea for Duck'. Members of the Wardroom commiserated with Squadron Leader 'Roly' Duck, the RAF liaison officer on board, about missing out on his seafood supper.

With the National Service officers now frantically practising their star sights, and their 'Sun-Run-Suns', the ship's position was plotted from each successive longitude to the next, and on schedule, on 4 March, *Warrior* reached landfall at Christmas Island. At this point a little ceremony took place. Commodore Gretton, who had been in command of the naval forces for the Task Force Commander, had just been invalided out of the Operation, and *Warrior*'s Captain Hicks was promoted to Commodore, 2nd Class, in command of all the Navy units under the Task Force Commander. At exactly twelve noon on the appointed day, the new Commodore's broad pennant was hoisted and the man himself appeared on the bridge with the broad gold band and circle on his epaulettes, which had been flown out especially by the RAF. Since a circle looks the same in either direction, no one could have said *he* had them on the wrong way round.

Commodore Hicks' broad pennant (Rowsell)

---

1 R A Begg, *One Man's Ditty Bag, A Naval Biography* [unpublished] Imperial War Museum

2 Oulton, p.209

MARCH

Christmas Island and Hawaii

March came in like a lion for Riches. While he was on post-Suez leave in early January, others had loaded the Christmas Island stores and supplies into *Warrior*'s hangars, piling them high and lashing them down and making them ship-shape for the passage to the Pacific. There had been time to allocate a place for everything and to make a note of where each item had been put. By contrast, all of the cargo, including those many crates of beer cans, would now have to be off-loaded and safely taken ashore within a matter of less than four days before *Warrior* embarked several hundred Army and RAF personnel for a well-earned jolly to Honolulu. One hangar had also to be completely cleared so that the ship could host a cocktail party there for an estimated 400 guests. As Riches remarked to his private diary, the ratio of guests to officers would be about four to one and, of those four, around 200 would *surely* be female and, of these, *at least* one hundred ought to be under thirty; so who knows? This thought had to sustain him through working watches round the clock to bring the stores up to the flight deck as *Warrior* came within twenty-four hours of reaching her destination, and then to prioritise everything for the most effective unloading. An earlier start was ruled out for fear of rough weather. Riches actually found he was enjoying this phase; one of the rare chances when Supply Officers get to work outdoors. However, among the Midshipmen enlisted to paint ship to improve the carrier's appearance ahead of its visit to Honolulu, there were several who would gladly have changed places with him. Later, however, when *Warrior* was at her Christmas Island berth, the off-loading began and the island's high humidity replaced the accustomed cooling breeze over the flight deck, hard work in the open air had less to commend it.

On 4 March *Warrior* reached Christmas Island, described as 'low and dangerous' on the charts, and sailed round to her moorings in the anchorage on the western, leeward side where she was fuelled and victualed in turn by two of the RFAs waiting for her. *Wave Ruler* ran more or less a shuttle service between Christmas and Singapore, where she took on great quantities of diesel; while *Fort Constantine* plied between several ports and Christmas bringing mostly frozen food. Fresh produce was usually flown down from Hawaii on a regular Hastings shuttle.

Apart from being the operational base for Operation Grapple, Christmas Island's other claim to fame is that it is the largest coral atoll in the world. On the chart, it

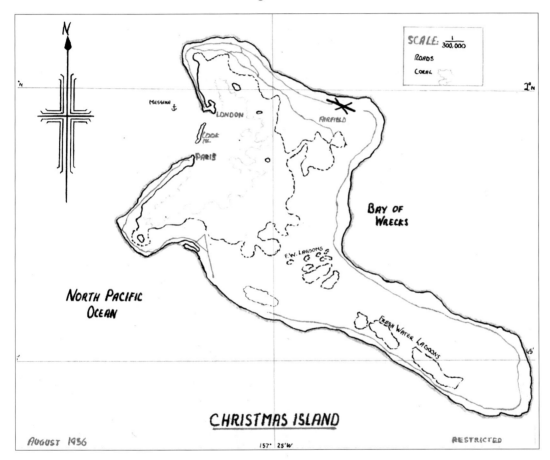

Anson's chart of Christmas Island (Anson)

looks like an adjustable spanner with the open jaws facing west and enclosing the main sea-water lagoon which takes up about half the area, with many other smaller, silted-up lagoons accounting for much of the rest. That part of the atoll is very roughly twelve miles square with the handle of the spanner running from the south-east corner for about sixteen miles and five miles at its broadest. This latter part is about half sandy dunes and half so-called fresh water lagoons which are replenished by rainfall; rainfall which varies from 6 to 100 inches per year. Apparently 1957 was an 'in-between' year. Daytime temperatures range from a spring-like 70°F to a torrid

100° and the humidity is generally high, some of the edge being taken off that by the easterly trade winds that blow fairly continuously.

Like all atolls, Christmas Island is low lying, generally not more than 10 feet above sea level, but the wind pushes the sand dunes up to around 20 feet with the occasional higher ridge. The bay on the windward side is called the Bay of Wrecks of which there was visible evidence. Along the northern coast, on the two-mile wide strip of land between sea and lagoon, the Royal Engineers had built the heavy-duty concrete and tarmacadam airstrip and the tented dormitory camp and hutted administration buildings. Not much grows on the island apart from some coconut palms in the north-west, the copra and coconuts from which were harvested by itinerant Gilbertese workers, and service personnel were not supposed to collect them as souvenirs. Surrounding the whole island are coral reefs that can be several hundred yards in width. These constitute a hazard to boat-running as the Midshipmen were about to discover.

Although the Gilbertese had visited the island, calling it Abakiror, or the 'faraway island', the reefs and the island were first discovered by Europeans on Christmas

James Cook, Naval Captain and explorer (1728–1779) (National Maritime Museum, United Kingdom)

Eve, 1777, led by the indefatigable Lieutenant (later Captain) Cook RN in his ships *Resolution* and *Discovery* and recorded in his Journal.

1777 December Wednes. 24. On the 24th about half an hour after day-break, land was discovered bearing North-East by East, half East. Upon a nearer approach, it was found to be one of those low islands so common in this ocean; that is, a narrow bank of land enclosing the sea within . . .

Thursday 25. At day-break, the next morning, I sent two boats, one from each ship, to search more accurately for a landing place; and, at the same time, two others, to fish at a grappling near the shore . . .

Sunday 28. On the 28th, I landed, in company with Mr Bayly, on the island which lies between the two channels into the lagoon, to prepare the telescopes for observing the approaching eclipse of the sun; which was one great inducement to my anchoring here . . .

Tuesday 30. On the morning of the 30th, the day when the eclipse was to happen, Mr King, Mr Bayly and myself went ashore, on the small island above-mentioned, to attend the observation . . .

Wednes. 31. Having some cocoa-nuts and yams on board, in a state of vegetation, I ordered them to be planted on the little island where we had observed the eclipse; and some melon seeds were sown in another place. I also left, on the little island, a bottle containing this inscription:

Georgius Tertius, Rex 31 Decembris, 1777

Discovery, Cap. Clerke, P.

As we kept our Christmas here, I called this discovery Christmas Island . . .

The 'small island above-mentioned' is now called Cook Island and lies across the mouth of the lagoon between the landing place called Port of London and the opposite tip of the main atoll called Paris. It turned out to be a good place for banyans; the Navy's name for picnics. No trace has ever been found of the bottle and inscription left by Captain Cook, but in 1835, F D Bennett, a visiting naturalist, noted the presence of yams, melons and coconut trees which might well be the descendants of those Cook planted.

Anson had the advantage of arriving nearly six months earlier than *Warrior* and he wrote a description of the island and his routine in a letter home. Since *Messina*'s arrival there, he was on watch every other day but with little to do other than boat running, daily rounds and rum issue, morning and evening colours, inspecting Libertymen going ashore and keeping the ship's log. The training programme had been pushed aside and they were off duty for the greater part of the time. Life consisted of waking up each morning to another cloudless blue and emerald green day, eating a great deal of good food plus a little washing and ironing – which Anson found to be a very satisfying task – reading a little more from the Pelican *History of England*, or perhaps a novel from the ship's library.

This would be followed by a quiet snooze after lunch with a cool breeze through the cabin. About four in the afternoon Anson might take a boat ashore and swim for a while in the lagoon, chasing the colourful tropical fish in and out of the coral, or simply enjoying a stroll along the beach, collecting cowrie shells. In the cool of the evening he might watch a film on the upper deck. Seen from afloat, the occasional walk in the sand might seem attractive, but for those who had to *live* ashore, the sand and its various life forms soon became very *un*attractive. The sand gets everywhere, the tents are hot and infested with huge land crabs which crawl all over the beds at night. A shower is a bucket with holes in it which you have to hoist up and stand under – short and tepid. The electricity goes off at 10pm every night. The food, although it had improved after a near mutiny, was not to be compared to the Navy's catering. As Anson wrote home, 'That seems to be the way the Army live, and the rougher it is, the better they like it. Thank God for the Navy.' His shipmates even managed to supplement and vary the ship's catering by catching tuna, and with one fish weighing 140 lbs there was plenty for everyone. 'The bass are good too and the flying fish sail right up onto the deck and are popped straight into the pan.'

Anson noted with pleasure the arrival of eight more Midshipmen whom he hoped to get to know quickly. Earlier, he had had the advantage of an aerial view of Christmas Island to help him restore his first more idyllic view, going up in an RAF Hastings to get a look at the island and take a few photographs. It was a most splendid sight from the air, such a maze of blue, green and red. The whole place was dotted with pools and lakes and looked much like a sponge from a height. It was quite cool above 3,000 feet and for the first time since he had come out there he had been in a temperature of less than 90°F.

Six months before *Warrior* arrived at Christmas Island, the problem of how to give the services a period of rest and recreation had been addressed by the Navy; first by the Royal Marine officer in *Messina*, and then taken over by Anson, who had to act more or less on his own initiative. When the island had been designated as the centre of operations for Grapple, there had been tricky negotiations with an American airline, South Pacific Airlines (SPAL), who had acquired rights to use the island's lagoon as a staging post for seaplane flights across the ocean and had constructed a base camp on the far side of the island that would make an excellent R & R base with a little hard work. The UK bought out SPAL when the Grapple project started and SPAL left behind several wooden huts filled with all the luxuries of living. The pongos [Navy slang for soldiers] pinched most of the beer etc. when they arrived here, but that was soon stopped and the idea evolved of turning it into a rest camp for the forces. As the Army couldn't spare the necessary hands to knock it into shape, Anson spent a week up there with another Midshipman from *Messina* and a few other bodies making the place habitable. The NAAFI provided some coloured sun umbrellas and chairs. It was a strange set-up of complete American luxury and roughing it at the same time with two fridges; washing, drying and ironing machines, toasters, a gas cooker for Calor gas and hundreds of small things like modern lamps, cushions, pillows, towels, etc. Anson's team had to connect up all drains, put in fresh water and salt water plumbing systems, make the electric generator work, fix incinerators and garbage pits, build a kitchen, and get enough stores, beds, food etc. for people to live here. In addition, the 20 tons of gelignite sitting in a tent outside had to be shifted as it was outdated and dangerous. The greatest problem was that all fresh water had to be brought from the ship, a good one and a half hour journey. On the Friday they shifted 5½ tons of gelignite down to a copra boat at the end of the jetty and took it out to sea and dumped it. Hundreds of these 50lb boxes had to be carried about a quarter of a mile – and they did it all before breakfast in case it should get too hot in the sun later in the day. Nothing went wrong (although Anson dropped a box and saw his whole life flash in front of him!) There were three permanent staff besides Anson: a cook, a stoker to work the generator and a shipwright to do all the construction. This last, a tiny dour Scotsman, reckoned that he was indispensable and tried to run the place. Added to which Anson caught him pinching bathroom fittings and had to have a serious talk to him. They had a first trial run leave party of twenty Army who had a splendid time – being served tea in the morning in bed (!) – and they behaved very well on the whole. While 'lights out' was at midnight on Saturday, the holiday makers took their beer out into the moonlight and sang songs and danced round the bushes until about 4.30 in the morning – and they were up at 8 a.m. the next day. They only broke two tumblers and departed with profuse thanks. The Army provided a very fine wireless. 'I think one of the most peaceful moments I have had since we started was last night – standing on the beach just outside the house with the moon shining, the waves lapping, the smell of warm palm trees and faint Hawaiian music coming from the wireless. It certainly makes life feel worthwhile!'

That Christmas on Christmas Island, the personnel there had the pleasure of sending home Christmas cards designed by the very much in fashion cartoonist, Rowland Emett.

Emett's 1956 Grapple Christmas card (Emett Society)

Meanwhile, back in March 1957, despite being called Port of London, the landing area had almost no other characteristics in common with its more famous namesake; and this was even *more* true of Paris! The steeply shelving sides of most Pacific islands meant that, by contrast with James Cook's ships, there was insufficient anchorage for large vessels like *Warrior* and the RFAs which had to be moored to the offshore buoys that had been laid for them by *Salvictor*. The reef surrounding the atoll afforded only a narrow passageway into the spit of land that enclosed the landing area. The water was shallow and the currents sometimes tricky with three rather ramshackle wooden jetties. Fortunately, the problems of unloading cargo there had been worked out by the earlier arrivals involved in setting up camp, off-loading men and heavy machinery to build the airstrip and keeping them fuelled, supplied and provisioned. *Narvik* and *Messina* had used their Royal Marine crewed LCMs and a DUKW to ferry personnel and supplies from ship to shore. There were also two or three pontoons made from six-foot-sided steel cubes, bolted together and fitted with outboard motors, which provided an invaluable area of flat surface onto which larger items of cargo could be lowered from the ship. However, there was no way of cancelling out the effect of the long rolling Pacific swell, which meant for boat runners and crane drivers the distance from the net of cargo being unloaded to the boat or pontoon could vary by much as fifteen feet in as many seconds. Furthermore, the speed at which the cargo needed to be taken ashore meant that it had to be a twenty-four-hour operation and not just during the twelve hours of equatorial daylight. There were other minor delays when two heavy fork-lifts were put on the hangar lift together with several crates of heavy stores and the lift blew a fuse.

Supply Officers had to separate out the scientific stores from the military and the naval, check off the stores against the inventories and ensure that each crate reached its correct destination. They did try to keep a running tally of what was leaving the ship, which was not too difficult for the large crates, but as the unloading moved to the smaller crates, they came up on deck thick and fast. Attempts to get these smaller objects passed through an administrative 'funnel' between the tally-checkers were only intermittently successful, with the fork lift drivers tending to 'hide' small packets for the weather ships behind huge army refrigerators. One or two items of cargo did not make it safely ashore. One crate slipped out of its net and went straight to the bottom, and on the last day of unloading, as Riches watched from the flight deck, completely unable to do anything to prevent it, a small crate slipped off the pontoon and splashed into the sea. It bobbed to the surface and had only just been retrieved with boat hooks and muscle power when it began to smoke and foam. Lest the gas were toxic or flammable, even as Riches checked frantically through the cargo manifest, the order was given to tip it back into the sea. As it foamed even more and slowly sank, he was able to confirm that the crate had contained foam-filled fire extinguishers.

While supply officers did the checking, deck officers were in charge of the lowering. Large reels of telephone wire were lowered by torpedo derrick onto a pontoon. Cooper felt the empty hook was being hauled up too slowly and he told the winch operator to speed things up. Unfortunately, the operator then hauled it up so fast that the hook was pulled right over the sheave at the end of the derrick, wrecking hook, sheave and the wire, judged to have been overstrained and in need of replacement. Cooper had a few anxious moments before he learned he would not be personally billed the £50 for a replacement wire.

Riches checking off stores (Riches)

As the troops and then the stores were being more or less safely taken ashore, the Midshipmen were learning not just how to drive but how to handle small boats as they took charge of the cutters and the motor boat running from ship to ship as the Commodore visited the vessels under his command, and from ship to shore with mail and libertymen. They also had to come to terms with the swell that could place the starboard after gangway platform anywhere from several feet below the sea at one moment to several feet above the boat's gunwales the next. The boom extending out from the ship's side for'ard of the gangway was where boats tied up, and their crews had to climb the Jacob's ladder before inching sideways along the boom itself to gain the safety of the deck; a good test for former Upper Yardmen. Sensing that the ship's roll was going to lower the boom so far that he would get a ducking, Robertson recalls scrambling up the ladder but losing his footing on a broken rung and falling backwards into the shark-infested waters. His crew hauled him out and then he had no choice but to climb the ladder again, this time more slowly, sodden wet and with his sandals slipping dangerously on the boom. It was clear to all the Midshipmen that taking small boats inshore wasn't going to be as simple as driving the car down to the shops.

Despite the haste to off-load and sail away to Hawaii, time was taken to establish cordial relations between *Warrior*'s Gunroom and the officers of the RFAs. By contrast to the warship, there were many fewer officers on the supply ships and they responded generously to the hospitality they received. *Wave Ruler* was the first in the queue and four Midshipmen enjoyed an evening on board before *Warrior* sailed for Honolulu.

Warrior was moored about half a mile offshore at the edge of the bluest waters imaginable, and in daylight the course to steer from the ship to the landing area was reasonably obvious. The channel through Cook Island passage had been marked with dan buoys and leading marks, but small boat operators had to be wary of cross currents and coral heads. Moreover, only two of the buoys were lit at night and one of them was out of position for a time, being directly *over* a strip of coral rather than marking its edge. The passage through the reef itself was fairly narrow which meant that any sea running would rush through the gap with the surf foaming on the coral on each side.

Once ashore, Christmas Island did not strike anyone as being an attractive place to stay. As Cooper wrote home, 'Army tents form what is called Port of London, with a lavatory right in the middle of Trafalgar Square.'

Beyond pure white sand, some beautiful sea shells and a few palm trees, the only attraction was the swimming in the warm shallow waters of the lagoon through which were dotted sharp-pointed coral heads plus the occasional non-threatening sand shark and huge manta ray. One did have to avoid 'fire' coral which could inflict an immediate burning skin rash. Cdr Begg, in order to point out the hazard, carefully speared some and waved it in front of his listeners. Unfortunately, the waving dislodged the coral and the water which splashed up was enough to give them a mild rash.[1] And if

'Trafalgar Square' (Riches)

Port of
London
(Riches)

that were not enough, going too far from the beach risked getting caught in undertows or even being swept out of the lagoon itself.

Hume's journal records the need to turn boats stem for stern at the jetty so as to drive straight out and into the channel, since there was insufficient water to go

Jetty at Port of London (Riches)

astern and turn, especially with the fairly steady 12 to 15 knot wind liable to blow the boat into the shallows or towards the coral.

From the port to the main camp and airfield there was a ten-mile road of sorts. Stretches were laid with blue lagoon sand which had dried hard and seemed impervious to the regular heavy rainstorms. Other parts, however, were pot-holed and rutted and these created axle-testing water-splashes for the unwary driver. Near the port was the Gilbertese village where the copra harvesters lived in native long-huts alongside a plain wooden building with a rusty corrugated iron roof, the whole edifice standing off the ground to prevent land crabs getting into the island's centre of civilian operations. This was the office of Percy Roberts, the New Zealand Colonial Service Officer, outside which a Union Flag flew beside a plain white noticeboard on which was neatly lettered the sum of his many responsibilities:

DISTRICT OFFICER
CUSTOMS AND EXCISE
AGRICULTURAL ADVISER
PLANTATION OFFICER
POST OFFICE

In several of his roles, Roberts sold the Warriors Gilbert & Ellice Island postage stamps and stamped a number of passports. He could also issue Christmas Island driving licences and even passports. Johnston bought some stamps and a copy of *The Structure of Gilbertese*. (He distinctly remembers reading Chapter 1; several times.) After the main Grapple operation was over, Roberts would hitch a lift to the UK in *Warrior*, sailing with the ship round South America. Whether he gave his agricultural advice on the subject is not on record, but the Task Force Commander had already taken action to combat a problem that was obvious as soon as one stepped ashore. Attracted by the odour of sweat which streamed from every human pore, flies abounded and plagued every new arrival. Their normal source of nourishment was dead land crabs, of which there seemed a never-ending supply, but before refrigeration equipment was installed at the main camp there was the plentiful addition of food waste and other 'gash'. When this was reported to him, Oulton recalled insect-borne epidemics of which he'd had unhappy experiences. He issued immediate instructions from London.

'I want an Auster aircraft with full agricultural pesticide spraying equipment purchased instantly – I don't care where you get it or how much it costs, and I want it flown to Christmas in a Hastings with as much liquid DDT insecticide as you can get on board. Jump to it! NOW!'[2]

Within two weeks, the suitably equipped Auster was flying dawn patrols over the airfield and campsites. Its pilot was immediately dubbed 'Captain Flit' and joined that small group of people like 'Harpic' who were only ever referred to by their soubriquet. (As an afterthought, so nearly nil was the radiation detected from fall-out that this regular DDT spraying may well have done more long-term damage to human health than the weapon trials.)

With the stores off-loaded in record time and in less than the five days allowed for in the programme, the ship's boats brought off nearly 400 eager Army and RAF holidaymakers for their jaunt to Honolulu. As *Warrior* prepared to sail, a met report came in saying that there had been an earthquake in Alaska which had triggered off a tidal wave that was due that night to reach the Hawaiian Islands. Reassurance was given that it would only be three or four inches high by that time. Few in those days had heard the word *tsunami*. Before she could finally sail, however, a party of Midshipmen was assembled, seven men with seven sacks and several shovels and sent ashore to collect sand and seashells from the seashore to be used as part of the ambitious décor for the on-board cocktail party in Honolulu. Riches had been involved as the assistant to the Captain's Secretary in the exchanges of messages about the visit to Honolulu. Both the Americans and the British, he told his Gunroom colleagues, seemed to be planning to make it a memorable event, such was the rarity of a British warship visit to Hawaii, or, as the several expert historians in the Gunroom wondered, was it that the 'Yanks' were hoping to expunge the memory of how Captain Cook had been so badly treated there some 180 years previously? One point was clarified to slightly anxious Midshipmen. There would be an Admiralty contribution to the costs of the cocktail party. This was important because Wardroom and Gunroom officers are generally expected to pay for any hospitality their ship extends on a 'per stripe' basis, and even a Midshipman's 'share' of a party for 400 could amount to a serious sum of money.

As *Warrior* steamed north, 'a painted ship upon a painted ocean', no one was allowed to forget she was a working ship training herself up for a critical role in the Grapple operation. The Midshipmen were by now expected to demonstrate their increasing competence and self-confidence by 'taking charge' while the Officer of the Watch, the Navigator and the Commodore looked on. Johnston was on watch as *Warrior* carried out a flying exercise which involved bringing the ship round into the wind, but for optimum take-off and landing conditions, the wind needed to be coming from about ten degrees on the port bow. He had brought the ship round and steadied it well enough but there needed to be this final correction. As he should have known, to bring the wind from straight ahead to 10° on the port bow, one needs to turn the bows to starboard but, given to occasional confusion under stress between his left and his right, he ordered, 'Port ten' for which he was immediately admonished by the Officer of the Watch, the Navigator and the Commodore, speaking in chorus.

Commodore Hicks in false beard (Rowsell)

At this point in the passage the beard-growing competition was judged. Riches was glad to shave his off; it had become so itchy, and despite Dennis's highly commendable efforts he had done likewise

*Prize winner
PO Bartlett
with Cdr Begg
(Rowsell)*

for the same reason. He did receive a mild reprimand from the Commander however! Shaving off a beard needs permission as well as growing one. The overall winner was 'Darky' Bartlett, a Petty Officer with a dense black growth from above which his eyes peered out beneath the brim of his cap.

Having become accustomed to horizon-to-horizon sunshine, it was a surprise to encounter heavy rain and high winds as *Warrior* passed through the Inter Tropical Convergence about five degrees north of the equator. Although the passengers were very put off by this turn of events, the Midshipmen, as veterans of Atlantic hurricanes, took it all in their stride. However, the rough seas had the disappointing effect of lifting a fair amount of the newly applied paint from the ship's sides. Nor was the Commander best pleased when the wind direction blew black sooty smoke from the funnel all over his cocktail-party-ready flight deck. After a couple of days, however, normal sunshine was resumed and by the time *Warrior* picked up the pilot on the morning of 13 March, everyone was keyed up to see and sample Hawaii and its legendary hospitality. On this occasion it was the Army Port at Honolulu where, at Pier 40, *Warrior* was brought alongside. The ship's band played manfully on the flight deck, its first public appearance, with Midshipman Kirchem, dressed like the others in 'square rig', on the euphonium. This involved some tricky manoeuvring with the assistance of tugs, and the considerable distractions of a banner proclaiming 'Welcome HMS *Warrior*', plus a US Army band playing 'The Happy Wanderer' and a team of young hula-hula dancers on the jetty waving their arms and swaying their hips in ways that had an aphrodisiac effect on men who, apart from the two motherly WVS ladies who ran the NAAFI, had not seen a woman for quite a while.

Warrior *entering Army Port, Honolulu (Rowsell)*

No sooner was the gangway run ashore than the dancers and their musicians streamed on board and continued their entertainment on the flight deck. As the Commodore stepped forward he was mobbed by the dancers who garlanded him with flowery leis and invited him to dance. If he seemed a little reluctant and not so agile, this was certainly not true of the ebullient Commander and the athletic Robertson, who both waggled their hips for Britain to wild applause from the spectators.

And then it was down to the serious business of shore-runs. The Commodore and

LEFT: *Robertson and friend (Rowsell)*

TOP RIGHT: *Reception Committee (Rowsell)*

BOTTOM RIGHT: *Begg and another friend (Rowsell)*

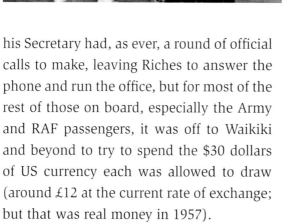

his Secretary had, as ever, a round of official calls to make, leaving Riches to answer the phone and run the office, but for most of the rest of those on board, especially the Army and RAF passengers, it was off to Waikiki and beyond to try to spend the $30 dollars of US currency each was allowed to draw (around £12 at the current rate of exchange; but that was real money in 1957).

Several of the Gunroom exercised their temporary entitlement to shop at the American PX (Post Exchange) which seemed to them rather more like Harrods than the NAAFI. Cooper treated himself to a fibreglass fishing rod, spinning reel and line for $10. He and Hume then took a taxi to Pearl Harbour where, as they expected, they were stopped at the gates by the Military Police. They were in civilian clothes and were at first refused entry. However, Cooper produced his identity card and the sentry snapped a salute and issued a pass immediately. They drove around for a while, looking at the ships and pausing to gaze at the wreck of the USS *Arizona*, now a war grave. It was a beautiful natural harbour but somehow smaller than they had imagined. With another flourish of his ID, Cooper was shown in to see the Officer of the Deck who drove the pair of them further round in his Jeep and then took them in to see the American Naval barracks which, all chrome and wood, compared very favourably with Victoria Barracks in Southsea although the sleeping quarters were more crowded. Hume noticed the 'help yourself' breakfast buffet and saw, for the first time, individual small packets of cereal which had not yet made their appearance in the UK. In the middle of an extensive lawn was a large swimming pool with translucent blue water. Finally, their guide showed them the 'brig', the prison cells, but told them these had now been converted into comfortable quarters for the Master-at-Arms and his staff.

When they returned to their cab, it was to discover it had been given a ticket for parking in a tow-away zone. However, the OOD bawled out the three MPs who had issued it saying they had 'as good as issued a ticket to the Queen of England' and made them take it back and apologise. On behalf of Her Majesty, Cooper graciously accepted their apology.

The flight deck cocktail party in the evening was judged a great success by the Navy since it led to an overwhelming number of official and unofficial invitations for the Wardroom and the Gunroom. It was only marred by one minor incident. A hot dog stand had been set up to make the Americans 'feel at home,' and the senior visiting US Admiral was invited to inaugurate it by enjoying the first bun and dog. Fried onions were strewn liberally along the cut bun and a piping hot dog laid on top, before, carefully wrapped in a napkin, it was handed to the unsuspecting guest of honour. Of course, the mustard pot had not been forgotten and no one was surprised when the Admiral picked up the long wooden spoon and dipped it into the bright yellow mustard. It was only when the Brits saw him slather a generous spoonful along his hot dog that realisation began to dawn that this was not the soft, sweet and gentle American mustard he was used to but the hot and harmful English variety he had probably never tasted before in his life. Fortunately he only took a small first bite and the Commander was there to administer a soothing drink to comfort the eye-watering senior officer. However, the feedback from Americans was that it was a 'swell party!'

That may also have been the verdict of the Officers' Stewards who acted as waiters. Afterwards, Johnston was on the for'ard gangway inspecting those going ashore and failed to notice Steward Smith swaying gently, allowing him to leave the ship somewhat less than sober. Unfortunately for Smith, and later Johnston, the Commodore was being driven off to an evening engagement and spotted the steward no longer swaying but staggering. He had his car stopped and ordered Smith back on board. Investigations revealed that he had managed to consume a fair amount of the liquor provided for the party. He was given a reprimand and Johnston was given a warning about his future conduct.

It needs to be recorded here how many of the other members of *Warrior*'s crew, both senior officers and lower deck (not forgetting Officer's Steward Smith who was generally good at his job and for whom the Gunroom officers had a very soft spot) provided the support, structure, guidance and backing, without which this group of young National Service officers would neither have been able to contribute very much to *Warrior*'s role in Operation Grapple nor had such a tale of their adventures to tell in the first place. This was especially true of – among others – the Navigator, and of the splendid crewmen in the ship's various small boats without whose seamanship skills some of the young officers could often have been in serious trouble.

Some of *Warrior*'s ratings who safely went ashore had discovered one interesting fact about America and began to take advantage of it. The British tradition of blood donors is not the American way. Hospital emergency blood banks *paid volunteers* for blood at a very reasonable rate per pint. Sailors queued up to give blood and later queued up at various bars to enjoyably replace their fluid loss with the local rum.

The British Consul had brought his daughter to the party, as had the local QANTAS manager, and it was Cooper and Riches who found themselves chosen as their post-party escorts. It was out to dinner and an exotic menu including teriyaki steak and ice cold rum *ad libitum*. The dinner bill – and the drinks with the dancing until 3.00 a.m., long after the parents had gone home – came, in Riches's estimate, to over £80, nearly six months' pay for a Midshipman, the tab for which was picked up by one of the fathers. Overall, the climate, the torch-lit beaches at night, the 'exotic' fish and fruit and the sheer size of the steaks, sometimes larger than the plates they sat on and unimaginably thick for Brits, all of whom could remember rationing, gave Honolulu an aura of paradise on earth.

Another difference that the then all-white British noticed was the multi-ethnic mix of the population and the seeming lack of discrimination or exclusion; although not too many white Caucasians seemed to be doing manual labour. This was especially obvious on the visit to the Libby's pineapple canning factory which was situated only

50 yards from where *Warrior* was docked. That was where the Navy visitors heard the somewhat cynical story that the missionaries came to the 'Sandwich Islands' to spread Christianity but many went into sugar and pineapple farming; in other words, 'they came to do good – and did well!' The industry had grown over the previous nearly sixty years to the point where seventy per cent of the world's pineapple crop was currently grown in the Territory of Hawaii.

On arrival, the visiting Warriors were greeted with chilled pineapple juice and fresh slices of the fruit before being taken on a tour of the cannery. By then, much of the process was mechanised, with the stalk and spiked top-knot sliced off and the fruit then peeled, cored and sliced to the standard size of the can. The only hand process was at that point where slices were inserted into the cans which went on to be topped up with syrup, sealed and labelled. A ripe pineapple is generally about two years old but they are 'succession' planted so that the farmer can harvest three crops a year in the benign and consistent Hawaiian climate. Libby's rival, Dole, almost next door, had a water tower in the shape of a pineapple which the Libby's workers said was 'overripe and ought to be harvested'. The Midshipmen returned to *Warrior* carrying fresh pineapples for the Gunroom.

The next morning, Riches worked with two US Air Force staff sergeants who bought fresh fruit and vegetables from Chinese wholesalers who brought their wares to the jetty. He was impressed by the high standards insisted on by the Americans before they would buy anything. The sergeants, both trained food inspectors, opened each crate and examined the contents scrupulously before they approved or, on occasion, rejected them. When they found several bruised grapefruit at the bottom of one crate, they rejected the whole consignment of fifteen crates, ignoring the protestations of the vendors and their suggestions that they inspect the other crates. It was on this visit that *Warrior* arranged to have a twice weekly air-lift of fresh produce sent down by Hastings from Honolulu.

Hutchinson had his own strong impressions of the visit. 'I remember the holiday beach where Cook was killed; the all-pervading 'stink' of pineapple; the loneliness and friendliness of retired people who approached us; eating and enjoying avocado for the first time and, more dramatically, the sight of the stricken battleships in Pearl Harbour.' Robertson recalls discovering the absolutely dramatic difference in taste between a slice of pineapple cut fresh on the spot from the field, in the warm sun, and the utterly different quality of the canned stuff.

Where the notorious attack on Pearl Harbour is concerned, undoubtedly the Japanese had planned ahead before they made their pre-emptive strategic strike, but Hutchinson had recently read critical tracts against imperialism, telling tales from retired Admirals and others claiming to be in the know. They suggested the US government knew the attack was coming. They had laid out the bait, the famous battleships with no air cover, past their peak as effective warships, but national treasures to be destroyed, rousing American public opinion to back a declaration of war. The modern and really useful warships, the aircraft carriers, were sailing around out at sea out of harm's way. As he realised from what he had seen and read, there were complex layers of significance in the Pearl Harbour memorial.

At the end of the day, Johnston met up with the journalist Larry Cott who ran the newsroom of station KHVH and whom he had met at the cocktail party. Cott took him to the roof of the station, which sat on top of the Hawaiian Village Hotel and afforded a panoramic view right round from Diamond Head along the Waikiki Beach and over to Pearl Harbour – but only if one went up onto the roof! From the studios themselves no window looked out at all! After that, the sight of American colour television was a disappointment, so poor was the colour quality. Cott, by way of a thank you for being allowed to record several bosun's pipes which he broadcast at the appropriate times of day, then presented *Warrior* with a hundred 45 rpm records for the ship's rediffusion equipment (SRE), including one by Little Richard entitled '*Wham! Bam! Thank you, Ma'am. I hope you're satisfied*' which would prove a very popular request item.

All too soon, but not before Reed posted off an orchid to his parents, the visit was over and *Warrior* was warped out of Pier 40 with the assistance of a tug and set sail due south to carry on with Operation Grapple preparations. Once back at Christmas Island, Johnston worked with Lt Calcutt in the studio of the ship's SRE to record messages to be sent back home to Portsmouth for playing to a gathering of families and friends of crew members with a record of their choice from the KHVH treasure trove.

The second half of March was an opportunity for the Midshipmen to put their boat-running skills to the test and, in the sense that one only ever learns from one's mistakes, one can say with confidence that a great deal was learnt. Some of the time for *Warrior*'s boats had to be spent assisting other ships in mooring to their allocated buoys. This process involved taking the ship's 'grass line' to the buoy and landing buoy jumpers on the selected mooring to thread this through the ring and pass it back to the ship. Then, as the ship nosed up to the buoy, she lowered a cable with a shackle which the buoy jumpers, including a blacksmith, had to secure to the ring. Manoeuvring could prove tricky. On the day when Reed was due to hand over his small boat running duties to Hutchinson, their boat was called away to assist the RFA *Fort Rosalie* to come to her buoy by catching her grass line and taking it to the buoy. Reed sat for'ard near the stem of the boat and let Hutchinson demonstrate his capabilities. Alas, a sudden jolt ran through the cutter as, somehow or other, the line managed to become wrapped round its propeller. On Reed's order, one of the crew dived into the sea to cut the boat free but it was to no avail. Helpless, the cutter tied up to the RFA. However, *Fort Rosalie*, noting that she was drifting towards the reef, started to go astern. A great surge of water came between the cutter and the ship's hull. The painter was pulled tight and Reed distinctly heard a splintering noise. He thought it was the stanchion but in the next moment almost the entire gunwale on the port side was torn away.

Warrior had seen their distress and sent another boat to the rescue. Since Reed was the officer still in charge of the cutter, he was the one who got it in the neck. 'The Commander sounded forth and, rocking back on his feet, asked, 'Are you aware, Mister Reed, that we can still flog Midshipmen in the Navy?' Then, looking down from his great height, he added, 'and your cap is filthy!''

Robertson went with the Navigator, the Boatswain and two local Gilbertese who knew where the significant coral heads were located to lay dan buoys in the lagoon so that sailing races could be held. The Gilbertese fished while the sailors laid the dan buoys, but all they caught that day was an unfortunate gannet attracted to the feather lure. Luckily it was freed without too much difficulty. The next day, Robertson, the Navigator and Cooper went to explore access to Cook Island through a gap they found in the reef so that leading marks could be placed for future visitors. As they approached the beach, in the wake of Captain Cook, they dropped a kedge anchor astern and paid out a line in order to prevent the cutter broaching to as the constant pressure of the waves pushed it forward. They grounded the bow on the sand and put out a line for'ard before setting up the leading marks. Then they explored the island, remarking on the number and tameness of the sea birds, especially the gannets, one or two of which could be persuaded to sit on the young men's wrists.

It was the nesting season and they had to be careful where they stepped. They decided to bathe on the lagoon side of the island but, as they waded into the sea, they saw some sharks wallowing in the shallows. Cooper was holding a camera and was attempting to photograph them when he happened to glance down and found another shark having a much closer look at *him*. He turned the camera on the shark, clicked and then ran back to the shore, shaken but not scarred! Alas, the image itself was too shaken to reproduce here. They spent around five hours on the island and the next day Robertson was taken into the sick bay with a reported life-threatening temperature of 105° F. His recollection of the events was affected by his illness but he had clear images of lying under blocks of ice as the medical team battled, quite literally, to save his life. He wrote home a week later saying that, as yet, no one had said definitively what had struck him although the MO was saying 'glandular fever,' and that 'a jugful of my blood has been sent off to Honolulu for laboratory tests'. The report came back from Tripler Hospital and it revealed 'hyperactive lymphocytes and pronounced heterophile antibody titer'.

Being cabined, cribbed and confined to the Sick Bay, he felt rather out of things but he did have a stream of visitors from the Gunroom and he was particularly pleased how often the Navigator looked in with magazines. The mystery illness was to keep him in the Sick Bay for three weeks before he was sent ashore to 'recuperate' and regain some of the 30 lbs he had shed. This was to lead to his having a different perspective on the events of Grapple from the rest of the Gunroom. He missed the Crossing the Line fun and games and did not get to see Malden on *Warrior*'s first visit to the 'operational area.'

Meanwhile, Hume had an alarming experience in his cutter. It was a planned late night run into the Port of London, but in the dark he made the unfortunate error of setting off from the starboard after gangway at the usual angle relative to the ship's side, not noticing in time that the tide had swung *Warrior* about sixty degrees from her earlier position at the buoy. Since the marker buoys for the channel were poorly lit, he did not notice until too late that there were breakers ahead and he was heading straight for the reef. Reckoning he had time to turn, instead of going 'full astern' and backing away from the reef, he put the tiller hard over. However, as soon as the boat came broadside on to the sea, the waves lifted it straight onto the reef where it was stuck fast in about two feet of water. Using the boat's Aldis lamp, they signalled for help which came in the form of illumination by *Warrior*'s searchlights and in the person of the Commander appearing on the crest of a wave bearing a line. He managed to paddle the inflatable surf boat through the foaming sea and attach the line to the cutter which was passed back to *Warrior*'s motor boat, standing off, which had sufficient power to pull the cutter off the reef, although it was badly holed and only its buoyancy tanks were keeping it afloat. They made it back to the ship under tow and a crane hoisted the damaged craft up onto the flight deck. Then Hume and his coxswain were given a fairly mild lecture by the Commander on the need to develop one's seamanship and with it an appreciation of how to handle changing circumstances. An inquiry, which routinely follows such incidents, decided not to reprimand Hume and he continued to run boats including taking the Commodore and other senior officers on an overnight fishing trip, well away from the reef of course. However, a message about the incident must have been sent to King Neptune as later events would reveal.

In yet another boating incident, Kirchem was sent off at 21.30 to collect a banyan party from Cook Island and managed to get completely lost and run out of fuel, while seven of his fellow Midshipmen were dining with some ceremony with the Commodore. When the apparent disappearance of Kirchem, his cutter and his crew was reported to the Commodore by the Officer of the Watch, as in accordance with standing orders it had to be when life and limb might be threatened, the dinner party drew to a hasty conclusion. As ever, the Commander went in search of them.[3] All the men and the boat were eventually found and the banyan party brought back on board, but it all took until midnight.

To set against this catalogue of calamities, all of the boat runners experienced and enjoyed seeing and hearing the various forms of aquatic accompaniment every time they made their journeys to and from the shore. There were the shoals of flying fish that would suddenly appear and skim across the bow, occasionally landing in the boat. At night, the sound they made as they smacked back into the sea was like a vast kettle boiling. Sharks and manta rays cruised below, ignoring the boats altogether, but by contrast the dolphins seemed to revel in being the boats' escorts. If one lay down on the boat's bow one could see one or more of them riding *ahead* of the boat, moving to port or starboard as the boat moved, using the pressure of the boat's bow wave on their backs to 'steer' with. At other times, they would leap out of the water and perform their own form of 'aquabatics' doing barrel rolls and even somersaults before smacking back down into the water. It was impossible not to believe the dolphins were actually smiling. They were certainly enjoying themselves, as were the Midshipmen. Not having a boat to run, and as if he did not have enough to do, Riches decided at this time to take up rug making and ordered a kit from Yorkshire. It is true that, while at Christmas Island, all members of the ship's company were encouraged to take up some form of occupational therapy, but with temperatures below deck only a little below 100 degrees a more unsuitable choice would have been hard to find, as Riches later remarked. He was partly inspired by discovering that a fellow officer made very attractive fancy waistcoats in his spare time.

On Monday, 25 March, a day without a breath of wind and with a temperature in the nineties, the Task Force Commander paid a visit to *Warrior* and gave officers and men a pep talk. On the Wednesday of that week, however, three storerooms flooded, with the loss of 5,000 lbs of flour and an unspecified quantity of puffed wheat. The ship's boxing competition culminated in the semi-finals on the Friday and the finals on the Saturday. Some Gunroom members performed what Riches's diary describes as 'a rather sordid sketch as part of a ship's concert, but an appreciative audience did laugh heartily.'

To round off the month, Cooper went snipe shooting with the District Officer. He compared this expedition – which was not very successful, seeing only two birds since the local Gilbertese had apparently frightened the rest away – with going after the same birds back in Dorset, where 'they are no good until there has been a good frost.' He also went fishing in the lagoon and tried to harpoon a manta ray,

Fijian member of King Neptune's Police (Rowsell)

which would have none of it, but did get sufficiently annoyed that it harassed an unfortunate swimmer who, having mistaken the tip of a manta ray's wing for the triangular fin of a shark, never went back in the sea again.

On 29 March a detachment of Fijian RNVR ratings arrived in HMNZS *Pukaki* and *Rotoiti* and joined *Warrior* for three months training. They brought colour and song and delightfully cheerful personalities as well as kava in full measure together with considerable natural seamanship, and sometimes specialist skills such as

*Manta Rays in
the swimming
pool (Riches)*

diving ability, which on occasion was to prove very valuable to Midshipmen in charge of the ship's boats.

While the colour and song may be self-explanatory, none of the members of the Gunroom had ever experienced drinking Fijian yaqona, made from the roots of the kava plant and found on many islands across the South Pacific. The ceremonial of preparing the drink by pounding roots with a little added water is as much part of the tradition as its serving. At a yaqona ceremony, the principal guest is offered a *bilo* of yaqona, a muddy brown watery liquid, in a half coconut shell. The recipient must clap once, drain the bilo and then clap three more times. Accordingly, the Commodore was invited to have the first bilo which he saw off with gusto. Drinking yaqona brings a numbing of the tongue and a relaxing effect. Comparing notes, the Gunroom consensus was that it tasted like liquorice water and was what they would call an 'acquired' taste. However, amongst the thirsty crew of *Warrior*, there was always a willing group of sippers and gulpers when the Fijians brewed up.

And then it was off again, crossing the equator to visit Jarvis and Malden.

1 Begg, R A, p.151

2 Oulton, p.159

3 Commander Begg was the complete seaman. Called away from a formal Wardroom dinner to deal with another boating incident, despite wearing full mess dress with medals, he could still produce his seaman's knife on its rope lanyard round his waist.

APRIL

Both Sides of the Equator

In April, the Admiralty finally agreed that *Warrior*'s crew were 'overseas' and therefore entitled to Local Overseas Allowance. However, believing that there was nothing at Christmas Island on which to spend extra money, their Lordships classified the area as zero-rated. Cdr Begg's papers show he felt that was mean.[1]

At sea there are no signposts, but Royal Navy ships usually know where they are, especially when they cross the Equator and move into southern latitudes. *Warrior* was to 'Cross the Line' fourteen times in the course of her voyage; but the first time, on 2 April, was marked by an event which started with ceremonial pomp but descended into utter chaos.

Neptune and his court, with the ship's band playing, rose from the depths (with the assistance of the after lift) and proceeded in state to the dais, attended by the Royal Barbers and Physicians. The Royal Bears closed up to action stations there. Conducting a levée, the Court invested the Commodore with the Order of Neptune (First Class) while the Commander was awarded the Order of Fish Head (First Class). Various other dignitaries received royal recognition for their efforts but one was foolish enough to make a face at the Royal Bears and was thrown to them for punishment. This led on to the

King Neptune and his Queen (Rowsell)

91

*The Royal
Barbers
(Rowsell)*

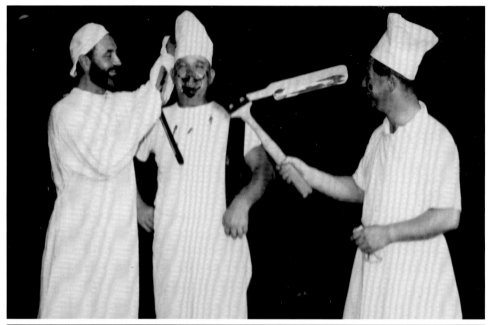

*The Royal
Mermaids
(Rowsell)*

Distinguished Courtiers (Rowsell)

Royal Guard reporting for duty (Rowsell)

*Royal Policemen
on Parade
(Rowsell)*

*Miscreant
thrown to the
bears (Rowsell)*

*Royal Musicians
(Rowsell)*

*Final scene of
chaos (Rowsell)*

Court, sitting now as a court-of-law, considering charges against a number of the crew for the injuries they were alleged to have caused to the many and various subjects of Neptune's undersea realms. Without exception they were convicted and awarded summary punishments.

Up to this point, Hume had been an innocent spectator; but then, with no warning, he was arrested by one of the Fijian Royal Policemen, conveyed onto the stage and heard the dread Warrant read out.

> *WHEREAS it has been represented to me that IAN MAITLAND HUME, Rating: Coxswain (u/s); Conduct: Regrettable; Character: Destructive; Leave: Broken; did on Sunday 24th March carry out a most unprovoked and brutal assault on 24 million of our most innocent and loyal subjects, to wit coral polyps, by deliberately and with intent, smiting them a resounding clout with a 32-foot motor cutter, thereby causing considerable alarm and panic among the 24 million polyps but also the stoker of the boat, the Boat Officer, the First Lieutenant, the Commander, the Canteen Manager, the Chief Gunnery Instructor, the Navigator's Yeoman, the Fresh Water Tanky, the Sea Cadet Liaison Officer, the Engineer's Writer and the PO's Messman,*
>
> *THEREFORE I hereby judge him, the aforesaid IAN MAITLAND HUME, to be brought before the Royal Physicians who will bisect, trisect, disect, infect, defect and disinfect him, open and clean his bickets, tighten his crutches and remove his rowlocks, after which he is to be shaved and thrown to the Royal Bears.*
>
> *GIVEN under my hand on the Equator, this Second day of April 1957.*
>
> *NEPTUNE, Maris Rex*

Fortunately he was wearing his swimming trunks; but for him that was perhaps all that was fortunate, since he was enthusiastically molested and had putty pills administered, washed down with sea water, was coated with an evil-smelling concoction, had sticking plaster applied everywhere and, worst of all for him, was tickled with malice aforethought. Then he was passed to the Royal Barbers who smeared him with glue and tipped him into the pool to be vigorously ducked by the Royal Bears. Finally he was tossed three times into the air before being allowed to stagger off.

He took it all like a man, but silently vowed to make sure his boat running could never again be faulted.

Hume was not alone in being indicted and punished. Lt Allen, the pilot who had made a heavy landing on the flight deck and woken up the barnacles on the ship's bottom; Lt Fogg, the ship's dentist, apparently for simply being the ship's dentist; a Chief Mechanic for venting avgas (aviation fuel) into the sea and causing nausea to certain fish – all had to endure the ritual. Those watchkeepers who could, with relative safety, look on from the bridge reminded themselves that, given the plans for *Warrior*'s various journeys, the wrath of Neptune might, one day, just as easily fall on them. As the official ceremonies drew to a close, a certain riotous spirit took hold. The 'rioters', led by one Midshipman plus many of the spectators on the flight deck, some armed with the remaining foam fire extinguishers, advanced menacingly on the Commander, in full dress uniform, and on Neptune and his Court, all of whom finished up in the pool. Arriving off Jarvis Island later that day was something of an anti-climax.

Discovered by Europeans in 1821, annexed by the US in 1858 while the guano deposits were extracted, and then abandoned by them in 1879, Jarvis was subsequently annexed by the UK in 1889 but never exploited. The island was occupied again by the US during World War II and then again abandoned. In 1956, a Decca Navigator master station was set up there, but the lonely souls manning it needed regular supplies of everything, including fresh water since there is scant rainfall and no natural water sources. In their time off, the Decca operators could walk round the cemetery with four graves and stroll along the remains of the tramway that was used to move the guano. The whole island is an oblong, roughly four or five square miles in size. *Warrior*'s helicopters landed the supplies and brought the 'islanders' on board for a bath and a good meal before taking them back and setting course for Malden, arriving there the next day, 4 April, a long way from anywhere. Anson, like Captain Cook, had been there already.

'Malden is quite a small island, only 3 x 5 miles and we lost our way and would have sailed right past it if the other Mid. had not spotted it! The trouble when we got there was trying to anchor, as the bottom was solid, smooth coral and there was no holding ground. We had one anchor up and down seven times! And you can't play with eight tons of metal like a yo-yo all day. Everything got red hot – tempers as well – before we managed to let go all our three anchors at once and somehow stayed put. [...] on the last day we beached the ship as a trial run for the next time we go there. It does seem a bit strange walking out of the bows of your ship and on up the beach. The island is quite flat, bare and lifeless and quite suitable to have three or four bombs dropped on it. The pigs are very thin and unfit for eating, and anyhow there was no time to go chasing after them.'

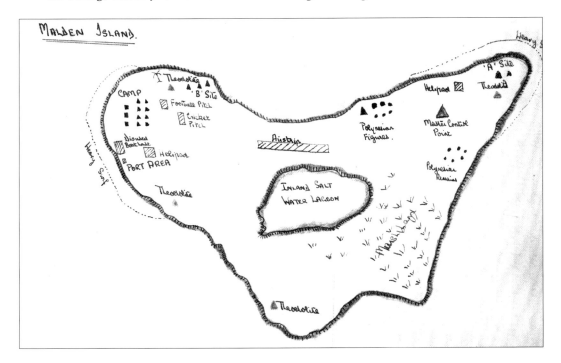

Malden Island from Riches's Journal (Riches)

Malden Island merits some historical and descriptive attention, given its role in Operation Grapple as Ground Zero for the nuclear tests. It was first discovered by Europeans when in July 1825 Captain the Rt Hon Lord Byron (cousin of the famous poet and inheritor of his title) sailed by in HMS *Blonde*. While the only living creatures he came across were birds, a species of small rat, and some copper-coloured lizards, he did find traces of human occupation, including the remains of ruined temples and other structures indicating that the island had at one time been inhabited. The ancient stone structures are located around the beach ridges, principally on the north and south sides. From the 1860s until 1927, the extensive deposits of guano were quarried and shipped out. A visitor to Malden in the guano-digging era, Beatrice Grimshaw, described the 'glaring barrenness of the island', declaring that '...shade, coolness, refreshing fruit, pleasant sights and sounds: there are none. For those who live on the island, it is the scene of an exile which has to be endured somehow or other'. She described Malden as containing 'a little settlement fronted by a big wooden pier, and a desolate plain of low greyish-green herbage, relieved here and there by small bushes bearing insignificant yellow flowers'. Water for settlers was produced by large distillation plants, since no fresh-water wells had been successfully dug on the island.

The five or six European supervisors on the island were given 'a row of little tin-roofed, one-storeyed houses above the beach', while the native labourers were housed in 'big, barn-like shelters'. Grimshaw described these edifices as being 'large, bare, shady buildings fitted with wide shelves, on which the men spread their mats and pillows to sleep'. Their food consisted of 'rice, biscuits, yams, tinned beef and tea, with a few cocoanuts (sic) for those who may fall sick'. Food for the white supervisors consisted of 'tinned food of various kinds, also bread, rice, fowls, pork, goat and goat's milk', but vegetables were hard to come by.

The guano diggers constructed a unique railroad on Malden Island, with cars powered by large sails. Labourers pushed empty carts from the loading area up the tramway to the digging pits, where they were then loaded with guano. At the end of the day, the sails were unfurled, and the carts were whisked back to the settlement by the prevailing south-easterly winds. While carts were known to jump the tracks more than once during these excursions, the system seems to have worked fairly well. Self-propelled railroad handcars were also used. This tramway remained in use on Malden as late as 1924, and its roadbed still exists on the island today. Although guano digging continued on Malden until 1927, no further human use seems to have been made of the island before the arrival of the Task Force in 1956. There are still some human remains in the little cemetery, including one very poignant tombstone recording the death of a youngster 'taken by the wild waves'.

The island has roughly the shape of an equilateral triangle, with five miles on each side. A large, mostly shallow, irregularly shaped lagoon, containing a number of small islets, fills the east central part of the island. The lagoon is entirely enclosed by land, but only by relatively narrow strips along its north and east sides. It is connected to the sea by underground channels, and is quite salty. Most of the land area of the island lies to the south and west of the lagoon. The total area of the island is about fifteen square miles. Malden is very low, no more than 33 feet above sea level at its highest point. The greatest elevations are found along a rim that closely follows the coastline. The interior forms a depression that is only a few metres above sea level in the western part and is below sea level (filled by the lagoon) in the east central part. There is no standing fresh water. A continuous heavy surf falls all along the coast, forming a narrow white to grey sandy beach. Except on the west coast, where the white sandy beach is more extensive than elsewhere, a strip of dark grey coral rubble, forming a series of low ridges parallel to the coast, lies within the narrow beach, extending inward to the island rim.[2] The nearest inhabited island is Penrhyn, (Tongareva) some 280 miles away, and Penrhyn itself is around 420 miles south of Christmas Island.

Chosen for its remoteness, this barren spot was to be the datum point for the first three H-bomb tests. At a Grapple meeting in London about a year earlier, Captain Guy Western RN had reported on the location and access to it.

> 'There's a reef right round the island, except for a gap of about 200 feet wide on the north side, and there is usually a strong tidal current between the reef and the shoreline. There's another hazard too. In the case of one visiting ship which put a landing party ashore, some of the oars were bitten off by sharks!
>
> At the gap in the reef, there are the remnants of a jetty and a few derelict buildings and part of a light railway used for the guano export, but nothing of any use to us.'[3]

Although Western's report initially convinced the Task Force Commander that there needed to be an airstrip for fixed wing aircraft, the LCMs and DUKW from *Messina* were in the end able to ferry heavy items ashore. By January 1957, Malden was operational.

By the time of *Warrior*'s arrival, scientists assisted by *Narvik* and *Messina* had set up their base for the telemetry that would record the tests, and Royal Engineers had created the leading marks, the southernmost being a fifty-yard sided concrete triangle liberally coated in luminous paint, which would be the final visual guide to the bomb-aimers in the Valiants as they came in directly over *Warrior* on their final live run.

Midshipman Dennis found the passage in to the island a challenge for his already considerable seamanship.

'Malden Island was an extraordinary place – a triangle of flat land with a solitary sun-blasted palm tree at the southern tip. The Landing Place, so-called, was a small gully in the stones between two spits of pebbles. This caused the rollers to break in an uneven fashion so that in the middle there was a small area of relatively still water where the sea wave motions met – it was probably this area of gentle back and forth motion which kept the boat in a stable position, assisted by frequent manoeuvring of the Kitchen rudder gear. The trick was to head straight at the middle of the gully and, at a certain distance off, throw a sea anchor over the stern to steady the boat in position in the slick of relatively still water. Then, by using the rudder gear, you manoeuvred the boat at the same time as watching the bearings you had made on your approach. You nosed the boat gently towards the shore, and when close enough but not aground you ordered the passengers ashore – they jumped into the breaking waves and strode ashore – obviously swimming rig was essential as it was a very wet landing and there were no drying facilities ashore. Once the passengers were landed, heaving-in on the sea anchor with the Kitchen gear in position 'astern', you revved up and went astern into the waves and made back for *Warrior*. It was a tricky operation but with the three good crew that I had (a bowman for'ard, a sternsheetsman aft and an engineer) – all went well. It was an amazing experience in boat handling and without the Kitchen rudder gear I do not think that landing using such big boats would have been possible. It was real Arthur Ransome – *Swallows and Amazons* – stuff.'

The 'Kitchen' rudder is the familiar name for 'Kitchen's Patent Reversing Rudders', a combination rudder and directional propulsion delivery system for relatively slow speed displacement boats which was invented in the early 20th century by John G A Kitchen of Lancashire, England. It turns the rudder into a directional thruster, and allows the engine to maintain constant revolutions and direction of driveshaft rotation while altering thrust by use of a control, rotating a wheel under the tiller, which opens and closes the metal quadrants enclosing the propeller and thus directs thrust forward or aft. Only the rudder pivots; the propeller itself is on a fixed shaft and does not reverse direction to go astern.

In terms of sheer numbers of islands visited, Anson has the edge. Having arrived earlier and given *Messina*'s role as something of a tramp steamer taking supplies, equipment and personnel to these further flung places, he probably saw more of them than the other Midshipmen. This month, ahead of *Warrior*'s visit, Anson in *Messina* travelled to Penrhyn (Tongareva), an atoll about ten miles across and the most northerly of the Cook Islands.

'We anchored just outside the lagoon and it took about two days to unload all the various bits of cargo we had brought for the place. The natives came out in their canoes as soon as we arrived and were all over the ship doing barter for grass skirts, pearl-shells and carvings which they make themselves. They use pearls instead of money ashore and bargain with them at the Trading Store to buy clothes and food. They are a most colourful lot but rather idle [...]. On Wednesday we held a party on board for the village children and had to cope with 250 of various sizes while they looked round the ship, played games and had a huge tea in the dining-hall. Some of the smaller ones got quite tired and fell asleep so we had sailors wandering round the ship with armfuls of sleeping babies looking for likely owners!'

The islanders laid on a dance in the Village Courthouse that evening and sailors had a splendid time doing semi-European dances with barefooted dusky partners in tow. Of course there was the inevitable display of hula-hula and local dances encouraged by guitars and ukuleles and a native beating hell out of an old tea chest. The crew got back to the ship late that night, and early the next morning the ship was hit by a fierce rain-squall. The terrific wind dragged the anchor right off the reef and *Messina* had to do some hurried manoeuvring to keep from going aground. One of their LCMs had its bow ramp torn off by the surf as it was coming through the reef, so the ship hoisted them both and left the island pretty quickly.

She sailed on, found a little island called Starbuck and had a look just to see that no one was living there. It was very like Malden without any trees and quite small. From there she sailed on to Malden where she met up with *Narvik* again. The ship spent a couple of days there and back-loaded some of the plant that they had brought down previously. Then she sailed to meet *Warrior* at Jarvis Island. This again is much like Malden, but has a small party of 'Decca' radio engineers living there to operate a Direction-Finding Beacon.

Cooper wrote in his Midshipmen's log on 9 April that the meteorological officers had now started producing weather charts with 'stream lines' rather than isobars. These are lines showing the currents of air at different altitudes. They draw 'stream lines' for the surface and about every 8,000 feet up. This gives a 3-D effect for the air currents. For the Grapple operation they are especially interested in the wind speed and direction, not only at weapon release altitude and below, but right up to 60,000 feet. The higher altitudes were important because of the need to forecast accurately the fallout pattern. Balloons to measure the wind were tracked by 277 radar to heights up to 100,000 feet. An understanding of the winds and temperatures in the upper atmosphere was essential since the cloud from a major thermonuclear explosion would almost certainly rise through the troposphere to the temperature inversion layer, at around 50 to 55,000 in the tropics, known as the tropopause, and go on up into the stratosphere, possibly reaching as high as 100,000 feet.

In the middle of April, now just a month away from the first megaton test, *Warrior* rehearsed the drills that would be necessary on the day itself. Everyone on deck had to wear full anti-flash gear – trousers tucked into socks, gloved hands and anti-flash hoods plus dark goggles.

Anti-flash gear being worn (Anson)

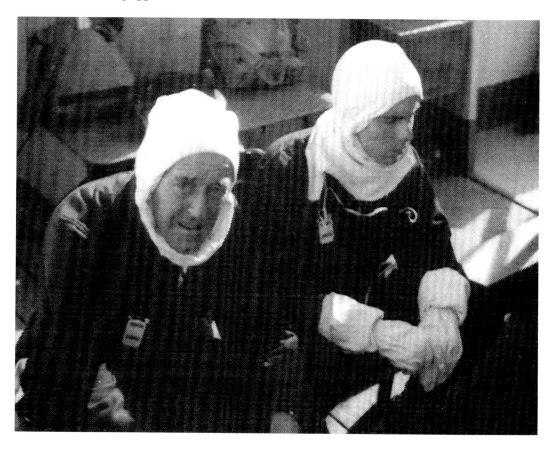

Then, acting out the possible scenario that the bomb had been released and successfully detonated but that there was some risk of radioactive fallout, everyone not on watch on the 'island' was ordered below. The so-called pre-wetting hoses were activated and water was sprayed over the island and flight deck. This was intended as a preventative measure to cause any radioactive fallout to be washed overboard before it had a chance to lodge; a more effective procedure than trying to wash it off after the event. For those below, in a metal box not far south of the equator on a hot day and with no ventilation, the conditions became harder and harder to bear. Temperatures rose in some parts of the ship to around the 100° mark and in the engine and boiler room spaces could reach 105 and even 110.

Other emergency eventualities had to be prepared for. For example, should the test be cancelled sometime after the Valiant was airborne, there was no viable procedure back at Christmas Island to receive the primed bomb back again to dismantle it, nor could the Task Force Commander have sanctioned the Valiant landing with the weapon still on board. It would have to be ditched at sea; making that whole test a write-off.

On the way back north to Christmas, *Warrior* refuelled the New Zealand frigate *Pukaki* abeam. This procedure, with the ships only about 20 yards apart and both travelling at 12 knots, involves a considerable feat of seamanship, made no easier by the long rolling Pacific swell. Lines are fired across and then jackstays rigged to support the hoses connecting the two ships. The lines supporting the hoses need to be tended continuously. Just to add spice to the operation on this occasion, the two ships were required by the Commodore to perform zig-zag manoeuvres such as would be essential at times of any threat from submarines. The operation was exciting for those off-watch to spectate, but rather more taxing for those in both ships doing the actual transfer.

Meanwhile, back on Christmas Island, Robertson was 'enjoying' sick leave. After three weeks in the Sick Bay, he had been sent ashore for a ten-day convalescence, to get some sunshine, do some swimming and put on weight. A tall young man, well over six feet, he had normally weighed around fourteen stone, but during the course of his illness he had shed more than two stone and all his ribs were showing. His first two days were spent at the RAF 'hospital' in the main camp near the airstrip, some five miles from the landing at London. He wrote home from there.

'The six bed "main ward" where I slept [...] is one of the few relatively solid erections on the island, and everything was really quite pleasant and comfortable.

(The plumbing, of course, is primitive in the extreme.) The people in there with me were a cosmopolitan lot, but we all got on very nicely together – a Squadron Leader who came in to have seventeen teeth out; a civil servant attached to one of the Fleet Auxiliaries who had a badly broken ankle and was waiting to be flown home; a Sergeant who had fallen asleep with a cigarette in his hand; an aircraft handler who had been "unwise" in Honolulu or Kingston (or possibly both); and last but not least a National Service Ordinary Seaman from *Warrior* who had fallen thirty feet down one of the ship's lift wells as a result of walking backwards without looking and came out of it with nothing worse than a couple of slightly fractured vertebrae.'

Robertson learned that this last patient was the son of a senior Admiral, and a little disappointed at not being selected for a commission which, sadly, may have been due to his most distressing stutter.

After a few days, Robertson was moved out to live under canvas. He was now attached to the main camp officers' mess, which had nearly 300 members and in consequence rather more amenities than the hospital. He shared his tent with one of *Warrior*'s Air Maintenance Officers who was based there to look after the ship's shore-based aircraft. The significant difference between living on board ship and on shore under canvas was the presence of other life forms. There were rats, smaller than the British brown rat, more like overgrown field mice, but the real enemy was the army of land crabs who seemed able to surmount whatever barricades were erected and came into the tents at night. Several of *Warrior*'s aircraft maintenance ratings were also ashore and had found from experience that land crabs who successfully made it into their tents would then burrow into the sand and die. This gave rise to a dreadful stench which could scarcely be dug out. It was better simply to pitch the tent somewhere else. The ratings devised other things to do with land crabs, however. They would capture a few and paint names (not ranks) and numbers on them and organise races.

Robertson's several employments were still reading and writing plus short spells of sun-bathing; almost enviable if it weren't so boring after a few days. He noted the old hands on the island who were by then a mahogany colour, which he compared with his rather pallid skin after three weeks in the Sick Bay. Away from Port of London, there was no swimming off the beach, which had been banned outright since a recent fatality resulting from the unfortunate victim disobeying orders and getting caught by the strong undertow. However, paddling was still permitted and was refreshing up to a point. He also visited the airfield to look at the considerable number and variety of aircraft involved in the operation.

However, as well as sun, there was rain; and when it rains on Christmas Island it can be like machine-gun fire. Apart from leaving an inch or two of standing water on the runway which takes time to disperse, it cools the atmosphere down for a while but it also gives the meteorologists, busy forecasting when conditions would be suitable at Christmas and over Malden for an air burst of a hydrogen bomb, additional working problems.

After three weeks, the doctors declared Robertson fit for 'light duties', but it had been decided at a higher level that there was need for a capable junior officer at the Joint Operations Centre on the island, the hub of the whole Grapple Operation. Robertson was seconded and found he was the only man working there who had not been 'security vetted'. The authorities decided that it was too late to bother with writing to ask anyone if he'd ever been a Young Communist, etc. and otherwise checking on his brief career to date. Besides, by then, Staff Officer, Operations (SOO) had given him just about every secret document on the operational side to read, learn and inwardly digest.

The place swarmed with senior officers, including the Task Force Commander, an Air Vice Marshal who, according to Robertson, looked astonishingly young and was an exceedingly pleasant person. He wrote home, 'You asked about the Japanese protest fleet. Certainly we are expecting them, and indeed as prepared as we can be; and as a matter of fact I may be flying up to Honolulu for two or three days later this week to help my chief with some enquiries on that score. I hope so, if only for the pleasant change! A short "jolly" is just what everyone longs for; especially the poor wretches who have already been out here for ten months.'

And there were other ways in which Robertson was able to relieve the tedium. One day he was given a lift back from 'Ops' by Wing Commander Hubbard, in command of the bomber squadron to be used for dropping the bomb. He was delightfully friendly and offered him a ride in one of his aircraft – needless to say Robertson accepted with alacrity.

Warrior returned to Christmas from that first visit to Malden and from the trials of men, ships and aircraft necessary to tune everyone and everything to a fine pitch in time for the first live test. This, it was generally assumed, would be around the middle of May. Actually, since he was privy to the messages exchanged by those in charge, Riches knew when the first test was scheduled and his fellow Midshipmen knew that he knew, but nothing could tempt or trip him up into telling them; and since Robertson was ashore he couldn't be pumped for information either.

Back at Christmas Island, matters of morale received attention. Johnston was the recording engineer for a number of 'Hello Mum' contributions from the crew to be sent back and broadcast or played to the Mums back home. Lt Calcutt did the interviews. The incoming mail included recordings made back in the UK of messages from their families for members of the crew. Johnston put these out on the SRE, and by all accounts they were very much appreciated. He wondered if there would be anything from Suva for the Fijian FRNVR sailors who were always singing and playing their guitars.

Lt Bagg and Johnston, as Divisional Officer and his deputy, took about half the junior seamen ashore to Cook Island for a banyan, sixteen and seventeen-year-old boys having the time of their lives and saying that if this is what the Royal Navy was like they would like to sign on now for twenty-two years. Lt Bagg told them about Arctic convoys and other less attractive aspects of a naval existence. The place teemed with birds, sufficiently trusting to move away only as one came very close and showing resistance or mild aggression only if one approached their pebble and seaweed nests. The birds swarmed in their thousands but only the occasional frigate bird showed any inclination to dive bomb the intruders.

Back on board, Johnston had received some LPs of classical music from his parents, and in order to play them added a classical hour to the SRE programme; but he let himself be carried away by starting to play Stravinsky's *Ebony Concerto*, which had been commissioned for and was played by Benny Goodman on his clarinet. However, its spiky rhythms and atonal harmonies provoked adverse reaction throughout the ship, and even a call to the SRE on behalf of the Commodore himself. *Ebony Concerto* was swiftly faded, never to be broadcast again, and, moments later, Grieg's *Piano Concerto* restored calm around the cabins and messes.

Hume was running his cutter on interesting trips like towing two whaler-loads of well-lubricated banyan sailors back from Cook Island to the ship and then joining four others from the gunroom for a spell of seine netting. They towed the net round part of the lagoon to enclose a patch of sea using one of the surf boats and were delighted with a significant haul of nearly four sacks of fish. Then it was a mad dash back through the rain to catch the cutter back to the ship. Alas, Kirchem managed to forget to deliver a packet of mail from *Messina* to shore and was formally admonished which also meant he was taken off boat-running until August.

The new Avenger to replace the one damaged on landing had to be rewired to conform to Royal Navy standards. When in due course this was complete, Lt Allen took off with his crew of three but the engine immediately lost power and the Avenger pancaked onto the sea. Allen was able to get out of his cockpit into his dinghy and onto the sea while his navigator walked calmly along the wing, blew up his life raft and stepped into it dry-shod. There was some anxiety for the radio operator who had to struggle to get clear, bleeding from a head wound and minus one shoe, but was then quickly pulled on board Allen's dinghy before the pair of them were picked up by the safety helicopter.[4]

Robertson could confide more of his work to his Midshipman's Journal than he could put in letters to his parents. 'As assistant SOO one is concerned mainly with movements of ships attached to the Operation – staff work at its most prosaic – but there are many different facets to this such as fuel-endurance, mail and fresh provisions, length of sea-time, and so on, which all add up to make the job more than just moving little letters around on a board and making sailing signals. Then there are the incidental offshoots, usually highly classified; dates, bombing details, radiation hazards and even important political considerations.' These included sometimes speculative and sometimes more concrete messages about, for example, both Japanese fishing fleets and Russian submarines.

Also ashore was a *Warrior* Concert Party, including Midshipman Riches, sent to entertain the troops. Their first performance was at the Port camp and was adversely affected by the amount of beer the audience and, alas, the band had consumed. The next day they moved on to the main camp at the airfield. There, the reception was completely different, with a packed house of 500 more sober but still enthusiastic and 'respectful' personnel. Afterwards, however, in the Officers' Mess, with the presence of many senior officers, the atmosphere was rather stuffy with precious few of the Army, RAF and scientific staff talking to them. Still, that night their accommodation was in a cool tent where Riches recalls he slept better than he had done for weeks. The following Sunday, Palm Sunday, the quarterdeck had been decorated with palm fronds from ashore. Riches enjoyed the service, but not the sermon, which was on divorce. It was the Padre's first communion service since his return from hospital. Riches felt unable to agree with almost anything he said and wondered to his diary why it was the Padre had not managed to win the confidence of the ship's company.

Warrior returned to Malden in the middle of the month and Hume was one of the Midshipmen whose watch keeping was now in *Warrior*'s Ops Room. This was an interesting place to see how the ship and its several radar systems kept track of the Valiant bomber carrying out its practice runs round the 'racecourse'. The run began north-east of Malden and the home straight was south-west, overflying *Warrior* and then the eastern coastline of Malden and the luminous triangle at the southern tip and on to the release point. Upon releasing the bomb, the pilot had to make a very tight turn to port, men and machine experiencing very high g-forces, so as to turn the Valiant's tail towards the imminent explosion. As the plane then flew off at maximum speed up the back straight of the circuit, the bomb would explode some fifteen miles behind it. The intention on the day of the actual H-bomb test was for the aircraft to complete an initial sighting run, to allow for all the instruments to log on to the telemetry on *Narvik*, *Warrior* and ashore on Malden. The next circuit would be another dummy run to make sure that the bomb aimer had seen the markers and that the routine had been well rehearsed. The third run would be the 'real thing,' and much would happen all across the Task Force as the fifty-two seconds from release to explosion were counted down.

That rehearsal of every facet was essential was well illustrated during one trial run by Cooper, on the ship's Tannoy, accidentally telling the ship's company to turn round and open their eyes *before* rather than after the detonation. No matter, he got it right on the day! So did the Valiant pilot; but during the week of practice for all the crews, who were dropping high explosive bombs, the difficulty of such precise flying became obvious, one bomb exploding 400 yards wide and 200 yards short.

When *Warrior*, with Commander Begg on the bridge, was slowing down prior to lowering two whalers that were going to sail back, at this very moment those on watch spotted a signal lamp flashing. Contacting the flag deck who confirmed they had seen it too, Johnston turned his back on the signalling light to tell the Commander, turning back to read the final word which was 'home'. No doubt, he thought, someone saying 'Welcome home' but in a moment a startled voice from the flag deck announced, 'Message from boat, sir, reads: "Stop H-bomb tests. *Warrior* go home".' Glasses came up but no one could actually pick out the boat and, as *Warrior*

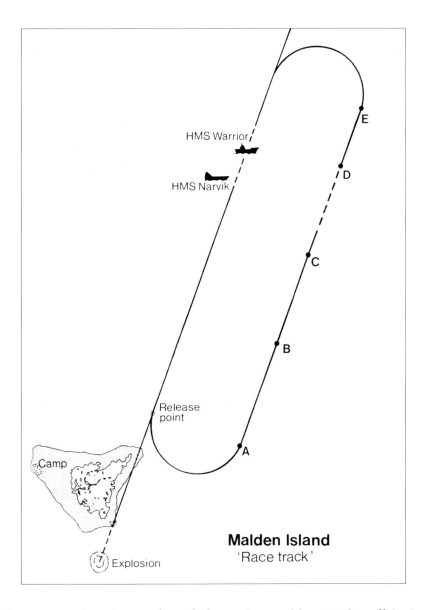

had by then stopped to lower the whalers, she could not take off in immediate pursuit. Commander Begg spoke: 'Chief Yeoman! Make to Task Force Commander. Have received following message from unidentified boat. "Stop H-bomb tests. *Warrior* go home." Am closing to investigate. Request instructions. Make that Operational Immediate.'

The ship had cast off the whalers and was moving off towards where the signal had come when it 'spoke' again. 'Sailor go home.' A lookout reported that the boat seemed to be flying a large Japanese ensign. 'Chief Yeoman, make to TFC, further to my last message, the vessel appears to be flying a Japanese ensign.' Moments later, came the reply. 'Sir, from TFC. Continue investigation. Do not go home.' As *Warrior* closed steadily, the tension rose. Johnston wondered about the safety of the many crew who were crowding the edge of the flight deck and hanging out of the sponsons, and made the mistake of asking the Commander, 'Sir, if they're armed?' To this day he feels he did not merit Begg's reply but, in the Navy, one does not answer back. 'Johnston, if you're scared you can go below!' Johnston could only sulk for the rest of his watch. Then came the rather bathetic denouement. Comments on the bridge came thick and fast.

'She's flashing again.'

'It looks like a cutter. It *is* a cutter.'

'I know him; it's Commander Spill from Port Camp.'

'Compass platform, from Flag Deck: signal reads, "Have mail from Tokyo".'

Warrior had been well and truly had!

This 'Japanese' incident was later revealed by Robertson as having been the brain-child of Captain Guy Western, the senior naval officer at JOC. Western inhabited an inner sanctum in JOC the door of which bore the hand-written legend 'Danger. Live wires'. The sign was somebody's idea of warning visitors that, as Robertson recalls, Western was a keen practical joker. He was thought to have personally hand-painted a large Rising Sun flag for the 'fishing vessel' to fly.

While the rest of the Gunroom was enjoying Easter Week adding to their collection of seashells, or going fishing, or working up a tan, Robertson was hard at work flying to and from Honolulu and having to put up with staying in Hawaii for several days at a stretch. His first visit had been with his chief, partly to look into the reported intentions of Japanese fishing vessels entering the operational area in protest at the tests, but also to learn about commercial 'long line' tuna fishing methods and to buy copious quantities of fishing gear. Then he was forced to go a second time to purchase additional supplies of fishing gear for use back at Christmas and Malden.

Robertson's significant involvement in fishing for tuna, which kept him apart from his Gunroom mates for many weeks, resulted from his persuading his Navy superiors at the JOC that his childhood experience of 'cuithing' (trolling for pollock) from a rowing boat in the seas off Orkney qualified him for the position of Assistant Fisheries Officer. A significant political concern about Operation Grapple was the need to persuade Japan and other nations carrying out major commercial fishing operations in the Pacific that the nuclear tests would not make their traditional fishing grounds radioactive. Together with the Naval Staff Officer (Materials), he flew up to Hawaii in a huge US Air Force Globemaster freight transport which had come in carrying supplies, and spent six days with the Pacific Oceanic Fisheries Investigation Board (POFI), staying with the amiable Herbie Mann and learning about yellow fin tuna and the 'long line' commercial deep sea fishing method. He purchased a good deal of long line equipment before returning to Christmas Island to assemble the gear and start fishing in earnest. With the first bomb test now scheduled for the middle of May, the fishermen needed to get in some practice.

Perhaps Robertson deserved some 'compensation' for the facts that his illness had caused him to be sent ashore, and that his proven usefulness resulted in his being detained there and so not being a witness to the first 'megaton' trial that was now fast approaching.

On 25 April, the Padre failed to return from a visit to Penrhyn and did not come on board until 27 April, for which the Commodore admonished him and a note to this effect was attached to the ship's log. For whatever reason, the Padre had completely failed to win the confidence of the ship's company and, not long after, he was replaced.

April drew to an end with the news coming back from the main camp on Christmas that the Scientific Director, Bill Cook, to his surprise, had been ordered to rest for several days due to letting his inner thighs become sunburnt. The explanation was that he had been wearing a pair of very wide-bottomed shorts and had taken no precautions against the glare of the sun's rays reflected up off the silvery sand. A particular case, it seems, of radiation sickness!

---

1 Begg, *op cit*, p.150

2 http://en.wikipedia.org/wiki/Malden_Island accessed 18 April 2014

3 Oulton p. 86

4 Lt Brian R Allen, *On the Deck or In the Drink,* Barnsley: Pen & Sword, 2010, p.104

MAY

....

On the Equator

For the first two weeks of May, *Warrior* and the Midshipmen currently on board were on station off Malden Island rehearsing the ship's role in the now imminent megaton trials. Robertson, left ashore on Christmas Island but afloat at all hours on the Pacific, was learning by doing how to catch tuna and other pelagic fish for important radiation tests. It was hoped these would give the major Pacific Ocean fishing nations, most notably Japan but also the Americans operating out of Hawaii, the reassurances they sought.

After his six days in Honolulu, Robertson returned at the end of April eager to put his new-found knowledge and newly-bought gear to good use. It turned out to be hard manual labour. While many would have welcomed the chance to go fishing, as the clock and calendar ticked down to D-day, no one else could be spared.

Fortunately, one of the purchases Robertson made in Honolulu was a special nicopress tool which allowed hooks to be compressed onto wires in seconds where the alternative would have required wire splicing; a tricky and time-consuming business. The one fathom wire leader had a pre-spliced loop at the other end with a rubber tubing sleeve. This obviated chafing when it was looped onto a further two fathom dropper at the other end of which was a swivel and a hook for clipping it onto the mainline sections, each of which was fifteen fathoms in length. Finally, each mainline section was connected to the next to create a ten-hook mainline of about 200 fathoms (1,200 feet) of pusser's codline with small marker buoys at both ends. The assembled line then had to be carefully coiled into a canvas skid, and several skids needed to be prepared. Around two miles of line was made up.

And once all that work was done, Robertson's small team had time only for a quick breather before they were out into the lagoon swimming among the giant manta rays, which turned out later to be their most regular companions, with a huge purse seine net, with which they caught plentiful quantities of bonefish to use as bait for the longlines. Finally they turned in, ready for a 0500 start on the morrow.

Early practice with longlines had yielded rather poor results. Later, when they got

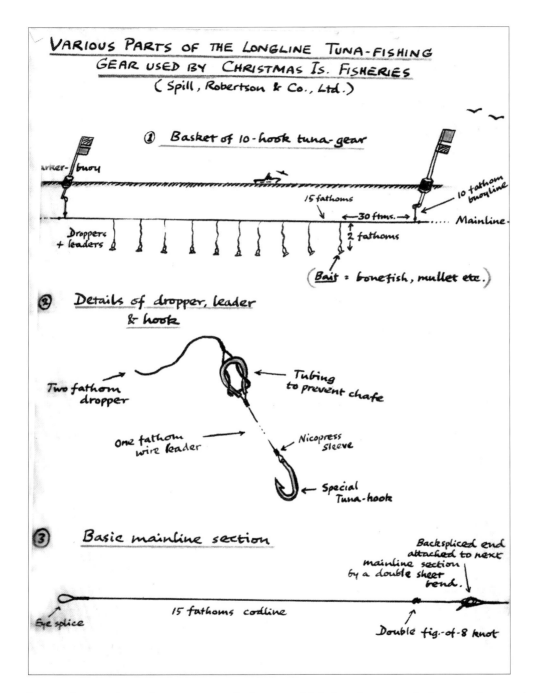

to know the territory better, a good day would bring in several thousand pounds weight of yellow-fin, with some individuals weighing up to 300 lbs. By the time of the first explosion they were regularly bringing in enough tuna for the troops on the

*Preparing for
seine netting
(Riches)*

island to wish never to see tuna on the menu again. The catch would be carefully tested to check for any signs of radiation, specifically changes in millisievert levels, both before and after a bomb test. Results were recorded daily and passed to the scientists and on to the politicians.

While out fishing off the north coast of Christmas, Robertson saw the survey ship HMS *Cook* which was 'sounding on passage'. In fact, all HM ships on passage are required to keep a record of depth soundings so that charts can be regularly kept up-to-date from the incoming reports. The seabed can be subject to great changes, not least from undersea volcanic activity and even the slow but steady movement of the earth's tectonic plates; a theory that in 1957 was not yet accepted as a reality. Cook seemed to be taking the word 'sounding' quite literally by firing her guns and sounding her siren. From those on shore unfamiliar with survey work, there was reported concern, but all was indeed well. The story got about, and Robertson noted it in his Journal, that Cook had been sent to establish the exact location of Malden itself in case the charts were wrong. In a marginal note in Robertson's Journal, however, the Navigator reassured him that Malden was indeed correctly positioned on the charts where Capt Cook had put it. That said, on passage in a direct line from

Malden to Christmas, HMS *Cook* had come across a previously undetected seabed mountain which is now recorded on Admiralty charts.

Once May arrived, certain operational steps had to be taken. *Warrior* set course on 7 May for the test zone and on the 9th some of the indigenous Gilbertese itinerant workers were taken off by the RFA *Fort Rosalie* to spend time on Fanning Island (Tabuaeran) some four degrees north of the equator, while the tests were under way.

Anson in *Messina* invited two of *Warrior*'s Midshipmen, Cooper and Reed, to come over for his birthday party which went on until 0230 the next day, partly because it had also been Cooper's birthday within the past couple of days. Anson and Reed had first met in 1955 in HMS *Theseus* while both were doing their pre-National Service training. Then Anson's workload as a photographer increased again. He wrote home: 'Our ship's photographer left us permanently today to go and help out *Warrior*. This means that I have now got the job of taking any official photographs we may require plus all the routine work. I am quite pleased as it will give me a chance to prove that we can raise the rather low standard of photography on board in spite of terrible working conditions. What with this and my private photography I almost have a full time job at last!' When *Messina*'s Captain entertained the Commodore and other senior officers, Anson was invited up to show off his pictures and all of those present ordered multiple copies. That coincided with a large order from officers on *Salvictor* taking Anson's running total of (purely private!) sales to over 3,700. More significantly, his reputation reached the ears of the scientists which would lead to even greater responsibilities later in the month. Meantime, he might have let matters go to his head since, on stepping briskly through a watertight door, he forgot to duck and required several stitches in his scalp. Was it an augury? A month later he would need more stitches elsewhere.

After delays and hesitation due entirely to Whitehall reluctance to alert the world to the increasing imminence of the first test, a Notice to Mariners (NOTEM) was published in April, in eight languages, together with a map showing that there was a danger area in the central Pacific due to the United Kingdom's forthcoming Nuclear Weapon Tests. This irregular oblong extended from 7° N to 8° 30″ S latitude and from 148° 30″ W to 164° W longitude, an area into which one could fit most of Western Europe. Leaflets with these details were printed off for the aircraft which, from then on, would regularly sweep the exclusion zone. The leaflet said that 'For your own safety, you should leave this area immediately, making maximum speed and in the direction indicated by the aircraft which drops this leaflet.' (See pages 118–119.)

Critical components for the weapons left AWRE in the UK on 5 May, being flown as fast as possible through several staging posts where crews stood by to take the loaded plane on as soon as it had been refuelled. The intention had been to deliver these components within less than forty-eight hours. However, headwinds over the Pacific were of such a strength that the Valiant was held up at Travis Air Force Base in California until these eased sufficiently and the mission-critical components did not finally land on Christmas Island until 9 May. There was still time to complete the weapon's assembly; just *less* time for what was a delicate and, if botched, very dangerous job. The components were handed over to the scientists and placed behind screens out of the general view. For the first time, armed sentries stood guard. On 9 May, TFC toured all the Christmas Island bases and delivered a pep talk. An embargo on outgoing mail took effect.

Warrior reached the operational area round Malden on 8 May. As well as final practice drills and rehearsals, last minute equipment was landed on the island from *Warrior, Messina* and *Narvik. Narvik* would be the forward operational control with the Task Force Commander due to arrive on board immediately prior to the test. Since *Warrior* was to all intents and purposes 'ready', some took time off to go fishing and Hume wrote home about having landed a splendid haul. For some of the night of 8/9 May, *Warrior*'s engines were on six hours' notice for steam to allow urgent maintenance to be completed while the aircraft carrier drifted slowly away from Malden on the current. That meant they lost the last remnants of the cooling breeze generated by steaming ahead and some found staying awake in the Middle Watch harder than usual. No sightings or soundings of Russian submarines were logged although rumours of their presence were rife. The silence and stillness seemed almost eerie.

In two senses, the middle of the Pacific on the equator should be the easiest place on the planet to do astronavigation. Not only are there many stars visible in the early evening when there is still a visible horizon down to which one can lower their reflections with the sextant, but also the distances represented by the seconds, minutes and degrees of latitude and longitude on the chart are the same length for both. Further north and south, measured longitude distances progressively narrow relative to latitude distances for which allowance must be made when trying to plot the necessary three sightings. Johnston had just been told by the Navigator that he

*Warning leaflet
(front)*

WARNING! DANGER AREA

1. You are in the Danger Area of the United Kingdom Nuclear Weapon Tests. This Danger Area which had already been announced in Notices to Mariners is bounded by the following positions :—

(a)	08° 30' South	161° 30' West
(b)	08° 30' South	148° 30' West
(c)	00° 00' Equator	148° 30' West
(d)	00° 00' Equator	150° 30' West
(e)	07° 00' North	150° 30' West
(f)	07° 00' North	158° 00' West
(g)	03° 30' North	158° 00' West
(h)	03° 30' North	164° 00' West
(j)	00° 00' Equator	164° 00' West
(k)	00° 00' Equator	159° 00' West
(l)	02° 30' South	159° 00' West
(m)	02° 30' South	161° 30' West

2. The dates between which it is dangerous to be in this area are 1st March, 1957, to 1st August, 1957.

3. For your own safety you should leave this area immediately, making maximum speed and in the direction indicated by the aircraft which drops this leaflet.

ATTENTION! ZONE DANGEREUSE

1. Vous vous trouvez dans la Zone Dangereuse intéressée par les essais d'armes nucléaires britanniques. Cette Zone Dangereuse, déjà annoncée par Avis aux Navigateurs, est délimitée par les points suivants :—

(a)	08° 30' S	— 161° 30' W
(b)	08° 30' S	— 148° 30' W
(c)	00° 00' Equateur	— 148° 30' W
(d)	00° 00' Equateur	— 150° 30' W
(e)	07° 00' N	— 150° 30' W
(f)	07° 00' N	— 158° 00' W
(g)	03° 30' N	— 158° 00' W
(h)	03° 30' N	— 164° 00' W
(j)	00° 00' Equateur	— 164° 00' W
(k)	00° 00' Equateur	— 159° 00' W
(l)	02° 30' S	— 159° 00' W
(m)	02° 30' S	— 161° 30' W

2. Du 1 mars 1957 au 1 août 1957 il est dangereux de pénétrer dans cette Zone.

3. Pour vous mettre hors de danger vous devez quitter immédiatement la Zone en vous dirigeant à toute vitesse dans la direction indiquée par l'avion qui lance cet avertissement.

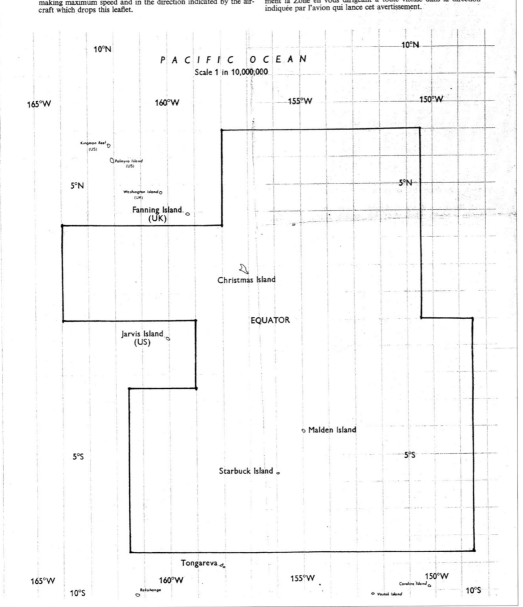

Warning leaflet
(back)

PERINGATAN ! LINGKUNGAN BERBAHAJA

1. Dengan maklumat ini diterangkan tempat ini letaknja didalam lingkungan terasing jang sedang dipergunakan oleh Inggeris untuk mengadakan pertjobaan sendjata2 peledak zarah, maka lingkungan ini adalah bahaja. Telah diberitahukan dengan perantaraan Berita Pelaut (Notices to Mariners) ketetapannja lingkungan berbahaja ini jang luasnja sampai undjung2 terdaftar dibawah ini —

(a)	08° 30′	Selatan	161° 30′	Barat
(b)	08° 30′	Selatan	148° 30′	Barat
(c)	00° 00′	Chattulistiwa	148° 30′	Barat
(d)	00° 00′	Chattulistiwa	150° 30′	Barat
(e)	07° 00′	Utara	150° 30′	Barat
(f)	07° 00′	Utara	158° 00′	Barat
(g)	03° 30′	Utara	158° 00′	Barat
(h)	03° 30′	Utara	164° 00′	Barat
(j)	00° 00′	Chattulistiwa	164° 00′	Barat
(k)	00° 00′	Chattulistiwa	159° 00′	Barat
(l)	02° 30′	Selatan	159° 00′	Barat
(m)	02° 30′	Selatan	161° 30′	Barat

2. Lingkungan ini berbahaja selama 1 Mart, 1957 sampai 1 Augustus, 1957.

3. Agar supaja tersingkir dari bahaja, seharusnja lingkungan ini ditinggalkan serta berlajar setjepat-tjepatnja menudju kearah jang ditundjukkan oleh pesawat terbang jang telah melemparkan surat siaran ini.

¡ ATENCIÓN ! ¡ ZONA PELIGROSA !

1. Vd. se encuentra en la zona peligrosa creada por las pruebas de armas nucleares británicas. Esta zona peligrosa, ya anunciada en los Avisos a los Navegantes, está comprendida entre los límites siguientes :—

(a)	08° 30′	S	161° 30′	W
(b)	08° 30′	S	148° 30′	W
(c)	00° 00′	Ecuador	148° 30′	W
(d)	00° 00′	Ecuador	150° 30′	W
(e)	07° 00′	N	150° 30′	W
(f)	07° 00′	N	158° 00′	W
(g)	03° 30′	N	158° 00′	W
(h)	03° 30′	N	164° 00′	W
(j)	00° 00′	Ecuador	164° 00′	W
(k)	00° 00′	Ecuador	159° 00′	W
(l)	02° 30′	S	159° 00′	W
(m)	02° 30′	S	161° 30′	W

2. El período durante el cual será peligroso encontrarse en esta zona, corre desde el 1° de marzo de 1957 hasta el 1° de agosto de 1957.

3. Por razones de seguridad propia, Vd. debe alejarse inmediatamente y a toda velocidad de esta zona, siguiendo la dirección indicada por el avión desde el cual fué arrojado este folleto.

ADVARSEL ! FARLIG OMRÅDE

1. De befinner Dem i fareområdet for De forende kongerikers atomvåpenprøver. Dette fareområdet som har vært kunngjort i Meddelelser til sjøfarende er avgrenset av følgende posisjoner :

a)	08° 30′	syd	161° 30′	vest
b)	08° 30′	syd	148° 30′	vest
c)	00° 00′	ekvator	148° 30′	vest
d)	00° 00′	ekvator	150° 30′	vest
e)	07° 00′	nord	150° 30′	vest
f)	07° 00′	nord	158° 00′	vest
g)	03° 30′	nord	158° 00′	vest
h)	03° 30′	nord	164° 00′	vest
j)	00° 00′	ekvator	164° 00′	vest
k)	00° 00′	ekvator	159° 00′	vest
i)	02° 30′	syd	159° 00′	vest
m)	02° 30′	syd	161° 30′	vest

2. Tiden det er farlig å oppholde seg i dette området er fra 1ste mars 1957 til 1ste august 1957.

3. For Deres egen sikkerhets skyld bør De forlate området øyeblikkelig og med størst mulig fart, i den retning som blir anvist av flyet som slipper ned denne advarselen.

VARNING FÖR FARLIGT OMRÅDE

1. Detta fartyg befinner sig inom farozonen för Storbritanniens atomvapenprov. Området, varom förhandsunderrättelser lämnats i " Meddelanden till sjöfarande ", begränsas av de räta linjer, som sammanbinda följande punkter :—

(a)	08° 30′	S.	161° 30′	V.
(b)	08° 30′	S.	148° 30′	V.
(c)	00° 00′	ekvator	148° 30′	V.
(d)	00° 00′	ekvator	150° 30′	V.
(e)	07° 00′	N.	150° 30′	V.
(f)	07° 00′	N.	158° 00′	V.
(g)	03° 30′	N.	158° 00′	V.
(h)	03° 30′	N.	164° 00′	V.
(j)	00° 00′	ekvator	164° 00′	V.
(k)	00° 00′	ekvator	159° 00′	V.
(l)	02° 30′	S.	159° 00′	V.
(m)	02° 30′	S.	161° 30′	V.

2. Det är farligt att vistas inom området från den 1. mars till den 1. augusti 1957.

3. Fartyget skall avlägsna sig genast med full fart åt hållet utpekat av flygplanet som kastat detta flygblad. Besättningens säkerhet beror på skyndsam handling.

一、貴船は、連合王国原子核兵器実験中の危険区域内に立入つて居ます。この危険区域については既に英國運輸省発刊「航海従事者に対する航海注意事項通告書」中に発表されてありますが次の諸地点がその範囲となります。

(イ)	南〇八・三〇度、	西一六一・三〇度。
(ロ)	南〇八・三〇度、	西一四八・三〇度。
(ハ)	赤道〇・〇〇度、	西一四八・三〇度。
(ニ)	赤道〇・〇〇度、	西一五〇・三〇度。
(ホ)	北〇七・〇〇度、	西一五〇・三〇度。
(ヘ)	北〇七・〇〇度、	西一五八・〇〇度。
(ト)	北〇三・三〇度、	西一五八・〇〇度。
(チ)	北〇三・三〇度、	西一六四・〇〇度。
(リ)	赤道〇・〇〇度、	西一六四・〇〇度。
(ヌ)	赤道〇・〇〇度、	西一五九・〇〇度。
(ル)	南〇二・三〇度、	西一五九・〇〇度。
(ヲ)	南〇二・三〇度、	西一六一・三〇度。

二、昭和三十二年三月一日から同年八月一日に至る迄の期間、右区域に立入るのは危険です。

三、安全を期するため貴船は、本書を投下する航空機の指示する方向へ、最大限度の速力で、すぐさまこの区域から立ち去られる様お推め致します。

警告！危險！！

(一) 這是英國原子武器試驗危險區。危險區的範圍已經通告海員週知, 危險區的經緯度如下：—

(子)	南緯八度三十分	西經一百六十一度三十分
(丑)	南緯八度三十分	西經一百四十八度三十分
(寅)	赤道零度	西經一百四十八度三十分
(卯)	赤道零度	西經一百五十度三十分
(辰)	北緯七度	西經一百五十度三十分
(巳)	北緯七度	西經一百五十八度
(午)	北緯三度三十分	西經一百五十八度
(未)	北緯三度三十分	西經一百六十四度
(申)	赤道零度	西經一百六十四度
(酉)	赤道零度	西經一百五十九度
(戌)	南緯二度三十分	西經一百五十九度
(亥)	南緯二度三十分	西經一百六十一度三十分

(二) 這區的危險時期, 從一九五七年三月一日起, 至一九五七年八月一日止。

(三) 爲你們自身安全起見, 應當立刻趕快離開危險區, 並應依照散發此傳單的飛機所指示的方向退避。

had been making basic mathematical errors in his calculations on the sheet provided for this. He had been ignoring fairly obvious clues, like + and −, as well as making, or was it *not* making, the Δ correction. When he reworked his calculations correctly, he found, to his pleasant surprise, that he had been making star sightings with more accuracy than he had realised. Once he had mastered the maths, and taken more time to avoid careless mistakes, he clocked up more sightings and he could 'fix' the ship within a mile or so of her real position which, given sight of Malden in the middle distance and its outline on the radar screen, he knew already.

The principle on which astronavigation works is that the navigator must first decide, usually by dead reckoning, approximately where the ship is when he takes his new sightings. (Dead reckoning requires an estimate of how far, and in what direction(s), the ship has travelled since the last reliable 'fix', allowing, where necessary, for the effects of wind, tide and currents over and above any course alterations.) For a fix using star sights, the drill is to observe three individual stars at twilight, when they are already visible and while the horizon is still a clear dividing line between sea and sky. He – and in 1957 it was invariably *he* – then selects, from those listed in the Admiralty Nautical Almanac, visible heavenly bodies which, for best results, will be located in different sectors of the sky; 120 degrees of separation being the ideal. The process can seem complicated since the three sights, inevitably taken at different times though differing by only a few minutes, need to be worked out and then plotted on a chart or plotting sheet and the earlier sightings 'run on' by the distance and in the direction the ship has travelled so as to adjust each earlier sighting to the same moment in time as the final star sight. For fixes using the sun, there will generally be two observations at intervals of around two hours. The calculations will either be based on a 'sun-run-sun'; which is two observations of the altitude of the sun at an interval of, say, a couple of hours with the plot of the earlier observation 'run on' along the compass direction of its course by the distance covered by the ship in that time; or a 'sun-run-mer-alt' in which case the second observation is taken at apparent noon local time.

For these sightings, *Warrior*'s Midshipmen used a sextant, which had been developed from the earlier 'quadrant', and had an arc of 60 degrees. This had been first introduced into the Royal Navy in 1757, exactly 200 years earlier. Today's more fortunate navigators can use the high-seas equivalent of Sat Nav and can plot their ship's position with relative ease and certainty on a computer screen. However, in today's Royal Navy, deck officers still have to learn about the 'old-fashioned' use of the sextant as part of their training; for those critical moments when, say, electronic silence is required, or the power fails in combat, or satellites stop transmitting, perhaps because they are being jammed. Likewise, today's charts are electronic and updated remotely like other forms of software. In 1957, the navigator had to manually update paper charts using violet ink to identify his markings as corrections. These corrections came in a steady flow from the Admiralty and kept Midshipman Anson busy every week, when he was appointed assistant navigating officer of *Messina*.

Holding the sextant in his right hand and adjusting the altitude of the body observed with his left, the trainee navigator, would stand on the wing of the bridge and bring a *reflected* image of the body down to the horizon (being very careful in the case of the sun to protect his eyesight by interposing tinted filters). When the object – whether the bottom 'edge' of the sun or the point of light that is the star – reached the horizon, he would gently rock the sextant with his wrist and note that moment when the moving arc of the image just grazed the line of the horizon. He would call 'Time' to his assistant who would record the precise time of the observation and then note down the altitude which he read off the sextant. In the case of meridian altitude (mer alt), the skill of the navigator was to judge the moment when the image just grazed the horizon due south of him (in the northern hemisphere) and when the altitude of the image had stopped rising but not yet started falling again. Practice, therefore, was essential.

Then the would-be navigators had to look up the various tables in the Nautical Almanacs for the current year, in *Warrior*'s case 1957, which tabulate the figures required in different latitudes and longitudes for the given date and time plus all the corrections that were then needed to finalise their calculation and tweak the final reading. Not least, these included the height above sea level of the bridge plus the height of the navigator's eye level. At this point he would need the local chart or a plotting sheet and the prescribed form the Navy used to record, tabulate and calculate sightings. From the final calculation of his two or three sightings, he would plot and run on each one, to achieve a fix which he would mark on the chart with a dot in a circle, noting the time alongside it. Having ploughed through all of this, having managed to get three lines on the chart to intersect, ideally in a point but more often in a triangle referred to as a 'cocked hat', the Midshipman would lay the results of each fix in front of the Navigating Officer for checking and approval. To be considered a 'trained' Midshipmen he had to do this a dozen times accurately. It wasn't easy and the sense of satisfaction when the magic dozen was complete usually merited a celebration.

Since he had not so far managed to get ashore on Malden, Johnston asked one of the chopper pilots in the Gunroom if he could fly in with him on one of their frequent supply trips. This was agreed and he climbed on board eager for his expedition. No sooner had the chopper touched down than he hopped out and gazed around at the arid landscape, eager to explore. Unfortunately, that chopper was delivering only one small package and this was off-loaded in less than a minute. When Johnston completed one glance round the horizon and turned round to look at the chopper he saw the pilot waving to him to come back immediately. His visit to the historic island had altogether lasted about two and a half minutes.

Riches had a more roundabout trip to go ashore on Malden with two RN officers. They went first by ship's boat to *Narvik* and thence by DUKW to the island. They

Riches on Malden to survey (Riches)

took with them theodolites that would be used during the practice runs to track the Valiant's accuracy as it flew over the south-west corner of Malden. He was fascinated by thoughts of the community that once worked the guano deposits on an island so

Survey work on Malden (Riches)

RIGHT: *Camp Coffee label*

remote. As he looked around, his eye landed on something glinting amid a pile of rubbish. On closer inspection it turned out to be a quarter-full bottle of Camp Coffee, coffee essence with added roast chicory that was still labelled with its kilted Indian Army officer holding his steaming hot cup with a turbaned coffee-wallah in attendance, dated 1925, two years before the island was finally abandoned.

Riches's earlier diary note reveals how much of an influence the weather had on the trials, for example 'A full-scale operation was expected today with a Canberra dropping a 5,000 lb bomb. However, it poured with rain all day – cloud ceiling about one to two thousand feet – and radio contact was lost. The operation was called off about 1500.' It may have been raining but the maximum temperature, recorded in his diary that day at Malden, was 81°. Hutchinson recalls playing a game of cricket on Malden at one point, apparently so well, that months later he would be selected to play for the ship.

Meanwhile, back at JOC on Christmas, Bill Cook, the Scientific Director of Operation Grapple called on the Task

Force Commander for a private chat and broke some rather disturbing news.

'I'm sorry to have to tell you this but the bad news is that the explosive supercharge shell which goes round the radio-active core of this first live round arrived cracked. Also the spare supercharge. The only explanation we can think of is that the bomb-bay heating in the courier Valiants didn't work properly and that with such a long time at such low external temperatures the cold cracked the explosive material.'

'Oh my God! We never thought of it! The bomb-bay heating, which had indeed given us some trouble earlier on but we had thought this was cured, was only sufficient to keep warm the space round a damn great bomb case filling the bay. With a tiddly little parcel like your package of explosive, there wouldn't be nearly enough heat. What the hell are we going to do now? Can you get a replacement?'

'No. We can't get a replacement in time – it would take at least six weeks. So we've stuck it together with Bostik and we'll just have to hope for the best. I think it better not to broadcast this in case it affects morale.'[1]

This was one of several pieces of information that did not become public knowledge until some time, often years, after Operation Grapple was concluded.

On 11 May there was a full-scale dress rehearsal and, just in time, a vital crystal for *Warrior*'s ILS emergency frequency radio reached the ship after mysteriously going missing on the way from the manufacturers in Wales. This was important as without it there was no way of breaking into the pilot and bomb-aimer's commentary during the final approach and, in consequence, no way at all to abort the bombing mission at the last minute. The story later emerged that the despatch rider sent to fetch it had been involved in a road traffic accident and had spent a couple of days in hospital in Cardiff before he was tracked down and the crystal could continue on its interrupted journey. Other new equipment had been installed in *Warrior*. To track the fall of the weapon from release to detonation, a new radar codenamed 'Avocado' was working well. It had, in fact, been developed by the Admiralty Signal Research Establishment (ASRE) and the Underwater Development Establishment at Portland for mine location, but it performed very well in this new role. To add to the capability of pin-point accuracy that these tests required, *Warrior*'s Decca navigation system meant that the ship, over which the Valiant would directly fly, could be positioned to within one hundred yards, less than the length of the flight deck.

Commander Begg's task was to keep the ship positioned exactly under the flight path of the Valiant at a distance of twenty-six miles from ground zero. He found that he could only just make out the two barrage balloons on Malden from the ADR platform and decided to make an urgent requisition for a pair of more powerful gunnery officer's binoculars. These were despatched from London as an airmail *letter* which duly arrived just in time smothered in £5 postage stamps, each one a fortune in 1957. Putting these to his eyes on the day itself, he could see the actual bomb falling from the aircraft before, like everyone else, he faced away and closed his eyes.[2]

On Christmas there was a rehearsal of the procedure to be adopted as the bomb-bearing Valiant took off on its mission. Personnel congregated at designated points so that, in the very unlikely sequence of events of a crash on take-off and a nuclear explosion, they could be swiftly evacuated up-wind. Clearly this eventuality had to be addressed since its consequences could not have been concealed. Not discussed openly, however, except on a need to know basis, were the drills to be adopted in the event that, perhaps due to an electrical fault (or some unanticipated consequence of Mr Cook's Bostik) the bomb would not drop from the open doors of the bay. There could be no possibility of returning to land on Christmas Island with such a live cargo. Instead, in *Warrior*, the choppers would be scrambled while the Valiant did another circuit at only 5,000 feet and the rear crew members baled out nearby. A Shackleton would be detached from other duties to follow the Valiant. Then, with *Warrior* in hot pursuit, the pilot would fly downwind of Malden for fifty nautical miles, some seven or eight minutes flying time. Setting the automatic pilot to fly on for a further thirty minutes, first the co-pilot and then the pilot would eject and hope that the Shackleton would spot them and *Warrior*'s choppers would quickly arrive to pick them up. The Valiant's systems would be programmed to shut down the throttles after thirty minutes, cut off the fuel supply and then put the plane into a nose down attitude so that it would quickly crash into the sea. There could well be an explosion but it would, the scientists confidently predicted, be low-yield with limited fall-out.[3] What would be unavoidable in such circumstances, but was never spoken about openly, was the complete and utter loss of face, the loss of valuable equipment and, with a test ban looming, the possibility that Operation Grapple would then have to be abandoned.

More prosaically, but just as crucial, steps had to be taken to provide backup for the air traffic controller on Christmas since, on one previous occasion, the officer on watch at a critical moment had gone down with a sudden attack of food-poisoning.

Before midnight on 10 May, the first Shackleton sortie had been launched and no untoward reports were coming in to JOC. Throughout 11 May *Warrior*'s helicopters flew twenty-seven sorties during which they evacuated all the remaining personnel from Malden. Once the rehearsal of the bomb drop had been completed, they would fly in the re-entry teams. This was not without incident, however, since the aircraft mechanics had had to work through the night of 10/11 May to change one helicopter's engine in time to have every aircraft serviceable at first light. During the day, *Warrior*'s Air Direction Room (ADR) had, under the eyes of several of the Midshipmen, maintained a continuous plot of up to sixteen aircraft operating within a sixty mile radius during the bombing runs. That day they had to plot two additional unscheduled circuits by the 'bombing' Valiant since, at that most crucial moment, the plane's gyro malfunctioned. The rehearsal included the ship going for some time into ABCD State 1A conditions; ABCD standing for atomic, biological and chemical defence with condition 1A being the maximum state of precaution. For a while, until this was eased, the temperatures for those locked down and even in the ADR thirty feet above the flight deck became hard to bear. After the test drop, Riches spent the remainder of the forenoon watch 'closed up' at the Health Physics Station, running his geiger counter over samples of fish and reporting the complete absence of any radiation. In the evening, by way of relaxation, officers hosted the Chiefs and Petty Officers for a session of Tombola on the quarterdeck. It is not recorded who won.

When the very successful rehearsal was reviewed, it was decided to draft in and position a further squadron of Canberras at Christmas and Hickam Air Base in Honolulu for the task of flying the air samples collected by the other photo-reconnaissance Canberras flying high and low around the detonation tracking the movement of radioactive fall-out. These samples needed to be back in the UK within twenty-four hours; no mean task, even today.

Given the invitation to travel back from Malden overnight to Christmas, making use of the Admiral's cabin, the Task Force Commander needed no persuasion and that was how Commander Begg and Surgeon Commander Pugh happened to engage him in a fairly typical Wardroom discussion. It started with the TFC remarking that it was a 'well-known fact' that bathwater going down the plughole in the Northern Hemisphere rotated anti-clockwise whilst the opposite was true in the Southern Hemisphere. Well-travelled and regularly-bathed senior officers, neither Begg nor Pugh was convinced that this was so and, in any case, what, they asked, would happen *on* the Equator. Would bathwater drain down the plughole without rotating? A couple of drinks later, an experiment was agreed in which the Air Vice Marshal would take a bath some ten minutes or so before *Warrior* crossed the line going north. At a phone call from Begg, on the bridge making use of the Decca Navigator's pinpoint accuracy, announcing the moment that *Warrior* had her bows in the Northern Hemisphere and her stern in the South, the TFC would pull out the plug and note carefully what happened. Reports from different sources give differing accounts of the outcome but the general conclusion was that in a moving ship, the water paused momentarily and, rather than flow straight down from top dead centre, waited just long enough to know which side of the line the bath was on and rotated in accordance with the principle enunciated by the Task Force Commander. As the highest ranking officer present, his account is of course accepted as correct. However, the Admiralty advise that no further experiments are planned. In the cold light of dawn, however, further jokes and japes of an inter-service nature were perpetrated. Oulton's account makes amusing reading.

> '... the next morning, when he was being shown round the Air Direction room [to] his shocked amazement, there was a Shackleton aircraft at about two hundred feet, wheels and flaps down, making an approach to the stern of the carrier as though in the process of "landing-on". It couldn't be true! – or possible, with the aircraft's wingspan greater than the width of the flight deck. Nevertheless, there was the batsman with his "Ping-Pong bats" on his little platform at the port corner of the round-down, signalling corrections to keep the aircraft level and on the right line of approach, all in accordance with standard naval aviation landing-on procedures. It took several seconds for the penny to drop, to notice that the batsman's signals were a caricature of the normal and that the whole thing was a well organised joke.' [4]

Back at Christmas after the rehearsal Johnston finally met his schoolfriend from the Scottish Borders, Pilot Officer Cartwright, whom he had known to be with the RAF at the main camp. RAF officers from all the squadrons on the island came on board for pre-lunch drinks and he was one of them. Johnston invited Cartwright to stay for lunch in the Gunroom then, afterwards, showed him around. They talked long, and even longingly, of home and mutual friends. Afterwards they went ashore together and borrowed a Land Rover in which to drive back to the Main Camp up by the airstrip. About seven or eight miles from the port, it started to rain and the vehicle had no roof. Even so, they wound up the side windows and soldiered on. Johnston visited Cartwright's well-appointed tent – camp beds, carpets and 230v AC power – to dry off and had a nostalgic read of his local weekly newspaper, the *Border Telegraph.* He deliberately chose to sit with his back to the WVS quarters where twin-sister volunteer ladies lived while they ran the NAAFI and 'mothered' the servicemen there. The Task Force Commander had been very much opposed to their presence but they seemed, overall, to have made a great deal of positive difference to morale. Because he did not see them he could still say it would be four months before he saw another white woman!

When the rain stopped, Johnston set off back to the Port. The road had become a series of water splashes of varying depth. Taking them at speed turned out to be a mistake. The splash of muddy water came up over the bonnet and windscreen, leaving him soaked. The engine then began to cough and splutter, and the rain started up again, so he guessed there would be trouble. As he drove slowly and carefully through the next very long, and deep, puddle, the engine died just before the Land Rover reached the farther end. He sat for a while, opened the bonnet and tentatively patted the battery with some sacking, all to no avail. Then, paradoxically he had to open the doors to let the rising water inside run out. In due course, the engine fired again, only to conk out after another three or four miles. By a combination of waiting, watching the rain fall and dabbing at the battery, he finally made it back to the port, thirteen miles from the camp. It had taken ninety minutes. He scrambled onto the last liberty boat and scarcely had time to get dry and properly dressed before he had to report for duty on the compass platform as *Warrior* slipped from her buoy and set course south again towards Malden. D-Day was imminent. Overnight on 14/15 May, as the Task Force gathered in the vicinity of Malden, the scientists there were completing their programme of readying their instruments and then evacuating the few remaining personnel in the hour before dawn. Oulton's account of the final moments of the evacuation are worth quoting.

'[The] two groups, having completed their tasks, then assembled at 'C' site on the north-east corner of the island, the only place where there was sufficient depth of soil to allow the excavation of an underground shelter for the last Land Rover, necessary for collecting the party together. It was also a completely flat and featureless piece of terrain, where there had been no concealment for the solitary Elsan chemical toilet which had to serve for all the men working there. To give some illusion of privacy for these private moments, the Elsan was positioned in a scooped out hollow in the ground, leaving only the occupant's head poking up above the skyline. Poor Peter Jones of the AWRE team, having rounded up all the bodies and delivered them to the improvised helipad, marked out with hurricane lamps, then parked the Land Rover in the underground shelter and ran to join the others as the helicopter came in with the dawn's early light. In the half-dark, he forgot and failed to notice Elsan Hollow, fell head over heels with a great clang and arrived at the helipad very fragrant and unpopular!'[5]

During the morning of 14 May the ship's company had been called to attention by an announcement on the Tannoy by Commodore Hicks. He advised everyone that the first H-bomb test would be held the following morning and that he expected everyone to carry out their well-rehearsed drills and to obey to the letter all the security procedures. Throughout the Grapple Squadron, on Christmas and Malden Islands and across the scattered islands with Decca transmitters, D-1 check lists were run through and not a few fingers were crossed. Despite the professionalism of the Royal Navy regulars, there was a perceptible increase in tension on board *Warrior* and the Midshipmen, accustomed to joking among themselves, became unusually serious. Everyone knew now that she would be the nearest ship to the explosion, NNE of Malden around twenty-six miles from 'ground zero' and that the RAF Valiant, with its bomb primed, would fly directly overhead as it made its three runs up to the release point. Commodore Hicks's official report said the weather was better for station-keeping on D-1 than on the day itself and such was the unexpected set of the current that *Warrior* had to steam back to her station only three minutes before the actual drop.[6]

On 15 May, *Warrior*'s entire ship's company were up and about in the early morning light and Robertson at JOC on Christmas Island had been on duty there since midnight, but would still have to go out fishing to furnish the specimens to test immediately prior to the first explosion. Dennis spent the first part of his day in the Damage Control Section, located in the middle of the ship for protection. He was assigned as one of his tasks to carry out a monitoring control of the whole ship before the drop to ensure that all hatches and DC doors as well as intakes and vents were tightly shut and/or switched off. He was equipped with a white protection suit (known on board as a 'zoot' suit), like a boiler suit but with a fitted hood, which covered him from head to foot and wore a pair of long sleeved gunner's anti-flash gloves. Attached to the suit was a film badge radiation detector as well as a pen-shaped quartz-fibre dosimeter. On his feet he had half wellingtons which fitted under a flap over the lower half of the trouser leg. In addition, slung over his shoulder in a carrier box was a gas mask with an anti-radiation filter attached. Across his back, printed in large black letters on the white suit were the words MID DENNIS and underneath that ABCD. Dressed like a man in a space suit, he was free to go throughout the ship carrying out his task of ensuring total sealing of the interior of the ship from the outside. Carrying out this task in a metal box sitting on or near the equator was a physical endurance test. The ship was sealed off in this manner for more than six hours. Fortunately, having completed his own task he was required to report his findings to the bridge and it was there that he sat and rested, his back to the imminent explosion, enjoying a relatively cool 85°.

By three in the morning, four Shackletons, their fuel tanks filled to the brim for maximum flying time, had begun their 'line abreast' sweep of the danger area looking for any surface craft that might be straying into the danger zone. A further two Shackletons headed for Malden to fly round and round at twenty miles from the island, looking first for intruders and then being ready to photograph the actual explosion.

At that time of year, just south of the equator, it takes about fifteen minutes from sunrise for metal surfaces, like the flight deck of an aircraft carrier, to become uncomfortably hot to touch. Johnston's duties involved assembling the junior seamen on the flight deck and checking they had all correctly donned their white coveralls including a hood with strings to pull them tight. One sees these coveralls nowadays in every news story where forensic teams are sent in to gather evidence, but in 1957 they looked outlandish and unearthly. He reported his charges all present and correct to Lt Bagg who then ordered the division to sit down and take the weight of their feet. However, the 'wait' was rather prolonged.

On *Warrior*'s flight deck it very soon became painfully hot on the backside but, rather than admit he could stand it no longer, Johnston pushed his bottom off the deck with the tips of his fingers. In no time at all, however, each finger felt like it had been stuck into a bonfire and he had to drop back onto the deck until he felt certain his backside was blistering. Finally, in Lt Bagg's temporary absence, he ordered everyone to stand up since the soles of their boots gave better protection.

From the compass platform over the Tannoy, the ship heard that the bomber was now airborne from Christmas Island. That must have been a tense moment for all in that area, and Johnston for one was not sorry to be 400 miles away but spared a brief thought for Robertson who was on the spot. V-bombers waste no time once airborne and in no time at all it could be glimpsed passing overhead on the first of its laps round the 'racetrack'. The manoeuvres had been practised many times but this time they would be in deadly earnest. All went well on that first run and Wing Commander Hubbard flew his Valiant on the second dummy run for the bomb aimer to be certain he had picked up the triangular marker on Malden and for the telemetry on *Warrior* and *Narvik* to lock on to the aircraft. There could be no further postponement and the Task Force Commander, now on board *Narvik,* gave the order. The bomber, flying on an exact course at its precise altitude of 45,000 feet, had to be sure of making a visual sighting of the marker on Malden which was the moment to press the bomb release switch. The Valiant then had to maintain its course and speed for a further eleven seconds until the weapon was automatically released, before making its very tight turn to port to take it out of range of the explosion. From release to detonation there would be exactly fifty-two seconds as the weapon fell to the burst point 8,000 feet above the Pacific, by which time the aircraft had to be heading directly away at maximum speed.

Midshipman Cooper, listening in on headphones to Wing Cdr Hubbard's commentary and other input from ships and aircraft, was broadcasting progress reports from the ADR as he stood there with the Commodore and the Commander. 'Bomb gone!' he announced. 'Pull down your goggles, put your hands over the goggles and close your eyes tight. … Ten seconds … five, four, three, two, one!' One second later there was a burst of light of such intensity that many of those who were there will claim to this day that they saw an image of the bones of their fingers as the brilliant flash imprinted them on their retinas, even through their gloved hands, dark goggles and tightly shut eyelids.

After only ten seconds those on deck were told they could turn round and remove their goggles. What they saw was more awesome by several orders of magnitude than they had been 'conditioned' to expect. For the past thirteen years everyone had seen photographs and films of atomic bomb explosions over Japan, in New Mexico, on Pacific atolls and the Australian Monte Bello islands but these had generally been fairly small, black and white photographs, or on relatively small cinema screens, and of smaller *atomic* weapons. Now, in front of them and taking up the whole sky was a kaleidoscopic display of all the colours of the spectrum though with a predominance of reds and oranges. The fireball was already being surrounded by a large misty mushroom of ascending cloud while blacks and greys were beginning to wrap themselves round the furnace door. Meantime, the downward blast of heat had vaporised the surface of the ocean more than a mile and a half below the air burst and a conical column of water vapour, growing steadily in height and density, was rising rapidly to form the stalk of the death's-head toadstool. They watched in almost complete silence, apart from a collective exhalation of expletives. Then, just as their defences were being lowered, and it began to seem that watching hydrogen bombs exploding was part of everyday routine, there came a rumble of thunder as the sound wave, travelling at a mere fraction of the speed of light, reached the ship. Many instinctively ducked. By this time, taking photographs was allowed and cameras were being passed from hand to hand so that their owners could be pictured standing in front of the mushroom.

Over in *Messina*, Anson was taking his own cine film of the event as well as taking many other still photographs for the Navy with the ship's large plate camera. Using the developing equipment he had ordered from Honolulu, Anson developed and printed his record of the explosion and, after approval by the Commodore and AWRE, was able to mail copies back home. He wrote home the next day, describing the event and his work.

'As you must have heard by now from the news and in the papers we have let off our first bomb out here. Most descriptions will be very general, so I thought perhaps you might like to hear what we saw and felt just over thirty miles away from the explosion. I shall enclose the special issue of the *Mid-Pacific News* which gives all the details. In actual fact I spent so much time photographing the burst I can hardly remember seeing the effects at all!'

Seen from *Warrior*'s flight deck, the Dantesque image of the mouth of Hell soon

*Five minutes
after explosion
(Rowsell)*

Fifteen minutes after explosion (Rowsell)

One hour later (Rowsell)

faded to the point when it became simply a cloud phenomenon, rather than the aftermath of an enormous explosion. That cloud, however, remained visible for around six hours. During that time, the staff of Christmas Island's own newspaper, *The Mid-Pacific News*, worked on a special 'Souvenir Edition' with the large red-top headline announcing:

BOMB GONE!
H-BOMB PUTS BRITAIN
ON LEVEL TERMS

The Mid-Pacific News, *15 May 1957*

Much of the copy had been written the day before, including the profiles of Air Vice Marshal Oulton and of Bill Cook, the Scientific Director. There was an inevitable jingoistic tone to the opening sentence of the exclusive report from the *Mid-Pacific News* observer on HMS *Warrior*. 'Wednesday 15 May 1957. A flash, stark and blinding, high in the Pacific Sky, signalled to the world today Britain's emergence as a top-ranking power of this nuclear age.' So they said! Given the time differences, *The Mid-Pacific News* could claim to be the 'only English newspaper to carry the news under a 15 May dateline'. Riches recorded his impressions in his diary the same day.

Riches's diary page (Riches)

It was many years before those outside AWRE senior staff would learn the truth about the size and scale of that first test.

Around the test site on all the ships, follow up exercises got under way to monitor the impact on people, all of whom had been wearing film badges, and some quartz fibre dosimeters. A few had Geiger counters that were meant to detect radiation from the seawater and any fish that could be caught from the sponsons. Johnston was called to one of the for'ard sponsons to run his measuring device over a poor fish, still flapping in hope of release and found quite alarming readings – until his Geiger counter was checked by experts and found to be malfunctioning. Within twenty minutes, *Warrior*'s helicopters were airborne and landing on *Narvik* to take on board the re-entry party. The chopper approached the island slowly, staying up wind and deploying Geiger counters. As they moved steadily closer, no increase in radiation was detected although fires were still burning and a long plume of smoke extended downwind for several miles. Some of the wild pigs had survived but were running around, clearly distressed. Once the chopper landed and readings had been taken on the ground, the overalled and hooded technicians were allowed to disembark and retrieve the vital instruments and records. These were immediately flown to *Warrior* and transferred to the waiting Avengers which flew them up to Christmas and the relay of Canberras tasked with getting everything back to AWRE in England within twenty-four hours. The Commodore's report states that there were no radiation problems apart from one momentary scare that turned out to be 'beta button markers' on the re-entry helicopter's life raft. However, the met balloon radar reflector recovered from the sea some five miles WNW of Ground Zero was found to have a beta count of over 1,000 p.s., which necessitated a member of the fishing party which recovered it being given health clearance in No. 1 Cleansing Station on board. The reflector was sent to the Scientific Director in *Narvik*.

Surgeon Commander Pugh was charged with dissecting and testing fish for radioactivity. He had already called Cdr Begg to express alarm at one reading before he discovered the clearly labelled sample used for training which Begg had earlier concealed. Their relations were frosty until the Wardroom bar opened that evening. [7]

Apart from some senior service personnel including one American observer, the Operation Grapple participants, civilian and military, had that first test to themselves. When it all happened again in two weeks' time, they would be hosting the world's press but not including Johnston's new friend, Larry Cott, at the radio station KHVH who wrote to him after the second test in very American terms; demonstrating the very positive PR effects of that test.

> 'Let me here and now welcome you fellows to the nuclear family of nations. It's really about time. I'm really about the only person around here who got excited about your detonations (the second one was this morning), but I don't think many people realize what this does for your military posture, your bargaining power and, most important, your prestige. Now at least the ratio is tipped … and it's two to one. And after the mess at Suez, and in Cyprus, you damned well had to come up with something quick to restore Britannia to a power position. Of course I know I'm speaking to a Scotsman, but after all you people have the Cross of St Andrew in the Union Jack. Incidentally, I hope you noticed that the Hawaiian Territorial flag has the Union Jack in it, too. Most Americans mistake the whole damned flag for a British ensign of some sort, and even, mind you, consider Hawaii a British possession. (I'm currently writing an article for a national publication based upon some Americans ignorance of Hawaii).'[8]

On the voyage back to Christmas Island after this first test, some twenty nautical miles from port, six of the Midshipmen in one of the whalers were dropped off with instructions to catch some fish and sail back home. As the one non-sailor of the six, Riches confessed to feeling slightly nervous as *Warrior* steamed away and was soon out of sight. Being the only Supply Officer, he was naturally charged with victualing the whaler. He had packed enough for three meals, including sausages, sandwiches, rolls and tinned fruit. (There is no mention of lashings of ginger beer!) Given the experienced sailors on board, Cooper and Dennis, all went well until they were in sight of Christmas but still two miles from home. At this point, the wind dropped to a complete calm which lasted for nearly four hours. Then, in the early afternoon, several squalls of torrential rain allowed the whaler to tack and move progressively closer to their mother ship. They reached the boom in the early afternoon, soaked to the skin and having caught no fish, which was a pity since the principal point of the exercise had been to catch fish and test them for radioactivity.

Warrior was back at Christmas Island for about ten days during which the Gunroom welcomed Robertson home although it was rumoured that his services might be needed again at JOC. Riches, who was privy to the signals coming in to the

Commodore, recalls that, around this time, there was some minor resentment felt by senior officers when they were advised that CINCSASA (Commander-in-Chief South Atlantic and South America) had decided to join the ship at Callao, thus stealing the thunder from *Warrior*'s ship's company and Commodore. However, in consequence, the Falklands and Puerto Belgrano had been added to the ports of call. It would later be realised that there was a pecuniary reason for the Puerto Belgrano visit.

Meanwhile, on shore at the assembly shed, the components had arrived for the second bomb, known as 'Orange Herald', and the task Force Commander was invited to see it all being put together; presumed beforehand to be a simple task – no Bostik required. His account follows:

> 'Then two copper hemispheres were placed round the explosive sphere to contain it exactly, one below, then the other on top. Round the diameters of the hemispheres were two small flanges, male and female, each with a fine screw thread. The Warrant Officer carefully fitted the flange of the upper hemisphere over that of the lower one and then gently rotated it clockwise to engage the screw thread. So far, so good. He continued to rotate the upper hemisphere delicately – one complete turn – one and a half – and then it stuck! It needed another six and a half turns.
>
> So he tried to reverse the movement to undo the flange threads and start all over again. Nothing to get excited about. But he could not move the top hemisphere. It was firmly stuck. Forwards again – no movement. Backwards again – no movement. The smiles raised originally by the small contretemps vanished. The situation was no longer amusing. Several times more the WO tried, gradually increasing the force applied to what was supposed to be a very delicate operation. [...]
>
> Time was passing and the two spectators, with other pressing commitments, felt they couldn't stay much longer; but neither could they go, leaving [...] this increasingly worrying problem unsolved.
>
> [Two hours passed in further vain efforts.] The WO stood back, wiped his hands on the seat of his shorts and turned to [Cook].
>
> "In my experience of this engineering problem, Sir, there's only one thing left to do – clout it!"
>
> Cook and [his deputy] looked at each other in dismay. The TFC, although only a visitor with no right to a voice, added:
>
> "I think he's right."

"OK," said Cook, less calmly than usual. "Clout it!"

[The WO] went over to his tool box, rummaged around and fished out a small seven-pound copper-headed sledge hammer [...] took a deep breath and gave the flange round the middle of the sphere a moderate thump [...] Sharp intakes of breath all round. He put down the hammer, put both hands round the upper hemisphere while the assistant did the same below and tried to rotate it. It moved as smooth as silk. Six and a half turns more – the assembly of Orange Herald was complete.'[9]

The day before the Grapple Squadron was due to sail south to Malden again, a flash signal was sent out by the Commodore. With only one hour's notice, ships at Christmas were ordered to raise steam since a 'tropical storm of fierce intensity but short duration' was forecast. This precaution was necessary since none of the ships in the anchorage was more than half a mile from the reef. The storm passed without any real incident at sea, but there was short term flooding of the Technical area at the airfield on shore, and on the Sunday, 26 May, *Warrior* set off once again to cross the equator as events began to build towards the second test. Robertson sailed with his Gunroom colleagues and had to learn how to be a sailor again after his spell at JOC. His Journal takes up his story:

'We closed [Malden] the next day, attempting unsuccessfully to anchor on the jutting 'shelf'. [Instead we] lay off, drifting gradually away with the wind. In the evening I was accorded the doubtful privilege of taking the first motor-cutter that Warrior had ever sent ashore through the surf. The fact that one of the leading marks had been burnt down by the first bomb, and also the news that an LCM had recently broached-to in the surf, did nothing to encourage me! However, crew and libertymen all donned life-jackets and we found the gap in the reef quite easily. Nevertheless, despite inching ourselves forward on the stern anchor, we were thrown onto the sand too heavily and violently for comfort, and I had all passengers out of the boat very rapidly. We got off again with difficulty, only to discover that the cooling system was blocked by sand, so, after clearing the reef amid clouds of steam, we had to stop and clean out the main cooling pipe. I made the same trip thrice more, but with the [Officer of the Watch's] consent I decided to remain some yards off shore and make the passengers swim in future.'

Meanwhile, *Messina* had arrived back at Christmas and Anson had been given added responsibilities. Word of the quality of Anson's photographs had spread, with two consequences. First, he received more orders, many of them 'private' and some from the very top of the chain of command. Secondly, an AWRE boffin came to visit and asked *Messina*'s captain if the ship could operate some of the recording equipment for the official record of the actual test. Her Captain, Commander H G Vere RN, inevitably gave the job to Anson. The necessary gear would be delivered by the 'boffin' when *Messina* arrived back at Christmas for a quick turnaround before setting off back again to the operational area. On the appointed day, the scientist turned up with the set of recording cameras that Anson would have to set up and operate – but with an admission that every one of the cameras, delicate instruments, and the stand on which they were to be mounted above *Messina*'s deck had fallen off the back of the lorry onto the pitted and potholed road from the main camp to the port. It took four or five days to make them all operational again. As good all-round observation was essential Anson had to build a high platform up for'ard where all the 'gear' was eventually mounted. Anson's account of that explosion, as reported in his next letter home, is worth quoting *in extenso*.

'It was all rather a last minute effort and so you can imagine I felt a bit naked sitting up there with a stopwatch in one hand, a press-button in the other and a Valiant flying overhead with a damn great bomb in it. I had left changing into anti-flash rig until the last half hour so that I could work on the machines and, imagine my horror – when I did go to change I found all my protective clothing was still at the laundry, with the ship closed down tight and everyone else on the upper deck. My fault I know, but it was a moment of slight panic! However, I emerged in five minutes looking rather like an entry for a fancy dress Ball, with some black trousers, silk socks, and a blue pullover tucked up under my ears. I had my own private countdown this time and I was listening to the aircraft the whole time. They seemed most unperturbed and you could hear the whole intercom system; the Navigator churning out courses, speeds, drift and radar bearings, the pilot checking up on his crew until the last half-minute when they went completely silent. "Five seconds to go ... steady, steady, steady, steady, bomb gone, turning now climbing; out." A few quick checks on instruments by me and the sharp jab of a button followed closely by the flickering flash of our second bomb.

In ten seconds we were round and looking at the fireball – much larger this time – as it boiled its way upwards. Then it was lost behind a bank of cumulus clouds for thirty seconds. The snow-cap re-appeared first, going up at an almost impossible rate, followed by the mushroom and the stem of the whole gigantic formation.

We were allowed to stay on the upper-deck for a change, although even that was a bit uncomfortable. There was a high wind and spray was going over everything. However most of us were already quite damp and preferred to be drowned rather than stifled.

The press were with us this time and I expect you have read what they thought about it. They were flown into Malden in a Dakota the evening before and taken out in a DUKW to HMS Alert. She came out here, from being the Admiral's Barge in the Far East, to be a grandstand for the press and VIPs. Anyway, she took them out to sea for the night. It was a bit rough and I heard that Cassandra and the rest of them spent most of their time hanging over the side wishing they were safely back in Fleet St! They were a bit further off than us and they also had trouble with clouds being in the way.

I took six official photographs of this bang and had to send them all to Warrior for processing and a security check. Today a letter came back saying that they had all been classified secret and sent to AWRE. I shall never see them now which is rather a pity. There has been a terrible flap about the photograph [of the first test] in the Express. The big slip-up apparently was made by the Ministry of Supply. They had the official photographs soon after the bang but were slack in getting them out to the press. One of the POs in *Warrior* had his processed on board, cleared by the Commodore, sent home in mail leaving for Honolulu the same day, cleared by Admiralty, and published for which he got £500! The rest of the papers didn't think much of this and the Prime Minister has asked the Task Force Commander to put his reasons in writing. So, thank goodness you didn't send those of mine to any other paper. Please be very careful of them and don't let them go astray anywhere. I have had some of my private ones back from the English firm now. The Manager sent me a letter which I will quote in part: "It seemed a pity that you did not mention anything about the Press as I could have readily got a handsome figure for you. The first pictures came out in the National Press yesterday when your order arrived – I may say yours are a hell of a lot better. It seems that one of your chaps has scooped the pool as it must be worth £250 to him if it was syndicated." It's easy to be wise afterwards, but I wouldn't have minded even a sniff of £250!'

It has to be admitted that there was a certain amount of mischievous glee at the trials and tribulation of the visiting press grandees who included the well-known, fat and peevish Cassandra (William Connor) of the *Daily Mirror* who was soaked on the boat journey over from Alert and had to be helped on board by a well-placed hand between his legs and a smart heave from Commander Begg.

William 'Cassandra' Connor

Later, he would trawl round the mess decks hoping to pick up gossip and, even better, scandal. There was also the redoubtable Chapman Pincher of the *Daily Express*, who died in 2014 aged 100, and Leonard Bertin, the Science Correspondent of the *Daily Telegraph*. Once they had all been given dry clothes and recovered their composure, various officers were detailed off to accompany them. Robertson found himself with Bertin whom he described as 'a terrible old woman of a man'. Johnston tried unsuccessfully to impress the BBC reporter with his experience as a freelance for the Younger Generation programmes on the Light Programme but found him curiously impervious and much more interested in the weapon tests! Riches remembers being interviewed in the Health Physics Section by reporters from Associated Press and the *News Chronicle* but the Commodore had laid down strict limits to what could be divulged so it was a fairly brief and uninformative conversation.

On board recollections of the day were unanimous in experiencing the second weapon, code name 'Orange Herald', as bigger, brighter and louder than the first. On the flight deck this time Reed 'watched the contrail streaking across the sky. It was just possible to make out the shining white bomber flying at 45,000 feet. We sat with our backs to the blast, and as the countdown began we put on the dark goggles [...], placed our gloved hands over our faces and closed our eyes. I saw the flash and felt the heat on my back and shoulders. After what seemed an age we were allowed to turn round. The fireball was still descending.' Cassandra's *Daily Mirror* report said, 'And there it hung before us, a boiling red and yellow sun above the horizon. It was an oil painting from Hell – beautiful and dreadful, magnificent and evil.' Riches told his diary that the flash was brighter, the burst of heat on his back more intense and the later soundwave much louder this time.

This was Robertson's first sight of a weapon burst and he was both sombre and lyrical in his Journal account. 'I had of course heard descriptions of the first explosion but I was sobered by what I saw. Like an orange herald[10] of destruction, a huge, fiery, mottled sea-egg hung seething in the sky, dazzling at first and then fading into an inferno of deep colour. Suddenly, the pure white cloud began to ooze out of the top of the fireball and pour down over its sides like cream over a blood orange, finally covering it until only a faint pink glow relieved the whiteness; while as we watched the shock-wave reached us as a quick double pressure on the ear drums, no more. At last, far below, the stem appeared as if out of nothingness, and silently and majestically a thin plume climbed the sky to meet the main mass of cloud as it mushroomed out into the stratosphere. The picture was complete. "Mean, moody and magnificent," as the Hollywood publicity agents say. [...] This was a hideous sight [...] but incredibly dramatic and powerful.' It was also the only test Robertson witnessed as his services were called for once again at JOC.

He wrote in his Journal:

'This will be something for my grandchildren to talk about, if they are not all deformed half-wits as a result of it.' Later, he recalled the safety aspects of the tests. '[My] reference to the safety aspect and the hideous effects of significant exposure to nuclear radiation reminds me that, from everything I heard and saw and experienced, we were genuinely and properly and meticulously protected and looked after by the scientists and civil servants who planned, and by the senior officers who helped the scientists carry out, this particular test programme. Radiation badges, protective clothing, special dark goggles, washing down ship's surfaces, hands over goggles and backs turned to the distant air blast, exhaustive water, air and ground sampling programmes, the fishing programme: the list goes on and on. [...] When we steamed under the remains of the mushroom cloud after Orange Herald, it seemed [somehow] disappointing that our beta-gamma probes showed not the slightest increase in background radioactivity.'

It's important to note here that *Warrior* and its Midshipmen were not involved in the second series of tests begun later in the year and staged *within sight of* Christmas Island. Most of the assertions of radiation 'damage' to personnel date from that period.

Newspaper accounts of the second test were an interesting combination of the bland and the bellicose. The *Daily Telegraph* used a four-decker headline and three photographs to tell its version of the story.

BRITAIN EXPLODES SECOND H-BOMB

DROPPED BY VALIANT HIGH OVER PACIFIC

'ROBUST' WEAPON FOR USE BY JETS

TEST WAS BIGGER THAN FIRST OF SERIES

From LEONARD BERTIN,
Daily Telegraph Science Correspondent

WITH NUCLEAR TASK FORCE, Central Pacific, Saturday

Britain exploded another nuclear device this morning. It was the second in the test series and was larger than that of May 15 [...] Another fact that was disclosed to me at the special briefing before the latest explosion was that the technique used for this detonation was different from that of the first test. Later explosions in the current series explore further possibilities. Mr. Cook said to me: 'Let there be no doubt we are dead serious and we are out to produce weapons, not just things that go off bang.' [...]

SCIENCE ADVISER 'HAD NO FEAR'
HIS HEAD SECURE

Sir Frederick Brundrett, scientific adviser to the Ministry of Defence, interrupted his speech last night to the annual meeting of the Agricultural Co-operative Association at Harrogate, to announce that the second British atom [sic] bomb had been detonated in the Pacific.

He made the announcement with relief and satisfaction, he said, because the Prime Minister had told him that 'I might easily lose my head' if the detonation were not a success.

But he had never had any real fear for his head, Sir Frederick added.

One is entitled to presume that one of the differences William Cook alluded to was the absence, this time, of Bostik – but one never knows! The fact that was not reported at the time and not public knowledge until thirty years later was the serious problem that affected the Valiant that dropped the bomb, captained by Squadron Leader (later Group Captain) David Roberts. The full drama was recounted in 1985, by Group Captain Hubbard, in command of the Valiant Squadron.

'What I did not know until Dave Roberts had landed and was giving me his initial verbal report, was that during the escape manoeuvre he had experienced an electrical fault in his accelerometer, which was vital in order to hold the accurate gravity pressure needed in the escape steep turn. This sensitive instrument failed to operate, and this in applying backward pressure on the control column in the turn, the aircraft suddenly reached the high speed stall point. To find oneself in a high speed stall in this configuration is an unpleasant experience, and it is to Dave Roberts's credit that he was able to recover altitude and resume the escape manoeuvre utilising the mechanical accelerometer which was not placed in a position in the instrument panel layout to facilitate easy reference whilst flying to the full blind flying instrument panel. To have recovered from this situation in a 60° banked steep turn, under full instrument conditions, was a supreme feat of airmanship, for there were only seconds in hand before the weapon would explode when it reached 8,000 feet. Even more credit to Roberts was the fact that [...] his voice never wavered during the commentary; certainly those of us listening on the ground did not realise the difficulties this crew was experiencing at a very critical period after weapon release.'[11]

Had Roberts failed to extricate his Valiant from the stall, and worse had the plane been caught in the blast, all in front of the world's press, there is little doubt that the test series would have been halted in its tracks and Britain's nuclear weapon programme set back significantly if not abandoned altogether.

There was another opportunity for some of the Midshipmen to sail back to Christmas Island from where their whaler was dropped by *Warrior*. Hutchinson recalls that, 'Most Midshipmen joined in the night-time fishing expeditions to catch tuna and barracuda, often a bloody massacre led by the Commander, for the scientists to measure radioactive fallout. Some Midshipmen caught a shark with the help of

Lieutenant Harland using a bent pin, while messing around in a whaler near the shore. Other Midshipmen with nothing better to do on another occasion were also put in a whaler several nautical miles out to sea as *Warrior* returned from Malden Island early one morning. We were told to sail back to Christmas Island in time for the afternoon watch. The crew included myself as recruitment officer, Midshipmen Dennis, Hume, Riches (the Suez veteran) and one other. The sea was dead calm with not even a light air, but one of us was soon agonisingly sea-sick. We made such slow progress that *Warrior* sent out a motor boat to collect Midshipman Hume to serve his afternoon watch. We came alongside slowly and carefully two and a half hours later.'

It had been both a busy and a momentous month, but *Warrior*'s Midshipmen could not yet relax there was one more test to be held before they could get down to the serious business of showing the flag and, not to put too fine a point on it, selling the ship, although that aspect of *Warrior*'s voyage home was not widely known outside a handful of very senior officers.

---

1 Oulton, pp. 303-4. Emphasis added.

2 Begg. P.149

3 Hubbard & Simmons, *Dropping Britain's First H-Bomb*, Pen & Sword Books, Barnsley, 2008, p.129

4 Oulton, page ref tbc

5 Oulton, pp. 311/2

6 ADM1/29346 in the National Archives.

7 Begg, p.153

8 Cott was right to call Hawaii a Territory. It did not become a State of the Union until August 1959.

9 *Oulton*, pp. 337-9

10 Robertson deliberately used the code name for the explosion, thinking that this information was probably still confidential.

11 Kenneth Hubbard & Michael Simmons, p.146

JUNE

. . . .

Penrhyn (Tongareva)

Warrior returned to Christmas Island on 3 June after the second Grapple bomb test. Although June is 'midsummer' in the northern hemisphere and 'midwinter' in the southern, no perceptible change of temperature or climate was noticeable on opposite sides of the Equator. It rained heavily, yet the temperature remained stubbornly in the mid-eighties.

Riches was having to spend hours on the apparently simple task of booking flights for several ratings due for release from the Navy and needing to return home, and for another needing to be sent to detention quarters in New Zealand. The problems were resolved; the rain stopped and a weary Riches managed to fall asleep in the sun with painful consequences. The next day, not feeling one hundred per cent, he and Robertson received an invitation to go bird watching with the Commodore. One does not lightly decline such invitations. They walked for miles on another blisteringly hot day.

The Commodore had just received another honour. The Fijian detachment on board *Warrior* had awarded him the Tabura, the Order of the Whale's Tooth, whose previous recipient had been HM The Queen.

By this time, some three months into the Operation, the heat and humidity of a less than perfectly air-conditioned warship meant that various infectious skin rashes were spreading through the ship, lower and upper decks without distinction of rank. 'Prickly heat' was the general term used in the Gunroom but when the rash was scratched, an almost unavoidable occurrence, it was very easily infected, leading to blistering, and often worst behind the knees. 'Worst' in this case was bullous impetigo which sneaked up on its victims since the symptoms were not visible for four or five days after infection. The visible evidence began with the sprouting of these blisters, large and fluid-filled, on the trunk or on the arms and legs. Fortunately the neck and face were spared. The blisters spread before bursting to leave a yellow crust which healed without leaving any scarring. They weren't painful, but were so intensely itchy that even the most saintly victim could not forbear to scratch. When he did, his 'contaminated' fingers touched uninfected skin and the process repeated itself. Victims were told in the Sick Bay that it would clear up in a week, but were given some creams to apply and told to wash their hands before and after touching (and scratching!).

For officers, there was an extra problem in the evening. Evening rig in the tropics, known as 'Red Sea Rig,' consists of a white, open-necked shirt, black trousers, silk socks and shoes, and with the midriff covered by a cummerbund. This meant, alas, that the black trousers became a 'vector of transmission', reinfecting the legs every evening and spreading the infection around. Surgeon-Lieutenant Davidson, assistant PMO, instituted the sensible practice of allowing those infected to wear their white tropical long trousers instead, which could then be hygienically laundered. Woe betide any RNVR officer, however, who presumed to act on this sensible advice without first receiving Davidson's permission.

RIGHT: *Johnston in the 'wrong' trousers (Rowsell)*

Heartier outdoor seamen like Cooper, Dennis and Hume seemed never to be bothered, while Supply Officer Riches had such an interest in meteorology and ornithology that he was seldom below decks when he was not on duty. It was in this climate, in several senses, that the welcome news of *Warrior*'s continuing travels was announced.

The rest of the 'cruise' would include the visit to Penrhyn (Tongareva); a very welcome return to Honolulu; a rescheduled call at Rarotonga, capital of the Cook Islands, plus a stop at Pitcairn; calls at Callao (the port of Lima) and Valparaiso; a voyage down the spine of the Andes, visible from far off shore, and through the Straits of Magellan so as not to expose the ship to the Roaring Forties round the Horn; then Port Stanley in the Falkland Islands and, nowadays mission impossible, from thence directly to Puerto Belgrano in the south of Argentina; on up to Buenos Aires via the River Plate; then back down the river to Montevideo; and, finally, briefly back into whites for a visit to Rio de Janeiro, before crossing the Atlantic to Gibraltar and home to Portsmouth.

First however, there was the matter of the third of the current series of megaton weapon tests and various visits to make around the Pacific islands. At this point, Hume handed over his first motor boat responsibilities to Cooper and reflected in his Journal on the pleasure and benefits of this work.

> 'The 3½ months have been enjoyable ones, for there is nothing better than to be in the open in weather such as we are having. I have learnt more than I ever expected to; confidence in one's ability, seamanship, capabilities of the boat and the handling of the crew were only some of the things. Above all else, I think the most valuable lesson was that of developing anticipation and learning through bitter experience how to foresee a situation, and to decide what form it will take when it eventually does arrive.'

The other point Hume noted was the news, from the Duncan Sandys Defence White Paper recently published, that there would apparently be 'no more Midshipmen serving at sea' which struck him as odd. Who would man ship's boats; how would they acquire the essential experience and training, such as the compulsory dozen successful star sights? 'Could it mean that HMS *Warrior* houses the last sea-going, genuine Midshipmen's Gunroom?'

Meantime, Cooper was becoming more skilful at dealing with that problem of boat-handling peculiar to single-screw motor boats. When going astern, the position of the propeller causes the stern to 'walk' in the direction of its rotation, causing the stern to move to starboard, while the bow turns to port. To come alongside the ship's starboard after gangway and hook on fore and aft, the motor boat's coxswain has to develop a slight swing of the bows to starboard which is corrected by going astern. Done perfectly, the manoeuvre should bring the boat alongside stationary and perfectly aligned fore and aft. However, if not done so well, the crew member in the stern, with his boat hook poised, not only cannot hook on but, as the boat goes further astern, the boat's stern moves further and further way from the gangway and the coxswain has to go round again – with everyone watching!

June had begun well enough for Anson. He had completed his training in navigation and his Captain had appointed him Second Navigating Officer, with the sting in the tail being that he was now responsible for chart corrections. *Messina* carried nearly 900 charts, and around one hunred corrections per week came in the regular NOTEMS (Notice to Mariners) from the Admiralty. Anson also felt appreciated by senior officers and scientific staff, as was evidenced at a cocktail party in HMS *Alert* which he attended on the one day *Messina* was at Christmas Island before sailing south again. 'I thoroughly enjoyed myself and met some most interesting people. First, Capt. Western and Air Commodore Weir came and thanked me for some photographs I had sent them, closely followed by the Commodore who had had some too; in fact "Anson's photographs" seem to be becoming quite a byword at Grapple HQ! I was then introduced to Mr Cook the Scientific Director and had a long chat with him about his bombs. An RAF chap came up and introduced himself; he was Wing Cdr Hubbard, CO of the Valiant Squadron and the pilot of the first plane to drop the bomb. He was most interesting but refused to take much notice of the romancers who insist that it was a difficult and dangerous mission.'

Tell that to Robertson! On 11 June, when he had more or less forgotten about the promised joy-ride in a Valiant, his phone rang at JOC. It was Wing Commander Hubbard in person asking him to be ready in one hour's time.

'That afternoon I spent 65 minutes in the air with Squadron Leader Millett, lying on my belly in the bomb-aimer's position, swathed uncomfortably in flying overalls, helmet, Mae West and parachute, and nervously breathing quantities of oxygen. Naturally, I saw little of what went on inside the aircraft, but had a magnificent view. My main impressions are of incredible acceleration at take-off, of silence and smoothness in flight, and of the thrill of cruising at 450 knots, 45,000 feet up in the air. Of the masses of instruments I glimpsed before take-off, only the familiar dials of a Decca Navigator meant very much to me. My position was the bomb aimer's. I had to lie flat on my belly looking through his narrow window as the runway rushed past me at ever increasing speed and then dropped away alarmingly. Just as we were airborne, the pilot came on the intercom asking me, "How are you doing, Middie?" I replied, "Fine thanks," but the intercom was faulty and he couldn't hear me. "Christ," he said, "he's fainted already." Not true, but they did not abort the planned one-hour flight to check up on me. Altogether an experience to remember!'

The next day, Robertson was airborne again, this time in a Hastings flying to Honolulu, charged with buying more specialised fishing gear and conferring with the Operation's American fishing advisers. However, when he asked to purchase some only-once-used long line, he was told that authority to sell US Fisheries gear really needed the prior permission of the American equivalent of the 'Min of Ag and Fish'. Fortunately, after further discussion, they agreed to provide ten baskets of almost new gear 'on permanent loan' to further the great task of research. Robertson promised full and comprehensive reports, especially if his fishing team managed to catch one of the US Fisheries 'tagged' fish. 'Then it was off to other shops to carry out the small commissions that inevitably fall to the lot of any lucky man sent up to Honolulu, before flying back to base.'

That same day, a medical drama was being played out south of the equator. Anson, at the centre of the story, had his first opportunity to write home about it three days later, following up the telegram that had been sent to his mother from *Messina*.

'I'm sorry that my letter yesterday was a bit short and cryptic. Anyway, as I know you'll want to hear the full story I'll go right through it. On Monday I was invited ashore at Malden by the AWRE (Boffins) to show them some of my NZ photographs. Doc [Gavin Taylor, Messina's MO] came too to show some of his colour slides. Well, we had a splendid evening and were invited to spend the night in some of their spare tents. It was a lovely moonlit night so I went for a stroll along the beach. Then I got the queerest feeling and kept wanting to sit down and rest. However, I thought nothing of it and went back to turn in. I was sharing a tent with a photographer chap and Doc was sharing another tent somewhere else in the lines. At about 3.30 a.m. it started to pour with rain and everything in the tent was getting wet because both flaps were open. We both got out to fix this and I was a little alarmed to find that there was such a pain in my stomach that I could hardly stand up properly. The rain stopped and I lay down and tried to think what it could be. At 4 a.m. I couldn't stand it any longer and went out to try to find Doc. I had to search through dozens of tents in the semi-moonlight before I found him.

He did a bit of pushing and prodding, told me not to worry, and so I went back and turned in. Unknown to me he then got busy and arranged for a signal to be sent to *Warrior* saying that I had got appendix trouble. She was 100 miles away, steaming from Xmas to Penrhyn at the time. But at 4.30 a.m. she altered course towards Malden, went up to 'maximum revolutions', got two helicopters ready to take off and generally woke everyone up rather earlier than usual. As soon as

RIGHT: *Anson in the chopper heading for* Warrior *(Anson)*

FAR RIGHT: Warrior'*s surgical team, Surg Cdr Pugh (right) and Surg Lt Davidson* *(Anson)*

she was within flying range the helicopters took off and I woke up at 7.30 a.m. to find them landing near the camp. In ten minutes the PMO Surgeon Cdr Pugh, from *Warrior* came over, talked to Doc, and in another five minutes we were all in a helicopter heading for *Warrior*.

I was a trifle shaken by this sudden turn of events, but couldn't help being grateful to all the hundreds of people who had suddenly taken such a lively interest in me. In fact I was feeling fine again and wanted to walk around when we landed on *Warrior*. But the PMO said that he'd had to get up very early for me and it was my duty to lie down and look like a good corpse! I was in the Sick Bay by 0900 and was "on the table" by 1000. They took about two hours over it and I came out at lunchtime. I must say I had secretly quite enjoyed it all up to then as everyone was terribly concerned except myself and the whole thing seemed a bit like watching a play being acted out.

I came round feeling OK and was told that is was such a beautiful appendix they had pickled it and sent it up to the Bridge for the Commodore to see. This struck me as being a bit funny, but I soon found out that laughing anyway was out for a bit.'

The story is complicated by the fact that Surgeon Commander Pugh wrote a long letter to Anson's mother which was never acknowledged, causing the surgeon to feel some resentment at being thus ignored, but the explanation was very simple. Anson's mother was a Christian Scientist who did not believe in medicines and surgery but rather in the healing powers of prayer. (One wonders, therefore, what might have happened to Anson had he been suddenly taken ill at home.) However, apart from his complete recovery from acute appendicitis and threatened peritonitis, the move to *Warrior* for the operation became, in a short while, a permanent appointment to *Warrior*'s Gunroom where he joined his fellow National Service officers for the extraordinary voyage home.

> 'I'm now firmly entrenched in *Warrior*. I've got a cabin of my own, quite a nice one too, and, of course, I'm living in the Gunroom. After the frantic rush and bustle of *Messina* it is really wonderful to live a quiet and ordered life again, to be able to speak to people of one's own age and be treated like a Midshipman and not a general 'run-about' for everybody else. There are twelve of us in the Gunroom: three Subs and nine Mids. The Mess is much larger than *Messina*'s Wardroom and very comfortable. We can listen to the wireless and have our own radiogram and records. I'm only hoping that I can stay here and never go back!'

Meanwhile, after fetching Anson on board by 'air ambulance', *Warrior* resumed her voyage to Penrhyn, the most northerly of the Cook Islands.

This was very much an R&R visit for *Warrior*'s crew, now tending to feel, and occasionally to express, their boredom. Before the 'jolly' could begin, however, there was the necessary ceremonial. The New Zealand Resident Commissioner for the Cook Islands had been visiting Penrhyn, and as he flew off in one of *Warrior*'s helicopters to catch the SS *Charlotte Donald*, the inter-island steamer, the chopper stood off the port quarter while *Warrior* fired an eleven-gun salute in his honour while hoisting his official flag on the starboard yardarm. Riches's diary records his first impressions. 'Hardly had we dropped anchor than the vendors came on board; nearly fifty of them.[1] It seems they want clothes more than anything and they have no idea of the value of money. I managed to get two small pearls in exchange for my old pyjama jacket which the buyer told me he was going to church in on Sunday!' Cooper wondered, as *Warrior* sailed round the much cooler South America, how many sailors would regret parting with their pyjama jackets. Hume recalls that:

> 'The men, wearing shirts and shorts, do all the trading, whilst the wives make everything. The young children look beautiful, but their looks seem to deteriorate as they get older.
>
> I was immediately asked what I had in my bag – my camera – and spent much of the time taking photos. Huts of palm wood and woven fibres on small stilts, all

*Children of
Penrhyn (Riches)*

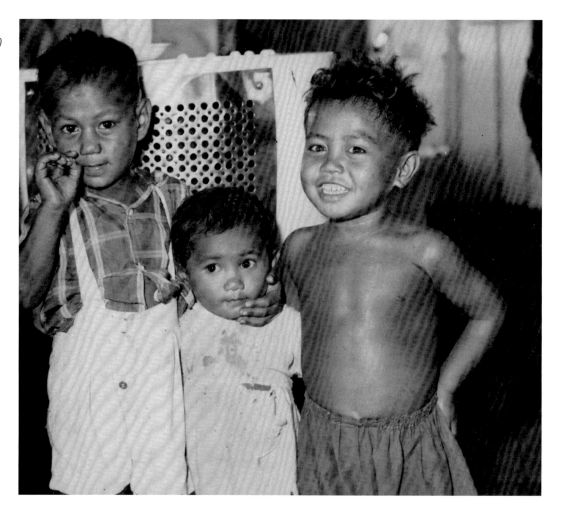

gave the village of Omoka a well-ordered look. The only piece of furniture is the bed, with sheets and pillows considered a matter of high social status; hundreds of children running around, many of them naked. The women wear bright print dresses. The whole place smells of coconut and fish. The men catch some fish and dive for pearls. Copra is produced and mother of pearl is sold by the pound. Interestingly, the price for this was 3s 4d on Penrhyn and a reported 3s 8d on Palmerston Island some 800 miles away; some islanders thought it worth making the long round trip for the extra fourpence! The islanders don't bother to catch enough fish to eat, so exist on imported canned food. All very chatty and friendly, but the smell! The fish the natives did catch was hung up to dry on clothes lines using plastic clothes pegs.'

Riches was ashore again next day with Dennis and Cooper and a large bag full of clothes to trade with. One lady was making grass skirts with a sewing machine. They wanted hats, and all the neighbours crowded in, with babies all over the place – one named after a ship, *Salvictor*, that had called there [about ten months ago]! Young women suckled children and eventually started bargaining, so finally they bartered a hat and grass skirt, just finished, for two shorts, two towels and a shirt. Time means nothing at all to the Polynesians, so negotiation is a long, slow business, but everyone seemed happy at the end. The visitors from *Warrior* noted with wry amusement that at the Council dinner entertaining the officers, native food was served: raw fish, stuffed coconut, breadfruit and fruit, whilst at the ratings 'do' they were served pressed beef and baked beans! Five Midshipmen sat down on palm leaves for the officers' *umukai* decked with floral garlands and, while they ate and drank, watched a wedding dance by the girls and a stick dance by the boys. Then everyone had to get up and dance at which point the girls all rushed to grab the Midshipmen as partners in the dance but not, in their cases, the wedding. However, there were three absentees before *Warrior* sailed; one had slept with a woman and so according to native law was now married to her. All three were brought back! The band had played for the people on Penrhyn, which thrilled them, and a chopper gave a demonstration. 'A very simple people,' remarked Anson, 'but the boys knew all about submarines and the Russians!'

Dennis described *Warrior*'s short stay with the eye of an experienced small-boat sailor and in glowing terms. Penrhyn, he said, [its European name; now called Tongareva, its Polynesian Maori name] was the most perfect Pacific atoll. It was a ring of coral-based thin islets covered with swaying coconut palm trees surrounded by a coral reef. In the middle was the lagoon which appeared very large. Access to the lagoon was through two passages between the islets. One of the major sized islets was broader than the others and this was where the main settlement was situated. Its stony water's edge on the lagoon side had a jetty jutting out into the lagoon and a rudimentary slipway ran up the stony beach. Beached on the shore there were a number of outrigger canoes. Lying off there were some broad-beamed short-masted sailing boats anchored or moored, used for fishing. They were about 20–25 feet long and had graceful lines with a broad beam in the waist to give them stability. They had a fixed keel and the rudder post passed through the deck and hull of the counter-shaped stern. The tiller was fixed, and when sailing one Dennis found they were easy to handle and there was no slack or play with the rudder. Each had a bowsprit and they were sloop rigged – a jib and a large gaff mainsail with a boom that extended slightly over the stern counter. All the rigging was primitive and improvised. Instead of blocks they used china HT cable insulators which must have been 'found' somewhere in the past among leftovers from visitors to the island, likewise the telephone wire was used as mainmast stays. They sailed well in the lagoon and Dennis remembered going out with Cooper and Reed and two fishermen looking for pearls.

'We sailed across the lagoon and at a shout the boat came head into the wind and the crewman tied a rather ragged piece of sisal rope to a large rusty hook which served as an anchor. Taking this in his hand he sat on the little foredeck and as the boat slowed to a stop he went over the side knee deep in the water standing on a coral reef. He hooked the anchor into a hole in the coral whilst his mate lowered and furled the mainsail and there we were, anchored in the middle of the lagoon. Before beginning their dive, the two islanders said a prayer in their own language and were pleased we said the Lord's Prayer. Fish were everywhere and the two fishermen dived into the water and swam around looking for pearl oysters. It was just like *Swiss Family Robinson* or *Masterman Ready* which I had read avidly many times as a young boy.

Up they came with oyster shells – each was opened carefully and, lo and behold, set in the mother of pearl shell was a half-formed pearl. We fingered it, we touched it, stroked it and smelt it – a real pearl in formation! They kept diving and coming back to the surface but the harvest was lean – not a pearl in sight. After an hour or so during which we also swam in the lagoon, there was great excitement. A small whole pearl was at last found which we proudly brought ashore. The trip was in our eyes almost a complete success. We had been pearl fishing in the coral seas in the South Pacific and had found one!'

Reed recalls there was one shell he opened which had two pearls. Cooper got one and he took the other which, back home months later, he had made into a tiepin.

The other adventure connected with the lagoon was the running of the ship's boats in and out of the lagoon, to and from the main settlement. The settlement, apart from the Polynesian islanders' own houses, consisted of a General Store, the

District Officer's house – it also had a radio station in an outhouse, the island's only connection with the outer world – and the school, which had an assembly hall where they proudly displayed a photo of Queen Victoria as they believed she was still alive in faraway Great Britain. There was also the only Church (Catholic) on the Island served by a Dutch priest who had lived there for over twenty years. Dozens of people spent their entire day gossiping on the veranda in front of the General Store which was set in the palm trees by the landing place. This looked out to the main gap in the reef through which *Warrior*'s boats plied back and forth. It was hot, the sky was blue and the sea in the lagoon was blue whilst, outside the atoll reef, the Pacific ocean swell heaved up and down in a slow rhythm day and night and, everywhere on the island, there was the background sound of breaking waves on the coral reef and the roar as the water ran across the reef. It was the real tropics – but was it idyllic?

'To ferry people in and out from the island, ships' boats were used with, as usual, the midshipmen running them,' reported Dennis. 'As boat midshipmen we had to follow the proper Naval procedures of driving the boats in and out of the lagoon to Omoka, on the edge of a curved inlet of the island of Moananui known as Gudgeon Bay. [...] The passage planning procedure entailed taking a large-scale chart of the lagoon and identifying the channel through the passage on the west side of the lagoon – the Taruia Passage.' Midshipmen-coxswains then had to plot a course noting the course to steer (CTS) and take into account the timings, currents and tides. There was a channel indicated in the lagoon by wood poles fixed on coral heads which one left to port or starboard when entering or leaving the lagoon. The passage plan was then checked by the Navigator who acted as Midshipmen's Nurse – in naval parlance 'Snotties' Nurse'. After all that, they had to do a trial run in with the Navigator, before it was over to them. The tricky part was going through the passage as there seemed to be a continuous strong current out of the lagoon. This necessitated creeping in near to the coral reef and keeping in as close as possible in order to get out of the main stream of the current, running at a good 2–3 knots particularly when entering the lagoon. This was especially difficult at night, in spite of the moonlight, and the launch's bow hand had to light the reef with a hand bearing lamp. At night the islanders lit a lantern which they hung from the flagpole by the store to act as a leading light.

'After half a day of using their passage plans as drawn up according to Naval procedures, Dennis was informed that the Island Chief had designated some of the locals (they were all boat handlers) to accompany *Warrior*'s boats on our trips and show the coxswains 'local pilot knowledge'. These islanders followed a much shorter route off the marked channel and, by showing the Midshipmen the bearings they used, the boats were able to halve the time of the trip. At night the bowman's hand lamp was important as it lit up some of the bearing marks they were using.

'All well and good,' reported Dennis. 'I followed the local pilot's instructions, and as neither the reef nor coral heads below water were hit, there was no problem. However, one evening on a routine run, I had to bring some officers back on board. Using this local knowledge passage, I set out, as it seemed to them, into the dark and away from the marked channel. Consternation ensued as they wondered what would become of them, followed by mutterings such as "He's not following the chart" and such like. The boat's crew performed with the lamp and all was well and we navigated the passage close into the reef and then across to *Warrior*. Happily, protests were by then muted and no more was said. However, I later discovered that the marked passage was intended for use by inter-island steamers which were much larger and had a bigger draught than our motor cutter. The islanders, who used either small outrigger canoes or their sailing boats which had a draught of, at the most, 3–4 feet did not need to use this deep draught channel. *Warrior* drifted on the current during the night and resumed station at dawn, while the steamers were able to use the deep draught passage and anchor in the lagoon, thus avoiding the long boat trip to go ashore.'

Hutchinson was also running the ship's boats but not getting as much pleasure as his fellow Midshipmen. 'I must pay tribute to the Fijian crew allocated to my motor cutter, members of a contingent who had joined the squadron for experience and training. They first showed their unusual value off Penrhyn Island in early June, diving repeatedly and for long periods under the cutter to untangle the reeds wrapped around the Kitchen rudder gear. Later that evening they gave more invaluable support when we faced much worse trouble trying to take the Squadron High Command from the shore back to *Warrior* through a narrow channel between reeds and submerged rocks. Dusk was falling.

'We had a local pilot, stationed on the starboard side. Dusk was falling rapidly when a very large landing craft entered the channel moving towards us and the harbour. The Commodore and other senior officers near the bow of our cutter shouted in alarm, exhorting me to steer the cutter to starboard and swearing at the landing craft, which had now seen us and was slowing down, full speed astern. I had slowed the cutter down too. I did not alter course to starboard as the pilot and the Fijians were gesturing frantically about reeds and rocks. Now our cutter and the landing craft, looming over us, were opposite each other in the channel, a cricket pitch apart, now in near darkness, their skipper was shouting at me to get out of the way. The Commodore was shouting at me and the skipper to get out of the way. The landing craft was not supposed to be there after 1800 hours at dusk. The pilot was still frantically agitated. I was pinned, motionless, frozen in the searchlight now shining from the landing craft, listening to the appalling language.

The Navigator, the Lieutenant-Commander in charge of Midshipman, told me that I had done wrong, not very precisely but emphatically. Later I wrote some sort of defence in my Journal (one of several reasons for destroying that evidence!) and he was even more critical of my uninvited and inappropriate apologia. On the day after the confrontation in the channel I had to deliver a package for the Commodore to a boat that was coming towards *Warrior* as it lay at anchor. I made a neat little manoeuvre to come alongside the other boat. The Commodore was impressed, or so the Navigator told me.'

Cooper recalls 'a pearl fishing excursion with John Marsters, a direct descendant of the original William Masters', whose name has been corrupted over the years to Marsters since this was how [the original West Country] William pronounced it, and who had settled on Palmerston in 1863 with a harem of four Polynesian wives. His descendants still populate the island and, as recently as 1954, had been granted legal ownership.[2] He also observed the curious Will o' the Wisp effects of flickering flames in the middle of the lagoon which the islanders said were the souls of the departed, but are almost certainly due to marsh gas released by rotting seaweed.

As a youngster, Johnston had attended a Congregational Church Sunday School which collected 'ship' halfpennies in support of the London Missionary Society's missionary sailing ship in the South Seas, the *John Williams IV*. Such a life seemed then very alluring. Now that he had actually reached the South Pacific, he had to admit he was rather glad not to have come as a missionary. He wrote to his parents that he had parted, reluctantly, with a tropical uniform shirt in exchange for a quite beautiful shell. 'I argued with the vendor that the shirt was not really mine to trade

Family group on Penrhyn (Riches)

Pua dancing (Johnston)

Islanders dancing on Penrhyn (Rowsell)

but the vendor promised not to inform Her Majesty. Then I wandered up into the village and took photographs as I went.

Eventually, after a look all round and about, I joined several others in a house where two local beauties (including *the* local beauty) were holding court, singing and playing the guitar. I came in as Pua was dancing the hula. A sight for sore eyes.

Islanders with empty glasses (Rowsell)

Her hips gyrated, swung and shook to the strumming of the guitar and her arms traced the most wonderful patterns.

After three months without seeing one woman, we all revelled in it.'

That night, on board ship, there was a concert and a troupe of dancing girls was invited together with island notables, both Polynesian and European. The officers entertained them nobly and at the bar on the quarterdeck the old women drank whisky and the rest of the crowd drank beer or lemon squash. The old women were not subtle. Holding their glass upside-down, they would say, 'Look, me finished!'

Finally, to get them down to supper, the officers took round some empty bottles, holding them upside-down and saying, 'Look, we finished too!' The Gunroom was allocated four or five people to entertain to supper but when they asked two of the dancing girls they all came down; nine of them and three men from the band. They found a little difficulty in coping with anything more complicated than a spoon but they seemed to enjoy the meal which they prefaced by a grace in Maori.

After supper came the concert and when the compère said, 'And now, the show all you sailors have been waiting for,' a shapely, slim, brown leg appeared through the curtains and waggled suggestively. The roar of all-male approval was immediately drowned by a gale of laughter as a young Fijian sailor appeared on the other end of the leg. But 'les girls' followed immediately and brought the house down. They stood in a semicircle with the 'prima ballerina' in the centre. Behind them sat the guitarists and drummers together with some singers. The dancers stood almost stationary, the movement being the swaying of the body and the weaving to and fro of the arms. At the height of the dance, one of the local elders who was conducting the band leapt into the centre and joined in with great gusto. This so excited one bald and fat old chap in the audience he got up and dragged his equally portly missus onto the stage where, backs to the audience, they performed dramatically if somewhat obscenely.

'At supper, I sat opposite Pua,' Johnston recalls, 'but she was on the verge of sophistication as far as we young officers were concerned. More receptive to our flattery and to the helpfulness that their inexperience with the knife and fork brought out in me – 'Here, let me show you. If I just put my arms round you and guide your hands!' – was Ka'a with the sweetest of smiles. She it was who taught me some Maori phrases while Pua corrected my pronunciation. 'Kia ora' – Good day. 'Pe'ea koe?' – How are you? 'E meitaki au' – I am fine.

'Word of my language lesson paid off at the gangway as we were bidding them goodbye. All the girls, especially Ka'a, said "Kia ora, Michael. Pe'ea koe?" to which I replied "E meitaki au" and handed them on to the suitably impressed Commander (probably the only time I ever suitably impressed him.) Afterwards, he asked me if I would go ashore the following day and collect some records for the SRE from an American lady who had been his dinner companion. Only *too* happy, I thought, but all I said was, "Aye, aye, Sir!" Next day, after collecting the records I was able to make tape recordings of Polynesian singing which I was later to play on the SRE. To my delight, I encountered Ka'a who beckoned to me (as I thought, seductively) to enter her hut – where she introduced me to her husband!'

During the day, an LCM ferried what seemed like the entire population out to visit *Warrior* where the main fairground attractions were travelling up and down on the aircraft lifts and riding round and round the flight deck on trailers towed by the tractors that normally towed the aircraft. Several old ladies had so many trips they had to be asked to step off and let the youngsters have a turn.

On both evenings at Penrhyn, *Warrior*'s concert party regulars performed. The first night was a bit of an under-rehearsed shambles and far too long but the star event was an outstanding rendition of Noel Coward's *We're three juvenile delinquents* by Midshipmen Cooper, Hume and Dennis, accompanied at the piano by the *Warrior*'s resident Rubinstein, Midshipman Reed and on the tuba by Midshipman Kirchem. Only Reed had any musical 'qualifications' and he had had the job of rehearsing the others for five days beforehand.

The second night was marginally less of a shambles but, due entirely to the participation of Penrhyn's dancing girls and brilliant drummers, the evening did not seem a moment too long. Sitting in the audience, Johnston found himself directly behind a charming young French woman on whom he cheerfully practiced his hard-learned skills in that language; until the Fleet Air Arm Commander, whose companion she was, sent him packing with *une puce dans l'oreille.*

Dennis, Cooper and Hume as three juvenile delinquents (Rowsell)

After two days in 'paradise' *Warrior* sailed again for Malden, but not before Riches bought his brother's birthday present: a whole coconut still in its hard outer casing on which he stuck the address label and the appropriate stamps. It duly turned up and was much appreciated. On the way north, the ship did its quarterly full power burst and registered 211 revolutions on the engine room counter. It says something about how soon one can adjust to prevailing circumstances that no one seemed much excited by the prospect of yet another H-bomb test in the middle of the following week; just the same old routine, really! On its course towards Malden, steering 030° at 15 knots, the ship passed close to the uninhabited island of Starbuck on the starboard side.

The Commodore and a few officers made a trip ashore by helicopter but others had to be content with using binoculars. *Warrior* arrived off Malden in the early evening of Saturday with the dress rehearsal for the final test planned for the Sunday.

'Rig of the Day' on 19 June, the day of the test, was No. 8s, long-sleeved blue shirt, blue jean trousers, tucked into socks, and shoes. Ratings on deck watch and on the flight deck wore the anti-flash hoods with dark goggles, gloves and carried respirators. All this was 'as normal' on these occasions. Station-keeping for the ships of the Grapple Squadron, to the north of Malden, was more difficult this time, due to the strong easterly set of the current which meant *Warrior* had to keep going slow ahead on one engine. Nor could the other ships take a visual bearing on Malden, since the low lying island over twenty miles away was below their horizon. The atmosphere on the compass platform and the flight deck was more relaxed than for the two previous bursts. Cooper's Journal describes the subsequent events.

'The Valiant was now overhead as she streaked towards ground zero on her first of two preliminary runs. She made these successfully and turned at the top of the 'racetrack' to make the live visual drop. At ten minutes to the burst no one seemed perturbed. At five minutes the compass platform was functioning as if on a station-keeping exercise. By this time on the two previous bursts everyone had been crouched and tense. Then the pilot's and bomb-aimer's commentary began and I relayed it to the ship. 'Bomb Gone! The weapon is falling. Close your eyes … 40 … 30 … 20 … 10 … five, four, three, two, one.' And then I didn't need to say anything, such was the brilliance of the flash. At +10 seconds, when we opened our eyes, we saw an intense white fireball. It was almost too bright to look at. Almost immediately the top half was covered with a thin white cloud cap, like a shiny bald head wearing a skull cap. A thin vapour stalk appeared. As the fireball developed into the familiar white, rose-tinted mushroom, the stalk almost touched the sand and dust cloud that was billowing on the horizon. Then a peculiar bulge appeared on the stalk about one third of the way down and at that point there was a sharp crack that made many duck instinctively, followed by a low rumble. This, for me, was by far the most spectacular of the tests and the shockwave added something which the two previous bursts had lacked!'

In the afternoon, *Warrior* closed Malden and went through the usual post H-hour routines. Damage to the island did not seem as extensive as one might have imagined. The one conspicuous tree still stood and the ruins of McCullough's settlement seemed to be in no greater state of disrepair. On this occasion, the Commodore was one of the re-entry team that landed on Malden in the aftermath of the explosion. The precious instruments and their readings, together with the air-sampling results from the Canberras were soon on their way to AWRE in the UK. Having had to fly through a tropical rainstorm, the Canberra's engines were reported as 'noticeably less contaminated than usual' and flying through such a 'plane wash' became part of regular decontamination procedure for aircraft engines.

With 'mission accomplished' the Grapple Task Force Commander flew off to New Zealand for official thank-you visits, taking the Commodore with him and leaving *Warrior* to the tender mercies of the Commander. Word was already coming through, however, that the scientists wanted to carry out further tests. Back-loading of equipment was halted and the question was raised whether some of the ships would require to remain on station. The scientists, it seemed, felt that such were the very low radiation levels measured during the tests so far that further testing could be carried out within sight of Christmas Island which meant there would not be the same need for an aircraft carrier to provide a forward 'airfield' and so *Warrior*'s plans to travel home round South America were not put in doubt.

Messina's plans to travel home seemed momentarily in special jeopardy as *Warrior*, under the command of Commander Begg, who sometimes handled the aircraft carrier like a destroyer, seemed to be bearing down on her at 15 knots. *Messina* signalled, 'Am stopped!' to which Begg, characteristically replied, 'Am not!'

Back at Christmas Island a couple of days after the test, Riches read an Admiralty Fleet Order which announced that all those who had taken part in the Suez invasion the previous year would now be receiving the Naval General Service medal. He confided in his diary, 'I suppose some of us deserve it but if I hadn't worked in the casualty ward for three days I'd have certainly felt a fraud!' A more general excitement for the Midshipmen was that now all the officers from the other services had begun to go home, there were cabins available for all of them. While all had enjoyed the camaraderie of the chest flat, the personal space and the additional privacy of a cabin was welcome. As yet, it was unresolved who would be travelling

The genial Percy Roberts with Grapple tie (Rowsell)

with *Warrior* as passengers for the journey back to the UK – apart from the genial Percy Roberts, the District Officer – so the possibility of having to surrender their cabins later on was always there. On the downside was the immediate obligation to paint ship again. The Commander's ambition was to turn a now somewhat travel-worn warship into '20,000 tons of shimmering bull!' HMNZS *Pukaki*'s parting signal to the Commander read, 'Hope you take the Horn by your Bull.'

Robertson finished his tour of duty at JOC to return on board, sad to leave the pleasant company of fellow officers but not at all sad to see the last of one creature. 'Memories are made of this. The obscene, ubiquitous, loathsome land crab, advancing lecherously into one's tent at night, doubtless encouraged by the swarms of cantharides beetles, otherwise known as Spanish Fly, swimming in one's nightcap, and patently intent on sharing one's bed.' For the first time in many weeks, Robertson did not go on a fishing expedition from the island using the new gear he had 'borrowed' from the US Government. But that happened to be the expedition when they caught something rather special: a superb 12 foot black marlin, on the longline. It weighed in at 950 lbs and had to be hauled in by hand; but not until it had itself towed the whole apparatus of buoys, line, the rest of the catch and the cutter for several hours. However, the team did finally have something to boast about that night. They took a photograph for posterity but, like the marlin, no trace of this can be found!

Although Hume thought his boat-running days were over, he was brought 'out of retirement' to instruct Johnston. Being a Sub Lieutenant, Johnston was rather in between the still youthful Midshipmen and the more grown-up RN Subs and had not done a great deal of anything except watch keeping, so he was grateful for the chance to drive the motor boat. At first he seemed a fairly capable pupil, but, not long after the Commander issued scarcely veiled threats to any Midshipmen damaging the ship's boats, Johnston managed to come into contact with the starboard after gangway with sufficient force to put a hole in his boat. More repair work for the Chippy! Then, no longer under Hume's supervision, but this time running a cutter in the early hours of the morning, he managed to go astern in too tight an arc and ran onto a sandbank at the port. On turning to head for the channel he found that his boat had grounded, with its propeller stuck in the sand. After a few fruitless efforts with boat hooks, he had to get out and push! The propeller was twisted and needed repair. He wrote home lamenting, saying that he felt he would never acquire the seamanship skills that seemed to come so naturally to his Midshipmen colleagues. Like Hume, he found himself spending his 'day off' painting the ship from a catamaran and getting filthy chipping rust off the hull. It was a relief afterwards to dive into the Pacific and swim back to the boom. In their filthy state, painters and decorators were not allowed to use the gangway. Hume could see the steady progress of the painting. *Warrior* did look more 'bullish' even if it didn't yet 'quiver'.

Fishing for sport rather than to provide material for checking radiation, Hume felt catching barracuda was a very good sport although they didn't put up so much fight as the tuna.

On 25 June a party of young officers went up to the airfield for a final look at the Valiant which had dropped the last bomb. The other aircraft had already flown home. They also saw the Canberras that had carried out the cloud sampling after the explosions and two of which were still too radioactively hot to fly home.

Johnston did not go on that trip as he had an appointment with the ship's dentist to remove an upper and a lower wisdom tooth. It was painful for a while until the Gunroom bar opened!

Sailing home too were the two New Zealand frigates, *Pukaki* and *Rotoiti*. Given the great support they had been to the UK H-bomb tests, it is somewhat ironic to note that the next time these two ships were deployed in the area was to lead New Zealand's official protest against the French nuclear tests at Morurua atoll. *Warrior*'s officers were welcomed aboard for their farewell RPCs. The frigates also carried away the detachment of Fijian RNVR sailors who had been such a decorative and musical part of life aboard *Warrior*. Captain Western had earlier asked Robertson if he would like to sail to Rarotonga in *Pukaki*, which was calling there, in order to 'get some small ship time in and wait there for *Warrior* to pick you up?' He was more than

Riches inspecting the Valiant that dropped the last bomb (Riches)

willing but higher authority was not persuaded. Instead, he had to put up with going back (again!) to Honolulu with *Warrior*.

News came too that Commander Begg had been officially notified that he was officially on the short list to be promoted to Captain in six months' time. There was a party to celebrate the start of his novitiate as well as the many other farewell rituals and libations. Quite a few of the older officers were, however, applying for the generous 'Golden Bowler' scheme aimed at reducing their numbers. Then it came time to say (almost) a last farewell to Christmas Island where *Warrior* would only stop briefly on her return from nearly two weeks up in Pearl Harbour. On the way north again, Hutchinson and Johnston were to begin their one month spell working in the boiler room and engine room. Given that *Warrior* was still in the Tropics, their natural curiosity about that part of the ship's working was tempered by a concern about the ambient temperatures in that working environment. Both, however, survived, although not returning to deck watches until *Warrior* approached the coast of South America. Meantime, there was much to do and see in Hawaii and then Rarotonga.

1 In fact, *Warrior* could not anchor satisfactorily on the steeply shelving coast of Penrhyn and needed to regularly steam back into position.

2 Although the whole island group is called the Cook Islands, Palmerston is the only one on which Captain Cook ever set foot himself. He discovered it on his second voyage in 1774, but it wasn't until Sunday, 13 April 1777, during his third Pacific voyage, that he went ashore. He named the tiny and remote island after Lord Palmerston who was First Lord of the British Admiralty and father of a future British Prime Minister. The ancient Maori name was supposedly Avarau, meaning 200 harbours. http://www.cookislands.org.uk/palmerston.html#. U6mAlrFMJx0 accessed 24 June 2014

JULY
....

From Hawaii to Pitcairn

With the Commodore back from his brief trip with the TFC, Commander Begg could focus even more on painting and primping his beloved ship for her visit to Pearl Harbour, her cruise through the Cook Islands and her brief visit to Pitcairn. Most important of all, however, would be her tour of South America, wearing the flag and the person of Vice-Admiral Sir Geoffrey Robson CB DSC RN, Commander-in-Chief South Atlantic and South America. CINCSASA was normally based at Simonstown in South Africa, but would be joining *Warrior* as she arrived at Callao, the port of Lima, in early August.

Few of those aboard escaped being roped in for painting parties. The emphasis was more on the painting and rather less on the party, and it took much of the time from Christmas Island to Pearl Harbour for some of the Gunroom to scrub off the traces of paint and patches of rust about their persons. They too wanted to look their best for the nine-day wonder of the visit, which promised to be a near continuous round of offering and accepting invitations to cocktail parties, picnics, dinners and dances. Some of the groundwork laid on the previous visit would bear fruit. For example, Cooper was summoned by the Commodore's Secretary to be told that a letter from the British Consul in Hawaii to the Commodore included the following: '... and I would also like to add that my daughter wishes to inform you that she is asking Rupert Cooper to partner her at a dance to be held here on Saturday, 13 July.' Fortunately, the Commodore had been amused that he was being requested/ instructed to pass on an invitation to one of his Midshipmen. Protocol is hugely important in the very rank-conscious armed services.

Warrior was called on to ferry the Task Force Commander and the Commodore round all the ships of the squadron so that each one could be formally thanked for all their efforts. It was Cooper who drove the Commodore's barge round the harbour area calling on eight other ships. The trip went off without a hitch and the Air Vice-Marshal congratulated Cooper on his seamanship, unaware that only two days previously he had managed to put a six-inch hole in the barge's side which nearly sank it. He asserts that the seas were rough at the time so he wasn't entirely to blame, but the Navy does tend to operate on the principle that someone, rather than something, is *always* to blame!

Robertson was now permanently back on board and installed in his own cabin. It had until then been a store for lavatory paper, not all of which had been removed before he took possession. It was the old-style paper, glassy and liquid-repellent on one side and something not unlike sandpaper on the other, with each sheet bearing the printed statement, 'Property of Her Majesty.' Anson was also 'permanently' on board, his transfer from *Messina* having been approved, much to his delight. The Gunroom complement of National Service RNVR officers was now ten; nine Midshipmen and one Sub-Lieutenant.

Riches's diary reports on 3 July that painting of the entire port side and the after half of the starboard side was finished. The for'ard half of the starboard side would be done during or after the visit to Honolulu, since the principal purpose of that visit was to complete the repairs to the starboard bow which had been so badly damaged crossing the Atlantic some five months earlier.

 The order 'clear lower decks' was issued on 4 July to bring everyone onto the flight deck to listen to the Task Force Commander thanking the ship's company and wishing them well on their fascinating voyage home. By then, it was known that *he* would not be going home. He was to continue in command of the next series of thermonuclear weapon tests, scheduled for later in the year and, probably, on into 1958. Partly because the three tests carried out at Malden had generated such a negligible amount of fall-out, the decision had been taken to carry out these later tests off Christmas Island, rather than Malden. This meant that an aircraft carrier to provide, amongst other things, a forward landing strip, would not be required, and *Warrior* could now return to the UK.

The return journey began on the same day, as *Warrior* slipped from her buoy at 19.30 and headed north. For a moment, it seemed almost that the ship was going the wrong way, leaving Christmas Island on the southern horizon; but by then it was dark, and only those who were reading the stars, or the ship's compass, could tell in what direction she was sailing.

Cooper and Robertson were busy star-gazing at dusk and dawn as they worked to make up their Midshipmen's dozen of astral fixes to the satisfaction of the Navigator. He had pointed out that they needed to polish these off now, in the Tropics, since cloudy skies off the coast of South America would make the task much more difficult. But they didn't need to wait for these overcast skies as, the very next day, *Warrior* encountered her old friend the Inter-Tropical Convergence which lurks a few degrees north and south of the Equator. The rain and wind were a nuisance for the two Midshipmen but a source of considerable frustration for the Commander. The rough seas managed to lift a fair amount of the newly applied paint off the hull and he was in no mood to appreciate having the task compared, by one foolhardy young officer, to that of painting the Forth Bridge!

Nor was the Commander best pleased when *Warrior*'s boiler rooms 'blew soot'. With *Warrior*'s funnels being in the island on the starboard side of the flight deck, it was customary to alter course while doing so, in order to bring the wind across the ship from port to starboard and allow the soot to be blown away. However, significant traces of soot were to be seen on the flight deck, leading to an exchange of words between Commander Begg and the Commander (E). After all, the latter argued, if the seamen on deck didn't alter course appropriately his stokers couldn't possibly see that from down in the boiler room!

Meanwhile, down on 4 Deck, the Gunroom itself was being given a coat of paint in anticipation of the entertaining on board (code-named 'Operation Smooch') during the visit to Hawaii. The ever-present heat and fug below decks, when combined with the smell of paint, made several Midshipmen queasy. Everyone was glad when, on the 7th, the outline of the Hawaiian Islands was detected on the radar. The following Tuesday morning, the US Pilot came on board and *Warrior* was guided alongside Jetty B17 in the historic Pearl Harbour.

By the end of the day, the rumour mill was reporting arguments between the two Navies, with the US team saying it needed more time and more money than the generally-supposed US$9,000 [then about £3,200 but the equivalent of around £70,000 at 2017 prices] budgeted for the work to repair the damage to the bows and to fix the permanently flooded for'ard trimming tank.

The round of official receiving and offering of hospitality got under way immediately as well as the formal calls made by the Commodore on the senior US Navy officers. These rejoiced in those classic abbreviations beloved by the services of both countries – COMHAWSEAFRON, CINCPACFLT, and COMPEARLNAVSHIPYD. A group of visiting Royal Canadian Navy Sub-Lieutenants came for lunch and it was noticeable that they were all older, often married, and significantly better paid, than

Warrior *entering*
harbour
(Rowsell)

their RN equivalents. Riches and Cooper had a tour of the dockyards which seemed very spacious with all the service families 'living in.' The bulk of the US Pacific Fleet was at sea so *Warrior* was the largest vessel in Pearl Harbour at that time. Since 1941, indeed, it had been US policy to keep the number of their ships in port at any one time to the necessary minimum so as never to be caught on the hop again.

None of this concerned the bulk of the *Warrior*'s crew, including the eager Midshipmen. The first encounter, an official cocktail party on the quarterdeck, was scheduled for the Tuesday evening. The RNVR 'experts' were swiftly called in to assist the Wardroom when Lt Harland, the Boats Officer, found himself unable to cope with *three* young beauties attending the party. Johnston managed to make an early contact with a USN Captain's daughter, Leanne, and he struck quickly, offering her an invitation to the Gunroom dance, which she accepted. It was a quiet pleasure for him to listen later to other (RN) officers being turned away disappointed, and seeing that, as they turned, some of them looked daggers at him. This was to be a momentous moment for Cooper too, who was destined to leave Hawaii heartbroken!

Here is what Cooper wrote home at the time. 'We arrived in Honolulu as I told you with the usual pomp and ceremony, and life seemed fairly normal until I met Frances. She really is an absolute honey. She is the niece of Admiral Olsen, who is in command of the Naval Shipyard, and I met her quite by accident at a boring 'cockers' party and really hit it off the second night in. On Thursday, Frances and I went out *à deux* to the Royal Hawaiian Hotel which is more than fabulous and is more suited to millionaires than Midshipmen. However, she made a hit with the head waiter and I am sure my bill was halved. We danced until 0200 and then returned to their home. She has an enormous Plymouth coupé of her own and I always insisted on filling it up with petrol wherever we went.

I got her invited to the ship's cocktail party and then six of us went off on a mad party returning [on board] at 0400!'

However, for Cooper and Riches a certain conflict of loyalties was becoming evident. Both had their already-accepted invitations to the Consul's dance, to partner the two young ladies they had met on their previous visit. Since both ladies, Anne and Judy, came to this cocktail party, there was no avoiding their duty to entertain them, which they took so seriously that they took them out after dinner to the Hawaiian Village Hotel on Waikiki Beach for drinks and dancing. The Consul was not altogether happy that his daughter did not return home until 0345.

On Wednesday morning, Cooper and several other Gunroom officers, including Reed, Riches and Johnston, had been met at the starboard after gangway by not just one limousine but a fleet of them that had come to take them, two per limo, to visit the US Marine Air Base at Kaneohe on the windward side of the island of Oahu. The visit included going up and over the Nu'uana Pali, a high pass on the shoulder of an extinct volcano.

This gave them a chance to admire the stunning view, take photographs, and hear about how the Hawaiian King Nu'uana had driven his enemies over the cliff, giving them the choice either to die in battle or to jump. Recent road excavation in the valley below had uncovered hundreds of skeletons. It had been a brutal civil war – in which *both* sides were using weapons supplied by the British!

On arrival at Kaneohe, the Warriors were taken aback to be met not only by a bevy of senior US Marine and Navy officers but also a battalion of the press corps. The tour of the base included a visit to a rifle range where crack US Marines were showing off their skills with .300 rifles. Expressing interest, Cooper was invited to fire one at a range of 500 yards. He was rather patronisingly reminded to take care as the rifle had quite a kick, and it was clear that no one would expect him actually to *hit* the target. Little did they know of Cooper's many talents, and they were somewhat abashed when the signal came back, 'Centre bull'. After that, the press had to take photographs of him lying down as if to fire another round.

Admiring the stunning view (Riches)

Although the Royal Navy were guests for lunch, such was the set-up, each guest paid 75 cents for their splendid meal. Since US Navy and Marine ships and bases are 'dry', there was no alcohol served, but at every place there were tankards of something that looked rather like Pimm's No. 1 in colour, and had the odd slice of fruit floating on it. However, some of the Americans were seen adding a spoonful of sugar and giving their drinks a stir. Johnston tasted his first and although it seemed vaguely familiar he just could not place it. He asked the Ensign at his elbow what was in his glass. The Ensign was astonished that a 'Limey' had not recognised cold tea.

Upon their return to *Warrior*, Riches and Cooper, maybe conscious of their earlier black mark, gave up the opportunity to catch up on sleep and atoned by showing the young brothers of the two girls round *Warrior* in the morning. Their penance was made all the harder by the fact that the youngsters asked 'such damned intelligent questions.'

Riches suffered a little less on this visit from the junior Supply Officer's usual problems when alongside, but on the day one his superiors still went off on their official visits leaving him to man the office, answer the phones and fend off fellow-officers (hard when they mostly out-ranked him) who wanted names added to the already vastly oversubscribed list of invitations to *Warrior*'s *official* cocktail party.

Johnston had successfully pleaded for an invitation to be sent to journalist Larry Cott. He came, but not without some difficulty at the main gate. The sentry, unfamiliar with British etiquette, argued that the printed invitation was for a Mr Esq, not a Mr Cott. It took a few minutes and a phone call to establish that Mr Larry Cott and Larry Cott Esq were alternative forms of address for the same person.

In due course Johnston arranged to meet Larry when ashore, and went with him to a record shop where he bought an EP (45rpm) of English fairy stories retold in Hawaiian Pidgin. Little Red Riding Hood became *Li'l Lei Pu'ahi an de big bad Pua'a who allatime lookin' aroun' for kaukau some pocky li'l Wahini*. Finally, Larry enrolled him in the 'Knock the Rock Club of Honolulu' of radio station KHVH, in return for taking this pledge: 'I hereby pledge my undying devotion to the preservation of good music (as heard on Swingin' Sunday) and will do all in my power to suppress that primitive cacophonous form of noise 'Rock and Roll.' I pledge to suppress and put down that decadent monstrosity the most.' A pledge he has kept to this day.

ABOVE:
Johnston's membership card, face and back (Johnston)

The lower deck hit town fairly hard, and *Warrior*'s shore patrol was kept busy. The ship's Regulators, plus a rota of conscripted ratings, worked closely with their American opposite numbers who had the legal jurisdiction ashore. Only one incident appeared to get out of hand, when the Hawaiian Police had to intervene with guns drawn to pacify a bar room brawl. The arrested miscreants were brought back on board and handed over to the Master-at-Arms, but not before some of them had even assaulted the Officer of the Day. That would later involve Riches in arranging some flights home to detention quarters in the UK.

Others from the Gunroom found time that day for a brief, but solemn, visit to the superstructure of the sunken battleship, the USS *Missouri*, now an official war grave in Pearl Harbour. Only sixteen years after that attack, the story and the images were still very fresh in naval and civilian memories.

The ship's log for 12 July records, without any other details, that 'at 2235 one underwater swimmer captured by US Marines whilst swimming near starboard screw during security exercises.'

On the Thursday evening, the Gunroom held its long scheduled dance, but some of the preparations were left to the last minute; so much so that some of the young men were still dressing or mixing fruit salad when their first guests were announced. It was the first time they had been able to wear their snazzy white mess jackets, white piqué shirts and single-end bow ties and they felt they were a bunch of real swells. However, not everything went as had been intended. Riches's diary reveals that he 'failed to get a girl for Laurance [Reed] and forgot to tell him,' and goes on rather cryptically to say that 'Rupert and I have achieved the smoothest of switches

LEFT: *'Dizzy' dancing (Riches)*

RIGHT: *Kirchem and partner (Riches)*

179

*Dennis
sitting out
the eightsome
(Riches)*

and the dance went accordingly well! 'X' isn't a live wire I'm afraid, but she's very steady and not temperamental like so many of them. The Commander ordered the proceedings to finish at midnight, rather I feel as a result of Tuesday, but that's mere speculation.'

Johnston's letter home describes a 'wild eightsome reel led by 'Dizzy' Robertson' and records the fact that he and Robertson were taken on afterwards to 'Kelly's, a snazzy coffee bar of the sort that are all over Hawaii. 'Dizzy' was on form and kept us laughing, especially the girls, to whom his peculiar accents and airs were something completely new.'

*Anson and
partner relaxing
(Riches)*

'Dizzy' keeping everyone laughing (Riches)

Perhaps it was as well for Riches that the dance ended at midnight, because he then went conscientiously to do some uncompleted office work before turning in at 0300, knowing he had to be up again at 0530. His diary picks up the story.

'Today has definitely been the climax of our visit so far. Twenty of us including the Commodore flew in a Dakota from Oahu the 216 miles to Hilo, the capital of "the big island" of Hawaii. The scenery there is real picture book and the flowers exotic. On arrival we went for a splendid lunch – again 75 cents at the PX cafeteria – the highlight (for me) being a glass of fresh milk, my first for five months. After lunch at the military rest camp at 4,000 feet, we became tourists, joining holidaymakers from California and Oregon and visiting the still very active volcano of Kilewa.

'The colossal craters and the steam holes fascinated me. I hate to think how many photographs I took. This really has been a wonderful experience. I'm certainly uncannily lucky how I always "draw the right ticket" for these outings.'

At that time, July 1957, the Gunroom officers did not realise how fortunate they were to be visiting the Hawaiian Islands when they did, just before the era of jet travel and mass tourism. One could say that, as yet, mainland American tourists had not really 'discovered' Hawaii and it was relatively speaking unspoiled. Then it was back to Honolulu and *Warrior* for a quick change for the dance hosted by the Consul and the manager of QANTAS that Cooper and Riches were required to attend. Another Midshipman who flew to Hilo was Hume, who found the views of Waikiki stunning but the flight rather uncomfortable, as the Dakota was actually rigged for dropping parachutists.

While others were visiting Hilo, Johnston and the Navigator went on an 'official' visit to Bishop's Museum to see relics of old Hawaii. As a textile designer, Johnston was fascinated by the intricately woven headbands and the beautiful bird-of-paradise feather cloaks worn by Hawaiian royalty. Back on board, Johnston had the task once again of recording greetings from some of the crew to their wives, families and sweethearts in the Portsmouth area. Then, too late to incorporate them smoothly into the reel of tape he had recorded, he was instructed to add in their choices of music to be played after each greeting. This meant bringing everyone back again to the SRE booth to make their choices, and then staying up half the night recording them with suitable credits and splicing them into the master tape.

Whatever his prior reservations, for Riches the dance went splendidly, and the Corbetts and Weatheralls were perfect hosts. For Hume, this had to be getting close to paradise on earth. 'We all turned up at the Consul's daughter's dance in aloha shirts. Great time and no one wanted to leave. Oahu is a sort of paradise where you can forget all your worries, cares and concerns.' For Cooper, who by this time had been badly smitten by the above-mentioned Frances, it seems to have been less fun, but next day he tried hard to make up for it.

> 'At 0900 Frances came aboard and after "seeing around" and drinking at yet another cocktail party at the Officers' Mess in Pearl Harbour we returned to the ship for lunch. Maitland Hume partnered her sister, Linda, who was another honey but only fifteen [as Hume only discovered later, after a passionate parting kiss]. After lunch we drove down to Waikiki Beach. This is just like paradise – palm trees, soft sand, splendid surfing and the water just the right temperature; Hula and Tahitian dancing everywhere. At six we met up with an American Lieutenant and his fiancée and went to a "Luau". This is a Hawaiian native feast. Whole pigs are baked underground wrapped in ti-leaves. One eats every sort of exotic native food until bursting point! Rum punch in vast quantities and so on. Dancing and singing

takes place all the time. It's all outside by torchlight underneath swaying palm trees. Aloha shirts and trousers are the rig. I bought some light cotton trousers for $3 made at a little Chinese tailors. These have proved extremely useful.

After this Luau we danced until one and then went and bathed in the moonlight (and our bathing costumes!) We then returned to their flat (sorry! – apartment) where we drank Scotch on the rocks and danced some more.

Frances came and saw me off when the ship left at lunchtime next day. I haven't been so near to crying since I was at Wellbury. It probably sounds rather pathetic but believe you me it was b****y awful. Frances is coming to work in the American Embassy in London at the beginning of next year! We have been at sea for forty hours and I am gradually recovering but I keep finding notes in my cabin signed "Love, Frances". I haven't yet discovered who's doing this. *If this happens at every South American port, I can see myself becoming a nervous wreck.'*

Robertson recalls the sad and lonely figure of Cooper at the ship's rail gazing back towards Hawaii. 'Take your filthy boots off my new paint!' bellowed the Commander at the love-lorn Cooper. Two particular thoughts had occupied some of Robertson's attention in Hawaii. 'First was an upcoming rugger match between the Cook Islands national team and the ship's fifteen on the island of Rarotonga, which we were due to visit *en route* to South America. I was chosen as a member of the side on the basis of having been in my school's first fifteen three years running. The second was another worry, having been told about the pending honour of my being appointed official Coxswain of the Admiral's Barge (the smarter but slower of *Warrior*'s two "fast" motor boats) for CINCSASA on our ceremonial visits to all the major South American ports.'

On the final Sunday, Riches had to make the tough choice between going to a service in the Anglican cathedral, or, being taken for an all-day picnic on a secluded beach on the island's north-west coast offered by the ever-hospitable Corbetts. He chose the picnic.

There was a chance to swim, sunbathe and gorge himself on a picnic lunch. Then, having slept that off, to return to the Corbetts' apartment for an English Tea, including 'real' tea such as he felt he had not tasted since leaving the UK. He returned to *Warrior* in the early evening loaded with pineapples and sugar cane for the Gunroom.

A fully repaired *Warrior* then sailed from Pearl Harbour at 1630 the next afternoon, heading south for a brief call at Christmas Island before beginning her long journey

The Corbetts'
picnic (Riches)

home. Riches, at the nerve centre of *Warrior*'s incoming and outgoing signals, learned that *Narvik* and the RFA *Fort Rosalie* had been recalled to Christmas Island to land further stores. This caused some speculation on board as to whether *Warrior* might suffer a similar fate, and fears were increased on arrival at Christmas when it was found that *Messina* had been retained for a further three to four weeks' service. It was with considerable relief, therefore, when *Warrior* sailed from Christmas finally – in notorious Christmas Island weather. During the six or seven hours stay in the anchorage passengers were embarked, stores landed, and the last minute paperwork cleared up in time to catch the mail.

The Commodore used the morning of *Warrior*'s brief stopover to tour all the other ships in the Port of London moorings. Robertson recalls, 'I was in charge of his boat, but Midshipman Cooper came too, having perhaps been asked to keep an eye on my seamanship as I had been out of small boats for some time.' A minor disaster struck when the propeller suddenly and inexplicably became detached from the prop shaft between two visits and the boat drifted alarmingly for a while. The intrepid Cooper, brimming as always with 'officer-like qualities', stripped off and went over the side

– 'a meaty target for any passing sharks' as Robertson's Journal recorded – to try and fix the problem. He failed, but they were rescued by *Warrior*'s pinnace in time to avoid real embarrassment or worse.

While the ship had been extensively repaired, as far as the Commander was concerned she had not been satisfactorily repainted. On the way south, and especially during the six brief hours moored at Christmas Island, painting went ahead with a vengeance. Nets made of 'orange string' were slung under the bows, and the painters lay back on them and thus got as much paint on their clothes and bodies as on the hull. It was as well not to glance down, lest one saw a hungry shark, jaws open, glancing back up. Each branch had its allocated area to paint. The clever engineering branch used spray guns and completed their task well before the others. However, as *Warrior* set off, it was raining very hard, and the following day there were the usual rough seas and wind as she passed once more through the ITC. A helicopter inspection revealed that most of the engineers' sprayed paint had come off. They were required to do the job again as the ship lay off Rarotonga, this time using brushes, and watching with envy the boatloads of libertymen going ashore.

On the way south, steaming towards the Cook Islands, the first of them picked up by the radar was Aitutaki, discovered by (the then) Lieutenant Bligh, a formidable navigator whose epic 4,000 mile voyage in an open boat saved the lives of those cast adrift with him by the mutineers of HMS *Bounty*.

At the end of the month, *Warrior* was planning to call on their descendants. Although *Warrior*'s crew had just come from the now rather 'civilised' Hawaii and had visited a more 'primitive' Tongareva, the sights, sounds, tastes and smells of Rarotonga, the principal island of the Cook Islands group, almost overwhelmed them. It seems a steamer calls there every two or three months, but *Warrior* was the largest ship the islanders had ever seen and the only aircraft carrier [before or since]. Riches told his diary, 'Approached from seaward, it must be one of the most beautiful islands in the South Seas, with volcanic mountains rising to 2,000 feet and covered with vegetation to the summit. We received a tremendous welcome.'

Early on the morning of 23 July *Warrior* arrived off Rarotonga – an island which should perhaps be marked on the chart as '*uninhibited*' for the edification of would-be visitors. As the ship approached, half a dozen towering peaks rose out of the morning haze to greet her, until drawing closer one could make out more details of this majestic green mass – occasional patches of bare cliff face against the dark

*Raratongan
skyline
(Rowsell)*

*Raratongan
hillside (Riches)*

foliage, and then houses straggling along the shore under the shadow of the 2,000 foot heights.

The sun came up over the port beam, flooding everything with soft rays; revealing the full beauty of this great volcanic pile reaching up out of the depths, its green shadows sifting the dancing sunlight, filling the stillness of early morning with grandeur. It was an impressive first view of the place.

Robertson wrote: 'My motorboat was lowered at 0945, as we came to anchor off the north coast [opposite the main settlement, Avarua] and, not long afterwards, I was provided with a rough map and sent inshore. Coming inshore in the motor boat on a bearing of 165° we soon picked up the black and white leading marks beside the jetty, and it was easy enough to see the channel in between the coral heads through the calm blue water. The gaunt ribs of an old wreck over to port and the rusty remains of a large ship's boiler to starboard gave evidence of the treacherousness of these island reefs in rough weather. Turning the motor boat round, one encountered the same difficulty as at Christmas Island jetty – a single screw boat will only go to starboard when making way astern under power, and the shallows were uncomfortably close.'

Meanwhile, a helicopter of the ship's flight had taken the Commodore ashore, where he was welcomed by a guard of honour formed by the Boys' Brigade, and by local officials, while Boy Scouts held back, or attempted to hold back, the excited populace. Previously there had been a demonstration flight up and down the coast by Lt-Cdr Bricker's helicopter, to the accompaniment of wild scenes of enthusiasm; and when he first landed there was an immediate rush up to the machine as people came to feel it and small boys vied with each other to try and swing on the rotor blades.

Riches went ashore in the afternoon and, with others, climbed one of the smaller peaks, as well as picking plenty of oranges, lemons and bananas at the invitation of the farmer. Hume went with him and then again on the next day; this time with Cooper who took his shotgun but, alas, found nothing worth shooting. They stayed overnight in the local hotel and enjoyed a breakfast in the fresh clear dawn. That dawn, like an English summer, lasted less than twenty minutes, however, before it once more became tropically hot.

The second day was declared a public holiday in Rarotonga. A memorable morning was spent watching the children of the island singing and dancing on the flight deck in a magnificent display. Graceful action songs alternated with throbbing drum dances.

*Stick dance
(Rowsell)*

*Boys and
girls dancing
(Rowsell)*

Boys and girls alike donned grass skirts and moved ecstatically to the rhythm of hide and wooden drums and old kerosene cans, often joined by their teachers or other spectators and camp followers carried away by the urge to get on their feet and give a personal improvised performance. The whole thing was irresistible, utterly unlike anything the Warriors had ever seen before.

Utanga Utanga greeting the Warriors (Rowsell)

As one Warrior to another, Utanga Utanga, an impressive personage dressed in foliage and brandishing a huge wooden spear, leapt and bellowed grotesquely before the Commodore making a 'speech' of welcome. *'Oro mai te Ika-Taurangi o te moana!'* (Welcome thou visiting sacred fish of the great oceans!)' Very likely Captain James Cook was greeted two centuries earlier in exactly this way.

While the morning had gone splendidly, the afternoon, when the ship was supposed to be open to visitors, was rather too chaotic. The crowd on the jetty, some said there were 5,000, went crazy with excitement; barricades were broken down, people injured and pushed into the water; police and Boys' Brigade officials ignored. At first, both the Trading Company's launches and lighters and the ship's boats were to be used for ferrying people out, but whenever the motorboat was brought alongside the jetty, within a few seconds she was loaded well beyond capacity and in danger of capsizing from the weight on one side. Robertson and his crew had literally to fight the people off and then drag out half the happily grinning passengers before they could safely leave the jetty. After two or three trips it was decided to secure, only to discover that three of the islanders' flimsy one-man outriggers were already bobbing jauntily at the boom, necessitating a complicated operation before the motorboat could tie up.

Others came out in local lighters, towed by a small motor launch. The bowman in the lighter casts off as he approaches his destination, and the coxswain then brings it alongside gracefully using a long sweep over the stern. On the way back, the motor boat comes past the lighter and throws it a line. The bowman takes three or four turns round a bollard in the bow and away it sails gracefully. Travelling in one is very pleasant; not too fast and, without an engine, very quiet.

As the guests arrived for *Warrior*'s official reception, drinks were handed out which, it was noticeable, the Maori women guests were very keen to have. Having white husbands gave them the liquor privileges of the whites. Many of them had what, at first, seemed incongruous names like Mrs Jones, Mrs Brown, Mrs Powell and so on, but their maiden names might have been Teokotai Kuruo, for example. It was intriguing to see the apparent westernising reflected in their European hairstyles and their use of make-up. Western clothes held their figures up and Western false teeth meant that few had toothless grins. The Maori men were, in the main, quite restrained in their drinking; but the whites and their native wives were noticeably less so.

As ever, Riches's interest in meteorology meant that it was he, rather than the sailor Midshipmen, who noted in his journal that 'During Wednesday night some alarm was caused by the wind backing from SE to NE, causing the stern to swing within 300 yards of the reef. Steam was raised for slow speed, but by the end of the morning watch the wind had veered to E and any danger there was had been averted.'

There was a 'return engagement' the next day when the Commodore and quite a few officers were invited to an Umukai [the Polynesian equivalent of the Hawaiian Luau] on shore where they sat round on coconut matting, shaded by palm fronds above, wafted by the cool breeze from palm fronds wielded by Maori maidens, and drank coconut wine copiously from one shell and sipped fiery coconut spices rather more tentatively from another, which was actually a 'dip' intended to go with the various meats (pig, chicken, goat) and fishes that had been cooking in an earth oven all day or hung up to dry in the midday sun. Johnston had his tape recorder running but, alas, it seemed to have developed an electrical fault and much of the music that he later used for a radio programme had to be recovered by something akin to a salvage operation. It was the rhythmic throbbing of the music and repetitive patterns of drumming that, coconut wine apart, were most intoxicating. Despite having gorged themselves, the Warriors were all pulled to their feet to dance while being garlanded with flowers. Local hosts looked after them assiduously. They were offered a choice of bananas, as one might offer a choice of cigarettes (Virginia, Turkish?): in this case 'this one good flavour; or this one fat and sweet.' With one old man and his student-teacher son, Johnston wandered a bit and had all kinds of trees and plants pointed out: kapok, hibiscus, coconut, yam, gardenia, tapioca, terawa, paw-paw, banana, tomato, oranges and lemons, pineapple, mandarin and chestnut. 'Too much fruit!' said the old man; but then he was a fisherman. He would go out when the mood takes him in his outrigger. The local outriggers are about five feet long and, in the hands of a Maori, they are wonderfully manoeuvrable.

The Warriors weren't offered any of the local orange beer at

Riches, Hutchinson, Kirchem and Dennis dressed to kill (Rowsell)

191

the Umukai. First, it's illegal, and second, it blows one's head off. The Commander had warned the crew not to drink it – a warning which had the predictable equal and opposite effect; with consequences that were just as predictable with sailors coming back from shore leave not so much headless as legless.

Entertainment at the dance (Rowsell)

More entertainment (Rowsell)

The next evening, many went ashore for a dance in aid of the Crippled Children's Fund where the music was provided by a curious band. One fat old momma pounded out the melody while the rhythm was provided by a double row of guitars and ukuleles. The touches of musical colour came from a strangely talented old man on the cornet; and the whole band sang!

Warrior hosted a 'ball' ashore for the local patricians with the officers dressed up in their white mess jackets again. Next door, there was a less formal 'dance' for the ratings. Many of them had a 'wonderful' time. (As an aside, there is a system in the Cook Islands of a two-year probationary marriage for couples from the age of eighteen and if it does not work out they go their separate ways. The arrival of any children does not seem to complicate matters, since another Cook Islands custom is to give the first child to its mother's family, its so-called feeding parents, and the second to the father's family. The third and fourth are also donated to relatives as tokens of esteem. Johnston tried to explain this to one of the Officers' Stewards but his only reaction was one of visible relief that the first child went to the *mother's* family.)

Then there was the rugger match between a hand-picked team of stalwarts from *Warrior*, including Robertson, and the local Rarotongan team who looked much fitter and stronger than the Brits. The final score was 44–10 in favour of Rarotonga. Their three-quarters played barefoot and their forwards had the knack of collapsing the Navy scrum onto the concrete cricket strip right in the centre of the playing field.

New Zealand's Resident Commissioner, Mr Nevill, hosted a cocktail party at his residence, during which the ship's band performed the sunset ceremony with the bugles sounding 'Taps' over the moving hymn tune. This was an event which could sometimes bring tears to the eyes of hardened matelots and at least one hypersensitive Sub-Lieutenant. Hume got into conversation with Mr Bateson, manager of the Cook Island Trading Company, who had travelled extensively round the islands. He explained why the Penrhyn people are so lazy compared with the Rarotongan islanders. He put it down almost entirely to the American occupation during the war, when the island became totally spoilt and the islanders lost the habit of working. He felt, however, that they might find it profitable to work harder soon, as the pearl shell beds at Manihiki were nearly exhausted after three years of continuous working, and the trade might shift its centre to Penrhyn.

Typical of the reception ashore were the experiences of Riches. 'That afternoon, five of us were lucky enough to be offered a trip around the island by the Deputy Registrar whom we had met the previous day – an Englishman from Croydon in Surrey. He had been living on the island for five years and, like so many others, had married a local girl so was informed on all aspects of the local history. He took us to a brother-in-law's plantation where we were given a free hand to pick what we wanted. Apart from the usual oranges, tangerines, grapefruit and bananas, there was a strange fruit the size of a walnut, pale yellow and round in shape. The flesh was soft and very sweet. Unfortunately I can't remember its name, but it is not common and is apparently peculiar to a few of the South Seas islands.'

Anson talked with Mr Williamson, another manager of the Trading Company, who invited him and several others back for supper. Night had fallen, the stars were out and, as it so happened, Mr Williamson was a very keen amateur astronomer, owning one of the largest telescopes in the South Pacific. They could not stay too long to admire the Heavens, since there was a dance to attend before spending the night at the Hotel Rarotonga, Anson's first night on dry land for quite a while.

As with the sand and seashells which the Midshipmen had fetched on board at Christmas Island to create decoration for cocktail parties, this time *Warrior* embarked about one hundred small coconut palms for use on the South American cocktail circuit.

Kirchem, as a key member of *Warrior*'s band, was kept very busy playing afloat and ashore, only taking a short refreshment break while the helicopters did an aerial ballet to entertain the Rarotongans who were fascinated by these giant mechanical dragonflies. Since *Warrior*'s first visit to Hawaii, when the band on the quay had played the popular 'Happy Wanderer,' this had become more or less the ship's signature tune, albeit under an alternative title 'Happy Warrior.' Its strains floated over the water as *Warrior* sailed off on the 26th, two hours behind schedule, having had to search for two deserters. It was surprising there were only two. According to Robertson's Journal, 'It was rumoured that when apprehended one had just been married and the other had to be dragged from the altar.' Riches remarked in his Journal, 'If I'm forced to emigrate, either New Zealand or one of the South Sea Islands would be my goal' and Hume, in his Journal, rightly predicted the importance that tourism, as opposed to horticulture, would play in the island's future economy.

Carrying with her crates of delicious fruit and nursing not a few broken hearts, *Warrior* steamed off towards the eastern horizon escorted for a short while by outriggers with men and women singing 'Now is the hour.' Those not on watch either got their heads down, or sat musing and reminiscing on a sunny sponson. As with Penrhyn, the island had not yet been 'commercialised' by mass tourism and Western values. For that reason alone, it can probably never be revisited. During the First Dog Watch, *Warrior* reached the southernmost of the Cook Islands, Mangaia, which is reckoned by geologists to be eighteen millions years old and the oldest island in the Pacific. The highest point above sea level is only around 550 feet, but the island rises some 15,600 feet from the ocean floor.

Since she had radioed ahead, *Warrior* was expected; and what could have been the island's entire population were on the shore gazing at the largest ship and the only helicopter they had ever seen. A helicopter took the Commodore ashore for a brief visit where, by all accounts, he was treated like a demi-god. There was a report that a New Zealand school inspector on the island begged to be taken off by *Warrior*. Due to inclement weather, the last six-monthly supply ship had been unable to land a boat, and in consequence he would probably be stuck there for up to another six months. Since *Warrior*'s next port of call with reasonable communications back to New Zealand was going to be Callao, the Commodore had to leave him 'marooned'.

Among the entertainments on board were evening film shows. The officers' cinema was the quarterdeck, where a screen was rigged aft and the audience sat in their cool Red Sea rig and watched various feature films. Smoking in those days was not only permitted but extensively practised. However, the cool breeze over the deck carried all the smoke away. One of the films that evoked howls of amusement and derision was a multi-episode serial recounting the adventures of young American aviators who were up against a deadly foe known only as 'The Dark Avenger', and dressed up in an all-black robe and hood while holding an axe, not dissimilar to the Ku Klux Klan. The Fleet Air Arm pilots and crew would roar with laughter as the bi-planes appeared to dive to their doom into the crater of a live volcano at the end of one episode, only to soar up safely at the beginning of the next.

A day after leaving Mangaia, *Warrior* came to a halt in the middle of the Pacific. There the ship's two remaining Avenger aircraft were brought up from the hangar onto the flight deck. On the lift bringing them up stood a tall, black-clad and hooded figure holding an axe. With the band playing a farewell tribute, he strode to the dispatcher's position near the bow, and at his signal, one after the other, the planes, stripped of anything reusable (including their crews) were catapulted into the ocean. Each created a very satisfying splash, lingering for just long enough to allow photographs, and then nose-dived into the depths. The suggestion in some publications that they were highly radioactive can be dismissed as without foundation.

LEFT: *Avenger launched by the Dark Avenger (Rowsell)*

*Avenger into the
drink (Rowsell)*

*Avenger sinking
into the Pacific
(Rowsell)*

Cynics, many to be found in the Gunroom, assumed the planes were being ditched purely to make room in the hangars for the many cocktail parties that stretched ahead of *Warrior* on her tour round South America. The official version, however, was carefully recorded in Hume's Journal. 'The Avengers had been provided under the American Mutual Defense Plan, but by 1957 they were becoming obsolete, [...] and, since the cost of overhauling them was not justified, the catapult was the answer.'

Later the same day, *Warrior* sailed close to the island of Rimatara, the westernmost populated island of the Austral Islands of French Polynesia. Rimatara was one of the last Polynesian islands to welcome European visitors. Captain Samuel Pinder Henry discovered the island in 1821. Two missionaries arrived in 1822 and established a Protestant mission. France established a protectorate in 1889 and annexed Rimatara in 1900. Rimatara is a much lower lying and less rugged island than Mangaia with pleasant looking beaches, whose principal industry was producing phosphates. An extraordinary looking top-heavy inter-island vessel, a power-assisted 'schooner' flying the tricolour, waddled erratically past, her upper decks and rigging crowded with cheering crew. It was reckoned the ship was returning from Bastille Day celebrations in Tahiti. Later in the afternoon *Warrior* sighted Rurutu, forty miles away to port, but Moses Reef, fifteen or so miles nearer, was not visible before sunset and did not appear on radar during that watch. Rurutu is the most northerly of the Austral Group. Owing to its unusual formation and the extensive caves in its fossilised coral cliffs, it is noteworthy for the fact that its earliest inhabitants were the only known cave dwellers in the South Pacific.

Apart from questions of time and fuel, calling on any of the Austral Islands would have needed diplomatic clearance from France, so *Warrior* sailed on past Tubuai and Raïvavae, where the local priest and his entire congregation came streaming down to the shore to wave, if not to bless! Tubuai was first viewed by Europeans when it was mapped by Captain Cook in 1777, although his party did not disembark. Cook discovered the island's name, 'Toobouai', from the natives who surrounded his ship in their canoes, but the next European arrivals there were the mutineers of HMS *Bounty* in 1789. Fletcher Christian, in looking for an island on which to hide from the Navy's retribution, had gone over Captain Bligh's charts and had chosen Tubuai as his destination. Upon arrival, however, a conflict arose while the mutineers were still on their ship. Several islanders were killed in their canoes, and Christian decided to sail further on; as did *Warrior*.

*Divisions
(Rowsell)*

On that Sunday, the ship's company paraded for Divisions in front of the Commodore for the first time since he had been elevated to that rank.

The officers and crew marched past him in single file, and according to Hume the manoeuvre was carried out with success. The ship's company would need some practice for the various ceremonies that would go with *Warrior*'s visits to five South American countries and the Falklands. Divisions over, *Warrior* came within clear sight of Raïvavae. The island seemed reminiscent of Rarotonga, but was surrounded by a wide lagoon enclosed by a reef; a place inhabited, yet seeming somehow to be out of civilisation's reach. The ship passed close enough for sight of the red-roofed, white-walled houses. Hume noted the principal 'industry' was coffee growing. Cooper's Journal mentions the continuous depth sounding by *Warrior* which alerted the Navigator and Officer of the Watch to the presence of coral ridges at around 25 fathoms, prompting the ship to steer to port to give the island a wider berth.

More exciting than yet another tropical paradise, of which the Midshipmen had by now seen quite a few, was the first sight of three whales on the starboard beam, spouting quite distinctly. For the next two days no ships were seen nor any land; 'water, water, everywhere' and the occasional shark. And then the solitary island of Pitcairn appeared on the radar. The entire Gunroom were telling each other what they remembered, or rather recalled reading, of the infamous *Mutiny of the Bounty* in 1789 and the images of Charles Laughton and Clark Gable sprang to several minds. Riches recalled a broadcast about the island he'd heard at his prep school and he had always been fascinated by the stories. His imagination ran riot and he pictured a desolate, windswept rock in the middle of the Pacific, inhabited by a few semi-civilised descendants of the *Bounty* mutineers. Afterwards, he felt he had got the bit about the rock in the middle of the Pacific just about right. What nobody in *Warrior* knew at the time was that the islanders had been hoping to meet and greet Britain's former Prime Minister, who had sailed past Pitcairn in February of that year, as an account from an Australian Seventh Day Adventist publication of May 1957 reveals.

Pitcairners Board Moving Liner

We are indebted to Brother and Sister P. P. Ward, who supplied these items of news on request from their Pitcairn correspondence:

Sir Anthony and Lady Eden were passengers on the *Rangitata*, which arrived at Pitcairn Island on 12 February 1957. The weather was bad – hard wind, rough sea, and dark night. The islanders had planned a programme of welcome (singing and other items) when the Government Secretary, Andrew Young, was to read an address and the Chief Magistrate, Parkin Christian, was to give some presents to Sir Anthony.

However, the islanders were disappointed as the captain did not stop, though the boats tied on to the ship and the men, with much difficulty, boarded the vessel. The boats were carried out some five miles, two of them, one at a time, breaking loose. A photographer on the staff of the *Auckland Star* was keenly interested. He had never seen anything like this before and took a number of flashlight photographs. Mr. Howe, the chairman of the shipping company, was fearful that someone would be hurt. It seemed a miracle that everyone got back safely into those little boats.

A few of the men had the good fortune to meet the former Prime Minister of Britain and his wife, but for lack of time they were unable to sing or to read the address, It was given to Sir Anthony for him to peruse later. The island-made souvenirs were presented also. They included a walking stick made by Fred Christian, a basket made by his sister Mimie, and filled with choice fruit, a fan made by Millie, and a set of stamps. How thrilled Lady Eden was after the long voyage from Panama to receive a lovely bouquet of Pitcairn Island flowers prepared for her by Bernice! An autographed copy of our little book *Come Ashore!* specially printed on art stock for just such an occasion, bound in black morocco and blocked in gold, made an elegant present for them both. In it the island's important people had written their names and the positions they occupy. This book was the same as was accepted by our beloved Queen Mother some time ago. For the islanders Sir Anthony Eden gave a signed photograph, and a telegram of thanks and good wishes was received from him later.[1]

The Royal Navy's account of the *Bounty* mutiny tends to highlight the considerable seamanship and navigational skill of William Bligh. Captain Bligh had previously served as sailing master with Captain Cook, and after a voyage of forty-seven days in the open boat into which the mutineers had put him, aided only by a quadrant and a pocket watch, safely reached the island of Timor.

Despite the romantic nature of the mutineers' story – sailing off into the blue with a clutch of beautiful Tahitian brides-to-be – mutiny is mutiny, and while Bligh

Warrior anchored offshore (Riches)

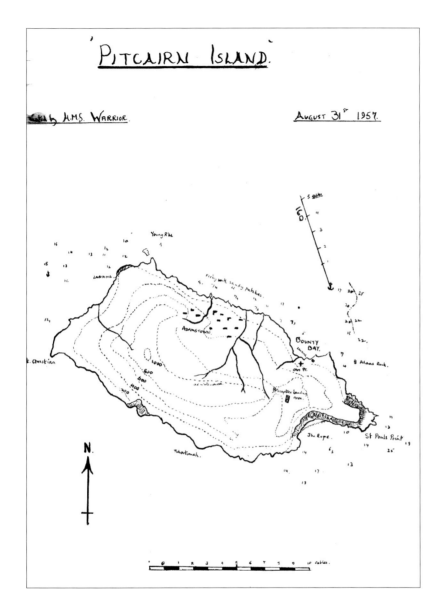

may have been a martinet, he was probably not much more so than the majority of 18th and 19th century Royal Navy commanders, thousands of miles from home and needing to ensure, by stern example, that their authority would not be challenged.

Warrior arrived off Pitcairn in the morning of 31 July at 0730 and by 0800 had anchored in a depth of 20 fathoms.

The island, on first looking at it, appeared far more mountainous and yet more rich in vegetation than had been imagined. No land appeared to be at water-level and the sea broke in foaming surf on the rocks all around. Under a Union Flag on a prominent piece of land and also on a hilltop several people were gathered to watch our arrival.

Around 0815 two very sturdy longboats rowed out from shore, about 50 foot long and double-banked. Their stem and stern are pointed making for adaptability in the surf but otherwise they must be the same in construction and in looks as the boats of the *Bounty* and similar naval boats of that period. The islanders seem to handle them magnificently. The boats came alongside and men from the island, of every different sort as far as looks went, came clambering on board with their wares. Many wore US Naval uniforms which they had ordered directly from the US Navy, and the rest wore bits and pieces; odd shirts, trousers, shorts and jackets. Everyone without exception was barefoot. Their feet seemed very large and stubby with well separated toes. They shouted and 'jabbered' in what, at first, seemed unintelligible English but, on listening closer, one could distinguish what sounded like a cross between New Zealand and Scottish.

Warrior's first wave of visitors were the traders, and it was reckoned they did between £800 and £1,000 worth of business that morning [£20/30,000 at 2017 prices], selling mostly wooden artefacts including walking sticks and carved animals and birds, much of very high aesthetic quality, together with great quantities of fruit and the local postage stamps. Meanwhile, the Commodore and an official party flew ashore by helicopter, another first for the island where no flying machine had ever landed before, and he would later bring off the Chief Magistrate, Parkin Christian, a direct descendant of the famous Fletcher, and other island notables. Christian was a weather-beaten, wrinkled man, possibly approaching seventy, but with a certain dignity of bearing. At his personal request, the ship's visit was extended from a planned three hours to a full day.

The mutineers, in the early stages of their arrival on Pitcairn, had

RIGHT: Parkin Christian holding the rudder band and gudgeon of 'The Bounty', the famous British naval vessel on which a mutiny occurred in 1790 (Kari Young, Dem Tull, Pitcairn)

salvaged as much as they could from their vessel, and then burnt it down to the waterline in order to conceal their presence from any pursuers. Within the past year, however, the Warriors were told, the islanders had 'discovered' the *Bounty*'s anchor near the one landing place and small pieces of that relic were now on sale to visitors. There was no 'certificate of authenticity': one simply had to take the islanders' word for it – and why would they lie?

There were not too many family names in use, given that the whole population is descended from a small pool of men who first of all mutinied against their Captain, then subsequently fought each other to the death over the Tahitian women they brought with them, willingly or not. When the internecine strife reached the point

LEFT: *King George VI 'Bounty Bible' stamp*
RIGHT: *Queen Elizabeth II 'Bounty Bible' stamp*

that only one adult male, John Adams, was left alive, he had a change of heart – or had a revelation – and started to preach Christian love and forgiveness and give readings from the Bible brought ashore from the *Bounty*. The original 'Bounty Bible' was there in the bare and austere church for visitors to see together with John Adams's Prayer Book. Adamstown, the 'capital' and only settlement, is of course named after him.

During the 1880s, after receiving literature from the Seventh Day Adventists, the entire Pitcairn community left the Church of England and joined that religious sect. American missionaries came, and the conversion of the whole population was used by the Adventists to great effect as propaganda. When *Warrior* visited, the population was 157, all Seventh Day Adventists, but since then there seems to have been a falling off in adherence to that sect. Several of the Gunroom were given copies of the Adventists' booklet about the island called *Come Ashore.*

There had been several fluctuations in population numbers over the years, and one or two attempts had been made to resettle in Tahiti and, later, Norfolk Island, but these tended to end with many of the expatriated islanders returning to the place they knew best. The community was now barely self-sufficient, but earned currency to pay for imported essentials from the sales they made to visiting tour ships over and above HMS *Warrior*; which explains the desperate eagerness of the traders who swarmed aboard. Having cut down most of the island's timber over the years, the wood they carve now is sourced by the islanders from Henderson Island, some one hundred miles to the east; a hazardous round trip. Pitcairn, Henderson and Ducie islands make up the Pitcairn Islands Group which is nowadays administered by New Zealand.

Another interesting example of local enterprise was exhibited by Floyd McCoy, the Postmaster on the island in 1957, who in his official capacity sold the new Queen Elizabeth II postage stamps at face value to many collectors worldwide, including several of *Warrior*'s officers. In his *private* capacity, however, it appeared that in late 1952, he had bought up the remaining stocks of King George VI stamps and was now releasing these slowly onto the philatelic market – at a premium.

After the trading was over, it was time for all of the young Gunroom officers to make the exciting and potentially perilous trip ashore. None could resist the opportunity to say they had actually set foot on Pitcairn. It was without question a hazardous journey. Such was the combination of the heavy ocean swell, which had *Warrior* rolling quite spectacularly when seen from the ship's boats, and the copious foaming surf at the base of the rocky shoreline, that it was not felt that the ship's own boats should risk attempting to land. Instead, the island's longboats met the ship's pinnace some fifty yards offshore and libertymen scrambled between the two. Then, while the pinnace went astern to move out of reach of the breaking surf, the Pitcairn oarsmen and coxswain navigated towards the narrow, barely ten foot wide gap in the offshore reef which could *just* be passed through at the right moment with the oncoming swell carrying the longboat into the foaming shallows. These were in front of an even narrower beach – less than four deckchairs' width one sailor remarked – where the boat had to make a sharp turn to port to enter the protected (up to a point) bay, at which moment passengers had to leap from the prow of the longboat. Few if any reached shore dry-

Bounty Bay
(Rowsell)

Bounty Bay
landing area
(Rowsell)

shod; and all who did reach shore were already wondering about the hazards of getting back off again! There were no attempted desertions on this visit.[2]

Thatched sheds at the landing place stored the island's ferryboats, including three for pulling and one with a motor. From here, a path led up the Hill of Difficulty to human habitation; the village of Adamstown. There was also an aerial ropeway from the shore to the top of the cliff, some 200 feet above, from which hung a trolley that was used to bring loads up from the shore to the village. It was hard to walk there without tripping over uncomplaining hens and dogs. The one modern building was the island school outside which children played an exhibition match of rounders.

Robertson wrote home saying that, 'What was fascinating in the people were the scarcity of signs of Tahitian blood, the slight West Country accent and old-fashioned dialect – *Bounty* had commissioned in Plymouth – the extraordinary mixture of clothing, and the total absence of any form of footwear. Another lasting impression, once one had reached the top of the island, was of the wonderful profusion of fruit. Recalling poetry learned at school, I called the prospect 'Andrew Marvellous' as his *Thoughts in a Garden* ran through my head.

> *What wondrous life is this I lead!*
> *Ripe apples drop about my head;*
> *The luscious clusters of the vine*
> *Upon my mouth do crush their wine;*
> *The nectarine and curious peach*
> *Into my hands themselves do reach;*
> *Stumbling on melons as I pass,*
> *Ensnared with flowers, I fall on grass.*

But all was not the profusion and plenty that it might seem. The ship agreed to send some basic food supplies, mostly flour, ashore, having learned from the one New Zealander on the island, the local schoolmaster, that the previous supply ship had arrived on a Sunday – the seventh day which the islanders advent and on which they may do no work – and had been ignored. In 1957, Pitcairn was on the main New Zealand–Panama shipping lane with some fifty to sixty ships passing each year. However, due to the fraught nature of landing on the island no one had yet found a safe way of getting passengers ashore. That said, the islanders' diet of fruit, fish and chicken, plus the exercise they all had to take as part of their daily lives meant they were generally fit. While the houses, set on terraced slopes amid trees, were basic in construction, the furniture had a more European look than what had been seen in the Cook Islands.

Hutchinson, Reed and others perched on the clifftop (Hutchinson)

Johnston took his precious passport ashore and persuaded Parkin Christian both to sign it and to give that signature provenance by adding an official stamp: one which read 'Pitcairn Islands School'. The view from the top of the island was dramatic in that, apart from *Warrior* in the foreground, there was nothing to see but sea in every direction.

At sunset, the ship's band performed the full ceremony and *Warrior* hoisted anchor and sailed at 1830, providing the delighted islanders with a farewell fireworks display. There was an exchange of messages between the Chief Magistrate and the Commodore. From Adamstown came, 'Your visit reminds us, small as we are, that we are not forgotten as a part of the great British Commonwealth of Nations.' From *Warrior*, the Commodore signalled that their message of loyalty would be sent on to the Queen and that *Warrior*'s visit would long be remembered by his ship's crew just as much as by the islanders.

Then, steering a course of 082° *Warrior* set off at a speed of 8 knots for an overnight sail to Henderson Island where landfall was expected at first light on the first of August.

---

1 http://docs.adventistarchives.org/docs/AAR/AAR19570513-V61-20__B.pdf

2 So far has technology moved on that it is now possible to bring up Google images of Bounty Bay, where tin roofs have replaced the thatch and to zoom in on detail that, even after sixty years, seems hauntingly familiar.

AUGUST

....

From Pitcairn to the Falklands

Warrior arrived off Henderson Island at first light on 1 August, and two helicopters took off to carry out an aerial photographic survey. There was 'idle talk' of assessing the island's suitability for having an airstrip. When one thought about having to build it and then man it, Henderson did not seem too appealing as a posting. That said, it is now a UNSECO World Heritage Site and the British RSPB have ongoing projects there.

It is the Pitcairn islanders' source of wood for their carvings, and they make an annual visit to harvest their requirements. Like Pitcairn, cliffs rise sheer on all sides, making landing tricky for all but skilled sailors.[1]

The Commodore was part of the visiting party. His particular role was to replace notices of British ownership of the island. The land, uninhabited and fairly bleak, might not seem like attractive real estate, but there was a growing international consciousness of the significance and potential value of territorial waters for fishing, and in more recent times for gas and oil reserves. Warrior then set off at 22 knots (204 revolutions) to ensure that she reached the other island of the Pitcairn group, the coral atoll of Ducie, while it was still light enough to take photographs. The first British sighting had been in 1791 by Captain Edwards, commanding HMS *Pandora* and hunting for the *Bounty* mutineers. Notices of ownership were placed there too. The shore party duly returned, and the Navigator plotted a great circle route from there to Callao. Attendance at Midshipman Dennis's Spanish conversation classes increased dramatically as anticipation of the next few weeks grew with each successive nautical mile.

Reading Midshipmen's Journals was part of a regular routine for their 'Nurse', the Navigator, and he would add his comments and occasional corrections. From time to time, the Journals were also submitted to the Commodore who would add his own remarks; succinct and pithy. For example, 'Excellent, though you omit a great deal of Supply Officers' ship's activities,' or 'This is better than before – but I hope journalism is not to be your trade.' Robertson was told bluntly: 'Curb your inclination to show off.' And the saddest remark, 'The tragedy of the "new-look" Navy is that RN ships will seldom, if ever again, visit the Pacific Islands.'

The Gunroom's diligent chronicler of the weather, Midshipman Riches, noted the daily temperatures, and his diary plots the progressive fall from the eighties and high seventies in Hawaii, Christmas and Rarotonga to a more bracing low seventies as *Warrior* left the Pitcairn Islands astern. The effects of the cool Humboldt Current were becoming evident. On the Sunday, Riches even started a streaming cold, spending a couple of energetic hours in the baggage room tracking down his trunk and unearthing warmer clothes. As a consequence, the air in his cabin was scarcely breathable for the next twenty-four hours, owing to the powerful aroma of mothballs. He escaped from that to play deck hockey.

A new deck hockey league was started soon after leaving Rarotonga, and during the passage from Pitcairn each team was able to play off at least two matches. Unfortunately, the long-awaited painting of the flight-deck took some four days, due to the adverse weather conditions upsetting the programme, but *Warrior* arrived at Callao with about half the fixtures completed. The practice was useful as there would be games to play at that very British establishment, El Lima Football y Cricket Club. 'More British than any modern-day British club,' opined Robertson later, 'with deep leather armchairs and copies of *The Field*.'

On Tuesday, 6 August, the temperature plummeted into the sixties, and the following day the officers and petty officers switched into their 'blues.' After so many weeks in 'whites', usually open necked shirts and shorts, these felt strange and uncomfortable for a day or so. The Humboldt Current is that cold, low-salinity ocean current flowing north along the South American coast from the south of Chile to northern Peru. This current makes itself most felt in Peru in late winter and early spring resulting in many grey but dry days in the months of August and September – as the Warriors witnessed.

The day before *Warrior* reached Peru, the Commodore spoke on the Tannoy to the whole ship's company. He stressed how much the officers and crew were the public face of Great Britain. As ambassadors they needed to behave well and diplomatically; always having regard to how their conduct would create an impression of the character of all their fellow Britons. 'And there's another thing. If you've absolutely got to dip your wick, for God's sake take the proper precautions. You can get them at the Sick Bay.' There was a momentary, somewhat pensive, silence in the ship. It was sound advice, but it was on a subject not generally spoken about in polite British company in 1957. However, as well as the potato, tobacco, llamas and gold, the early European invaders had brought back a new and terrible disease from South America – syphilis. The ship's barber, who incidentally never set foot on shore throughout the whole voyage, did a roaring trade in what in those more inhibited days were known as 'something for the weekend'. He reminded his customers, however, in his capacity as a Leading Regulator, one of the ship's policemen, that 'getting the clap is a punishable offence, as well as making you go blind!' Perhaps it was some of the already evident results of the Hawaii visit which stimulated the Commodore to speak out.

The same day, signals were exchanged with CINCSASA. The gist of these was that all the arrangements *Warrior* proposed were approved, but that 'Breakfast [is] essential.' In the early morning of 9 August, *Warrior* approached the coast of South America, with first sight of Isla San Lorenzo at 0439 before making landfall at Callao. The weather was not as inviting as the people would turn out to be. The hilly shore could be seen through low misty cloud and a light but biting wind made everyone glad to be in blues. Hutchinson recorded that 'The Navigating Officer was pleased to arrive off Callao on course and on time, over 1,000 miles, with no assistance from radar.'

It was in even more foggy conditions that another British sailor, at that time also Vice-Admiral of the Chilean Navy, had approached Callao in 1818 with the intention of attacking the Spanish ships in the port. This was *Almirante* Cochrane; hero of the Napoleonic wars and real-life model for novels by Captain Marryat, C S Forester, and, still in the future in 1957, the Jack Aubrey novels of Patrick O'Brian. Cochrane had been enlisted by Chile to advise and assist them in their struggle for independence from Spain. During his blockade of the port, Cochrane earned the nickname 'El Diabolo,' which pleased him very much since, as he knew, Sir Francis Drake had raided Callao a couple of hundred years earlier and had been christened 'El Dracone' (the dragon).[2] When it became known that Cdr Begg was the great-grandson of Admiral Cochrane, it added hugely to his prestige all round South America.

At 0815 the flag of the Commander in Chief, South Atlantic and South America was broken at the mast as Vice-Admiral Sir W Geoffrey A Robson KBE, CB, DSO & bar, DSC, landed on the flight-deck in one of the ship's helicopters.[3]

The Admiral was received by the Commodore. As they were inspecting the Guard of Honour, one of the rating's caps blew off and, instinctively, the Commodore chased

*Arrival of
CINCSASA
(Rowsell)*

*CINCSASA
inspecting the
guard of honour
(Rowsell)*

CINCSASA inspecting the ship's band (Rowsell)

after it. Unfortunately, he tripped over a wire, cut his knee *and* his best trousers; his medals flew off with a clatter and his smart white cap landed in a patch of soot! However, these things happen in the best arranged families and soon the Admiral was thumping him on the back for taking the ship alongside so well. After inspecting his guard of honour and the band on the after end of the flight-deck, the Admiral came up to the bridge, and was then escorted to his quarters [where breakfast awaited him!] Vice-Admiral Robson would remain in *Warrior* until she departed Rio de Janeiro.

At 0830 *Warrior* fired a National Salute of twenty-one guns which was replied to by a shore battery and the guns of the fifty-year-old British-built cruiser, *Coronel Bolognesi*. Then, at 0835 she fired a thirteen-gun salute to the C-in C of the Peruvian Navy. This too was replied to, immediately followed by a fifteen-gun salute from the shore battery to CINCSASA's flag. No one within a ten mile radius could now be unaware of *Warrior*'s arrival.

All too often a Midshipman's job can deny him the hoped-for opportunity of being a tourist on a sea cruise. Robertson was disappointed that his 'Special Sea Duty position', one's assigned station when entering and leaving harbour, was to be on the cable deck throughout the South American voyage. 'Although, from a seamanship point of view, it is an extremely interesting place to be, and I have learnt a great deal there, yet when one is entering or leaving port it is galling to be able to see practically nothing. So it was with Callao.'

In another respect, *everyone* on board from the Commodore downwards was aware of the Admiral's arrival. Writing home, Hume commented on the downside of visiting Admirals. 'The poor old Commodore is being turfed out of his cabin, and the Commander in his place has been chucked out of his; extra people have to be found to stand outside his door, room has to be found for his staff; in fact he is a nuisance in every respect.'

At 0850 the Officer of the Guard came aboard, and with him the Peruvian Pilot, the Admiral's Liaison Officer and the British Naval Attaché. Slowly *Warrior* steamed through a small gap in the breakwater into the outer harbour, watched by a gaggle of scruffy looking pelicans. Tugs came out to help the ship turn and back into an even narrower gap in the basin, where she was to secure just ahead of a large tanker. It was a delicate manoeuvre for a ship of her size, with an offshore breeze against her, but even so *Warrior* was secured alongside the Muelle Marginal by 0950. Once the carrier was alongside, all the berthing wires were doubled up with manila hurricane hawsers, as a certain amount of Pacific surge was expected. Even so, the gangways would move from side to side on the jetty.

Riches summed up the look of the port. 'Callao is the principal port of Peru and the third largest port on the western seaboard of South America. As a port it is impressive, buildings going up fast and the whole area gives a sense of urgency for the need to expand.' He also revealed some youthful and perhaps rather British prejudices. 'Officials are efficient, but like all of Latin American temperament subject to bribery and useless at making up their minds.'

Robertson, who was to drive the Admiral's barge, was introduced to him that morning. 'Impressive, he was, although somewhat deaf and far from sharp-sighted. Also, he had a habit of calling me 'Snotty', the old-fashioned term for Midshipman which I did not really appreciate; but who was I to object?'

Callao itself, while not very exciting as a run ashore goes, had the appearance of a well-ordered and well-equipped seaport. In harbour were most of the ships of the

Warrior
entering Callao
(Rowsell)

Coming
alongside the
Muelle Marginal
(Rowsell)

Peruvian Navy: the *Bolognesi* and her sister-ship *Almirante Grau*, two light cruisers built by Vickers and completed fifty years earlier, modified from coal to oil-burning in 1925 and re-boilered by Yarrow in 1935: several ex-USN and ex-RCN frigates: a tank landing ship, a depot-ship and one of their sizeable little fleet of submarines. The 'original' Almirante Grau was the Peruvian hero of the 'great Chilean War' and a wreath-laying party was sent to honour his monument, accompanied by the C-in-C who actually laid the wreath.

Laying a wreath at Almirante Grau's monument (Rowsell)

INSET: *Almirante Grau (Rowsell)*

Hume was a part of that ceremony. 'On Saturday morning Admiral Robson laid a wreath at the monument of Almirante Grau, who died in the great naval battle of 1879 against Chile. Both the Peruvian Navy and HMS *Warrior* supplied a guard and band, and the ship acquitted itself admirably during the ceremony and afterwards when the guard and band marched through the streets. Midshipman Reed and I had to hold the wreath for the

Admiral and the organisation was such that, although we had been told what was to happen, we only just managed to arrive with the wreath in time.' In only a few days' time, *Warrior's* officers would lay a wreath at the monument to the Chilean, Arturo Prat, who had opposed him!

Among the varied tasks that befall Midshipmen, it had been Hume's responsibility to look after the Ambassador's six-year-old son while the ship entered harbour, which gave him the opportunity to look around. From his British perspective, it was rather depressing to see German ships unloading car after car onto the dockside. Once, the car market had been entirely in British hands, but because the several firms had been reluctant to supply a spares service, the Germans stepped into the market with ease, having first built up a three-year stock of spares. Hume's was the first of frequent comments made by, and to, the RNVR officers during *Warrior's* South American visits to the effect that both the British Government and British business had an open door for better relations and better trade and would neglect this at their great cost. Meantime, Hume wrote, '[the British community] is well represented and much emphasis is being placed on trade and industry, [where] there is much room for development. The first vessel to be built in Peru is nearing completion; an 8,000 ton tanker being constructed under the guidance of Cammell Laird, who have sent fifty men to help with the work, and when it is completed it will be a major contribution to the Peruvian oil industry which is largely in Peruvian hands.'

On the recurring theme of Britain's reputation in South America, Robertson recollected later, 'Both the leading politicians in each South American country we were due to visit *and* the British communities were very conscious that this was the first visit by a capital ship of the Royal Navy since World War II. Was Britain's erstwhile global power in terminal decline? Of course it was, but in small ways everyone we visited wanted to hear the old lion roar a little [...] one more time. Peru proved no exception. Both the hospitality and political/professional interest in *Warrior* – and her doings and capabilities – came our way in equal and always generous measure.'

The feelings evoked by one's recollections are coloured by the circumstances of that particular time. Johnston was experiencing some of the penalties of his rank, having been put in charge of seeing a reasonably fair distribution of the very attractive as well as the frankly unattractive invitations to the Gunroom RNVR officers which had come flooding in, including the chance to make an excursion by train to the interior. He was going on watch and on his way encountered Lt Harland, in plain clothes and ready to set off on an interesting trip. 'The previous day [he wrote to his parents] I had been on the list for that trip, but then came a demand for ten officers to walk round the naval base and lunch with the Peruvian Navy. Places had not been "snapped up" as happens for the more attractive outings. Alas, these less attractive ones are usually the obligatory ones, and to spread the burden each group of officers was asked to provide a body. My group could only provide one with any ease and we were asked for two. I had either to detail a Midshipman and thus stop him going to the Andes, or drop out of the Andean trip myself!' However, Johnston worried that his letter would intrigue and alarm his parents, since he continued on another rather different note. It seems that what had hit Cooper in Honolulu had now collided with Johnston in Callao.

'I first saw Cata at an upstairs window looking every inch a lovely girl. Strange, I wasn't immediately infatuated, but once we arrived at "Lima Cricket" (as the locals call it) we spent the rest of the evening together, talking and dancing. I arranged to meet her at Lima Cricket at 6.30pm (*hora inglese*) on Sunday […] Cata arrived there at ten past eight! She had a car, and when she asked where I would like to go I suggested she knew the town better than I did.

Cata drove a few kilometres down the coast. All the time there was something going round in the back of my head. When we pulled up on the sea front opposite a fish restaurant, I leant across and kissed her. […] I am returning to Peru as soon as the Navy and my money permit to marry Cata and she has said she will wait!'

Meanwhile, two other *Warrior* Midshipmen, who shall remain nameless, met up during their run ashore with an old school-friend of theirs who lived in Lima. They had got into bad company! They finished up in a high-class bar-cum-brothel, masquerading as a place for 'tea-dancing'. After plenty of alcoholic refreshment, one of the extremely beautiful and thoroughly 'nice' looking girls at the bar had attracted both young men to the point that a discussion of her 'availability', *and* her price, ensued. It turned out that to meet the current tariff they had to pool their meagre resources. They tossed a coin. After the inevitable disappearance upstairs by the winner, he was asked if he had taken the Commodore's advice about suitable precautions. 'Yes' was the answer, 'but it came off half way through!'

As soon as *Warrior* had docked in Callao, the official, unofficial and private round of giving and receiving entertainment got under way. Riches was on duty the following day and witnessed the arrival of the President of Peru, Manuel Prado. He was given the full ceremonial treatment, with a ceremonial guard of honour, and the band making a good job of the Peruvian anthem.

President Prado being introduced to the Commander and the Commodore (Rowsell)

Inspecting the guard of honour (Rowsell)

This, according to the informative Embassy First Secretary, was Prado's second presidency. Prado, a conservative patriarch of a wealthy and powerful family, had reached the Presidency of Peru with the help of the left-wing APRA party. Prado then announced that 'one of the first acts of my government will be to declare a general political amnesty and put an end to the proscription of political parties.' The only significant proscribed party was, in fact, the APRA (American Popular Revolutionary Alliance). A bill was later passed and APRA's famed founder and revolutionary, Víctor Raúl Haya de la Torre, returned from foreign exile. *Warrior*'s Midshipmen heard several mentions of that name. Riches gleaned more on this as he spent a good part of the day showing Embassy staff and the British community round the ship, getting an invitation to lunch on the Sunday for his troubles.

LEFT: *Miss World 1957, Gladys Zender of Peru*

The Midshipmen learned many other things about Peru and Peruvians in their short stay. It was frequently mentioned with pride that the latest Miss World, Gladys Zender, was a Peruvian.

But there was a darker side to their observation of Peruvian society, 'Such as,' recorded Robertson, 'the open racism of the Spanish-speaking urban upper and middle classes towards the remaining "Indian" native peasantry who had not been wiped out centuries earlier by the *conquistadores*.' Johnston's family friends, the Stewarts, entertained him and commented from their British perspective on the inequalities of Peruvian lives. Even some men with 'respectable' jobs in, for example, a bank, would have to go home to their *favela* (slum) and put their business suit into a biscuit tin to protect it from vermin damage before donning it the next day to go to work. Riches too noted the wide gap between the haves and have-nots. 'One is either living in a fine mansion with servants, two cars and plenty of money or living in a mud hut and barely able to support life.' While attending a lunch at the home of a charming Anglo-Peruvian family he was shocked at the way the hostess shouted at the servants treating them like dirt. Robertson opined that 'the Indians should have stayed up in the mountains around Cuzco, capital of the old Inca civilisation, and never come down to the sea where they found worse poverty than before.' Unfortunately for the Warriors, Cuzco was simply too far away to visit, but some of their purchases brought a breath of the old 'mountain' life with them: rugs and slippers of llama and vicuña wool, necklaces, bracelets and brooches and other ornaments of Peruvian silver featuring mythical figures from their own history.

The hectic life was beginning to tell on some of the officers. Hume and Dennis came back early from the Embassy cocktail party with another officer who was going down with Asian 'flu. Illnesses like that would run quickly through the ship. The next night Hume was off to dinner with the Embassy's Second Secretary. 'I did not want to go, but the Gunroom had to supply three people, so that was that. In fact, that is how it is going to be all the way round; all the invitations have got to be fulfilled and anybody not on duty is liable to be roped in for them. But then the whole cruise is a duty cruise as the Admiral pointed out in his address this morning. We are really a trade mission to these countries – Buenos Aires has not seen a white ensign for five years. Last year a cruiser visited Rio for a week and it is reckoned that the visit was worth £1,000,000 in trade to the UK. The dinner itself was very pleasant if a bit boring. The hostess was a charming French lady; the husband a very small man beside her. After dinner we all felt rather sleepy and it was with the greatest difficulty that we kept Richard [Dennis] awake at all!'

But it was not all dinners, dances and cocktail parties. During his time off, Hume took a trip into the capital. 'The cheapest way into Lima is by the tram which is almost as fast as an electric train. Lima is a fairly modern city but does not possess many very modern buildings (as do the other South American capitals.) Life centres round two Squares and the two main streets. One square has the cathedral and the palace and the other has the big hotels, both of them! We saw round the cathedral, being guided by the very enthusiastic and wizened old caretaker. He showed us round the monastery which had the most beautiful mosaic floors but was, on the whole, very shabby. We also entered the palace of the president, passing the sentries in their very colourful but completely shabby and badly fitting uniforms, past more guards until we could go no further.'

After the President had made his official visit on board and been entertained to lunch, *Warrior* was opened to the public. In no way could the officers and crew manning the gangway have anticipated the crowds that turned up, and their eagerness, one might even say desperation, to come on board. Hume recorded the events in his Journal.

'The ship was open to visitors and throughout the afternoon they poured onto the ship in so great a number that at 1600 it became impossible to take any more. On being told this, the waiting crowd, which still numbered some thousands, tried to storm the gangway which was gallantly defended by the Officer of the Day and the gangway staff. Eventually the mob was dispersed, the police having spared no one with their truncheons, and from the riot emerged a bent and battered gangway. However, we did notice the corruptness of the Police who did allow some of their own friends through.'

Crowds 'storming' the gangway (Rowsell)

In addition to the crowd control problem on shore, it turned out that not enough precautions had been taken to lock offices and cabins, and a fair amount of Government and private property disappeared. Similar scenes were to be repeated at later ports of call, but on board the ship was rather better prepared.

One group of officers made the fascinating train trip up into the Andes. Hume's detailed account was recorded in his Journal.

'As we pulled out of Callao in a comfortable if slightly antiquated train, we could see, stretching for miles, thousands of mud huts, some built fairly solidly, others quite the opposite. [...] But as the train took us further away from Lima and began following the valley, the houses assumed more solidity and the villages we passed appeared quite well built. Suddenly we burst out of the pervading mist into bright sunshine and almost immediately began the long ascent up to Rio Blanca. This particular railway, British-owned until last year and now in Canadian hands, is a remarkable feat of engineering. The track follows the mountain round, climbing very slowly, and passing through a great number of short tunnels.

At several points during the ascent we passed only 30–40 feet above a section of track which had been travelled over some thirty minutes earlier. [At times, in order to negotiate difficult obstacles the train would reverse into a single siding and the locomotive would move to the other end of the train and haul it up the next stretch of track.] After four hours of steaming at what might seem an incredible speed considering the load and the nature of the countryside, we arrived at Rio Blanco, a small town nearly 14,000 feet up in the Andes. Whilst the engine changed ends, we were given the opportunity to stretch our legs. At this altitude one feels very light-headed and any violent exercise had an exhausting effect. Wandering around the tracks and past the houses, we could observe the Indian women occupied with knitting, or spinning the cotton into yarn between their fingers, or leading a small train of mules up a mountain track to fetch wood. They were very shy of the camera, as opposed to the children, four of whom posed on their mule for me. Eventually, the time of departure came and we started a very rapid descent; the vistas opening up one after another from our viewing platform in the rear carriage. Very dramatic were those moments when the rail track clung to a narrow ledge cut into the side of the mountain. It really displayed the beauty of the Andes and the skill of British engineers.'

While the trippers were up in the Andes, *Warrior* moved to the oiling jetty and took on fuel. It turned out to be both expensive, some twenty-five per cent more than the going rate, and so thick that the Commander (E) had to mix it with diesel to be able to pump it from tank to sprayers. As Hume remarked, 'This is one of the reasons why the Admiralty is having to reduce the number of ships in commission. Fuel is becoming too expensive.'

During the evening cocktail party, the Peruvian Minister of Marine presented the British Admiral with the Grand Naval Cross, the highest naval award in Peru; a great honour to him and HMS *Warrior*. Many of the guests at the party were members of the expatriate British community, some having been in Peru for several generations, yet most in their dress and their tastes and in their attitudes seeming more British than those whom the Warriors had left back home.

Cocktail party with Lt. Peter Rowsell, Warrior's photographer (left) (Rowsell)

Altogether, *Warrior*'s stay in Callao was a pleasant one and relations with the Peruvian Navy most cordial. She left on the morning of 13 August, well enough satisfied with the results of the 'First Round', and set course southwards along the coast for Valparaiso, well down the Chilean seaboard. Such are the distances which have to be covered, it took *Warrior* four days to reach her next port of call; time enough for the eager party-goers to recharge their batteries and get ready to represent their country once again. The Admiral's Barge coxswain, Robertson, was also bracing himself for a busy time, since *Warrior* would be moored outside the harbour at the next port of call.

'During the passage down to Valparaiso, my main concern was my motor-boat, which had been singled out for use as the Admiral's Barge. In spite of the fact that the other boat was a good deal faster and had recently had a new coat of paint, the

Boats Officer decided to make use of mine as it was generally cleaner and more respectable. Both boats are standard 40 feet, hard chine, single-screw motorboats, powered by Perkins 6-cylinder SGM engines. The Barge is particularly difficult to handle, as her lack of power, due to broken piston-rings, makes it virtually impossible to attain a satisfactory planing trim, and she tends to handle sluggishly at all but top speed. However, it is the most enjoyable job being in charge of her, and I suppose the best possible kind of training. It is tantamount in fact, in a very small way, to being in command of one's own ship. Even a mere £4,000 worth is no small responsibility. Unfortunately, hard chine boats are by no means seaworthy, being at their best in the smooth waters of a calm harbour. In the heavy cross-swell in between the reefs at Christmas Island when we first arrived I had some distinctly unpleasant moments.'

While Robertson mused on deck, Hume had gone below. All the Midshipmen had to spend four weeks in the Engine Room and Boiler Room. Work and conditions there were in total contrast to watch-keeping on deck. Up to then, he had never really given a great deal of thought to the Engine Room. However, every bridge watch-keeper should have some idea of what happens below when an alteration in speed is signalled and of all the associated machinery which has to be kept running. One of the first things he noticed was the scarcity of information from the bridge about what was happening. The Engineer Officer of the Watch complained bitterly, saying that whilst manoeuvring he liked to be able to picture what position the ship was in. It would help him should an emergency stop be ordered. After the first few days Hume managed to raise quite an interest in what was going on around him and gradually his 'deck officer' prejudices disappeared. One important difference he noticed was the number of senior rates on watch. Where a watch on deck might consist of one petty officer and a leading seaman with twelve to fifteen seamen, as quartermaster, helmsman and messengers, the Engine Room alone had a Chief Engine Room Artificer and a PO Mechanic plus two Leading M(E)s and two Ordinary M(E)s while the Boiler Room had a Chief and a PO M(E) together with four or five stokers, one of whom would be a Leading hand.

Another difference was in the work of the Officers of the Watch on deck and in the Engine Room. Whereas the former keeps his watch in one place, on the bridge, the latter spends much of his time personally checking every bit of running machinery and every space in which machinery is situated. Fans, shaft bearings, hull and fire pumps, generators, steering gear, refrigeration, steam glands and auxiliary machinery all contribute to making the Engineer Officer's watch a constantly busy one with, it might seem, little variation from his routine. By contrast, the seaman Officer of the Watch has to be on the alert for every eventuality and it is never the same, never consumed by routine. Hume was on the throttle plates as *Warrior* entered Valparaiso, and although unable to see what was happening, it was not difficult to form an idea of the alterations in the ship's position from the sequence of orders received from the wheelhouse. The rapidity with which these were executed by the throttle watch-keepers was impressive.

After firing the salutes *Warrior* moved in onto a course parallel to the right-hand mole and some 300 yards away.

Gradually coming closer, she stopped just before the harbour entrance and let go the port anchor. Swinging round on this she brought her stern about until it

Warrior *firing a salute (Rowsell)*

Warrior *secured astern to the mole (Rowsell)*

was facing the breakwater, and then a berthing party which had been lowered in the motor-cutter, secured two wires from the quarter-deck to heavy cables on the breakwater. There was a bilingual burden thrust on Dennis to make sure that *Warrior* did, in fact, become securely attached to the mole. He recalls:

'The carrier had to approach the breakwater, drop anchor and then turn so that she was stern on to the mole and then pass two hawsers to the mole which were attached to bollards on the flat top of the mole. Set into the sides of the mole were metal rung ladders for men to scale up the sides, which the landing party used to gain access, having been brought alongside them by the ship's boats. Arriving early in the morning just after sunrise, *Warrior*, with officers and crew at harbour stations, in the Pacific swell, slowly approached the allotted berth. On *Warrior*'s foredeck, the anchor party were at stand by and ready to drop anchor. On the quarter deck aft, the quarter deck party prepared the two steel hawsers to be taken ashore.

The plan was to carry the hawsers, one at a time, ashore to a landing party on the mole. They had to attach each hawser to a bollard and make good before returning on board. Each hawser eye had a heaving line attached to it so that as the cutter reached throwing distance to the mole, a sailor would throw his line at the landing party who would catch it and haul in the hawser and place the eye round the bollard. The landing party was chosen – there were six to eight hands, a Leading Seaman and the only officer being myself, a Midshipman with a small command of "Pidgin Spanish". As we were leaving *Warrior* and boarding a cutter to be taken to the mole, I was informed by the Officer of the Day (OOD) that the Chilean Navy would be providing a squad of sailors to assist in this berthing operation. The meaning was clear – use them!

We arrived ashore and within five minutes our Chilean colleagues arrived. A mixed lot of about fifteen to twenty sailors with a couple of Petty Officers. They were a disorganised shambles as they stood about talking, gossiping, banging each other on the shoulder in their Latin way as well as a few having a good smoke, including the petty officers. I thought, "Right! Men, fall in!" Taking the Leading Seaman (LS) as marker, I ordered them to form two ranks on the LS. I brought them to attention, stood them at ease and then easy. The Chileans were slightly open mouthed. One of their POs came to me and asked in Spanish what were they to do as we all saw the cutter leaving *Warrior*'s stern with the first hawser. In "Pidgin Spanish" I explained that the heaving line came first and then we all heaved the hawser – Chileans and British. Long palaver in Spanish and I put my party ready to catch the first line. One, two … Woof … and it was on its way being caught smartly by the British sailors. Then to my slight surprise the Chilean colleagues quickly backed them up. We had seized and held the eye of the hawser with all its weight as it stretched one hundred or so yards back to *Warrior*'s stern. We definitely needed muscle power and it was clear that the Chilean POs knew the rules of this game. Acting as cheer leader, I got them heaving in rhythm to my cries of "Uno, dos, tres!" which was soon taken up by the mixed Anglo Chilean shore party as they heaved away.

It took a good five minutes to get the first eye round the bollard. The problem was that the Pacific swell was unremitting, which added to the weight we had to pull as *Warrior* was rising and falling with the movement causing the hawser to tighten up and slack off all the time – no easy task when you are hauling it in by hand, especially a steel wire hawser. The second hawser was transferred in the same way. When all was "shipshape and naval fashion" there was a distinct display of mutual respect. This was expressed by many handshakes, pats on the back, smiles and lots and lots of "muchas gracias". Our Chilean colleagues this time marched off as a squad commanded by their two POs all in smart order and unlike the party outing atmosphere in which they had arrived.'

It was altogether an elegant naval solution to the lack of space in the harbour, and the journey from the starboard after gangway to the Muelle Prat was not more than a quarter of a mile; but it was still far enough for things to go wrong as Johnston was going to find out.

Owing to the rough and misty weather on the passage south, the coast had not been visible to the naked eye and the Midshipmen had not seen Chile until the moment Valparaiso came into view. Anson's Journal records his arrival and almost immediate departure for Santiago.

'When I emerged from the engine room after "special sea duties" the securing operations had been completed. Valparaiso harbour is an attractive sight. The town is built in a rising semi-circle round the bay and in the distance the snow-capped tops of the Andes could be seen. We had little time to speculate on the scenery that day, however, as shortly after the Chilean C-in-C of the first Naval Zone had called on the Admiral, I left the ship in a party of twenty officers to spend the weekend in Santiago.'

The journey took three hours by train even though Santiago is only about fifty miles away as the crow flies. The route lay through many little towns and villages as they slowly climbed higher and higher into the Andes. Just outside Valparaiso the railway makes a sweeping curve through the flat-bottomed valleys where cattle graze and elderly farmers till the land with ox-drawn ploughs.

At Santiago station they were met by a number of British families who had offered to put them up. Midshipmen Kirchem and Anson were the guests of the Shaws and their two daughters. The first evening they attended a delightful Ball, given by the British Ambassador, which lasted until the early hours of Sunday. On Sunday morning they were driven up to Colina, high above the snow-line in the Andes. Scattered over the mountainside were a number of Alpine-looking ski lodges with a ski-lift leading to the upper slopes. It was bitterly cold and gentle snow fell listlessly from a leaden sky. In

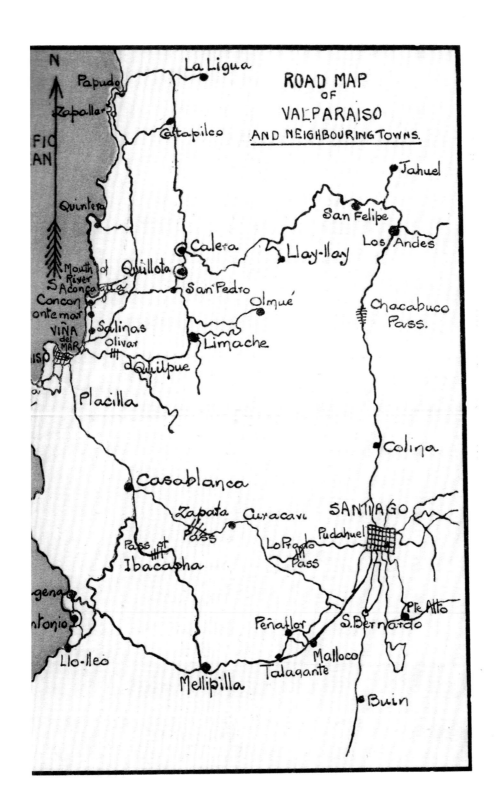

Anson's Journal map of Chile (Anson)

such a place it was hard to recall the boiling tropics they had left so recently.

Cocktails had been arranged at lunchtime with the American Naval Attaché, and after this came a quick drive around Santiago to capture a few points of interest. The most impressive viewpoint was undoubtedly from the top of San Cristobal, a small hill near the edge of the city. From here the vast panorama was spread out below on the valley floor. In the centre was the old town and the small hill on which Pedro de Valdivia built a fort and so founded the city in 1541. In those days the river used to run on both sides of the fort and so made it nearly impregnable. It has since been diverted and runs down one side of the city only. The main Plaza and widest street are named after General Bernardo O'Higgins, the first President of an independent Chile. And then it was onto the train to return to the ship. The British sailor who so ably helped Chile win its independence, Admiral Lord Cochrane, is still held in high esteem in the country and there is a memorial to him in Valvular to which passing Midshipmen raised their hats in salute.

The late hour of dining in Latin America – dinner at midnight being not uncommon – put a certain strain on the diurnal rhythms of the young European officers, but they wielded their knives and forks gallantly for Queen and Country. Riches in his ship's 'Entertainments Office' dealt with, and dealt out, the shoals of invitations that poured in from the moment the ship dropped anchor. It was a steady stream, mostly for parties of two or three to go to dinner or for a day trip to the country, all of which, needless to say, were taken up. Riches and two other officers accepted a very vague invitation on their first evening to dine with Sr and Sra Ramirez. 'They would *probably* collect us from the jetty at 2100!' They duly went ashore on time to be met by a station wagon into which they climbed and were taken to a house on one of the many hills overlooking Valparaiso. It turned out to be a purely family party to which relations had come from within a seventy-mile radius. They were all made to feel most welcome, the 'language difficulty' proving no barrier. Thirty people finally moved in to dinner about midnight after which dancing commenced. The local Chilean wine, which Riches thought to be superior to many French ones, flowed like water, and the quantity of 'piscos' even the grandparents consumed was quite astounding. Apparently it was the Chilean custom that all guests had to either sing a song or perform a sketch during the evening. Whether this was a genuine custom they never discovered, but their hosts managed to convince them it was so, and they did their best to oblige! 'The great enjoyment of the evening,' he recalls, 'was derived from being at a Chilean party so typical of the country; for however hospitable they are one soon tires of the British Community, and HM ships don't visit foreign ports to meet only them.'

Cooper had followed Robertson in 'choosing' this moment to be laid low with *la gripe*. 'I naughtily got up yesterday to drive the Admiral in his barge. There are only two of us who can drive it, and the other chap wanted to go on a trip to Santiago for the weekend. The Ship's Doctor got a bit cross and made me go to bed eventually. Heaven only knows who will drive the wretched barge now.' In fact, it was Johnston who had to take over barge duty. Robertson, who as official Coxswain should have had the principal if not sole share and indeed had done so for the first day or two, was already in his bunk, laid even lower than Cooper.

Johnston recalls:

'I had to go ashore to pick up the most senior officer in the Chilean Navy who was also the Vice-President of the country. Our boat hook drill as we came alongside the jetty was perfect and I snapped a smart salute as he came on board. Again we carried out the drill with style as we set off back to the ship. My destination was the ship's starboard after gangway where officers and distinguished visitors came and went. I had to pick my way with care since the harbour thronged with unlit rowing boats and mooring buoys that were no more than a plank on a rope.

As I came up to the gangway, developing my necessary swing, a pleasure boat came unexpectedly under the stern of *Warrior* and created a significant bow wave which struck my motor boat just at the wrong moment, pushing it a few inches, maybe just a foot away from the ship. It was enough to make it impossible for us to hook on and so I had to circle round again. The trouble was that the bugler had already sounded the Alert, the Petty Officer of the Watch had already announced "Attention on flight and weather decks. Face to starboard. Vice-President of Chile." The coxswain had already made the first pipe and everyone on the ship was standing to attention saluting. They had to stand like that for what, to me, seemed like a lifetime while I circled round and, the second time, managed to hook on and discharge my precious cargo. As he climbed out of the boat onto the gangway, the Vice-President of Chile smiled, winked, and said thank you. Once aboard and the second pipe had shrilled and the bugle had announced the event was over, the Commander leant over the rail and glowered down at me, threatening unspeakable torments.

Admiral Robson and the Vice President of Chile (Rowsell)

Hutchinson took on his share of being entertained.

'Lieutenant Bagg, Midshipman Hume and I were detailed off to go to tea with a Chilean Admiral at his home in nearby Viña del Mar. There we found three young ladies who may or may not have been daughters of an Admiral but they could not speak English and we could not speak Spanish so we never found out. I forget how it all ended but it did. I returned to my duties and the late liberty boats, returning with several parrots and small monkeys. Another invitation to tea took us up into the hills on a verandah with a kind English family gazing at the distant Andes, capped with snow, fifteen times higher than any other hill I have seen, like the Wrekin.'

Robertson wrote home to say that:

'Almost the only things I remember about the place are driving the boat disgracefully badly [he was well on the way to a raging bout of 'flu] and making polite conversation to hordes of Chilean cadets in the Gunroom. The cadets were dressed in a quaintly outdated uniform, wearing high wingless stiff collars, with black "French bandleader" style bow-ties and extraordinary nineteenth century monkey-jackets, topped by long, flowing black capes. Their training ship, the *Esmeralda*,

Memorial to Arturo Prat in Valparaiso (Rowsell)

233

Royal Navy
tribute to Arturo
Prat (Rowsell)

came into harbour our second day in. She is a most handsome schooner, four-masted, displacing, I should say, some 2,500 tons.

'I don't remember seeing much else of the Chilean Navy, although we heard plenty about *Almirante* Prat, who was Grau's opposite number in the Chileo-Peruvian war, and died while leading a boarding party onto the Peruvian ship as she rammed his command. It was his jetty where our boats came alongside, and a wreath was laid at his statue with the pomp and ceremony due to a Chilean hero.

'I kept going as long as I could despite how I felt. My memories are largely of ceremonial duties, but one incident involved my stopping a drunken libertyman trying to pour the contents of a bottle of beer down the throat of an unfortunate penguin which he had somehow captured and was leading by a makeshift collar at the end of a rope as he returned to *Warrior*. Earlier, CINCSASA himself, returning from some much higher level but I suspect equally bibulous party ashore, had refused to accept my slow pace as I picked my way in darkness through the harbour, seeking to avoid huge balks of timber and other dangerous debris all around us which his poor eyesight and/or generally jolly condition prevented him from seeing. "Open her up, Snotty, for Heaven's sake!" he kept grumbling.'

Steeped in naval history and the tales of Cochrane in the service of the Chilean government as they sought their independence from Spain, the Gunroom officers had hoped to see and hear more of the dashing sailor. They knew he had sailed the fifty-gun *O'Higgins* on several successful raids on the Spanish ships and ports. His night-time small boat raid on Callao when, risking the guns of the forts, he cut out the *Esmeralda,* is not only an example of his derring-do but a classic of the art of surprise in naval encounters. This man who almost single-handed cowed the Spanish into submission and departure from the west coast of South America was later to fall out with the newly independent Chilean government over the payment of his dues as a mercenary. He left Chile behind to go on to 'free' Brazil from the Portuguese, where money and its non-payment were to be the cause of further argument. In consequence, he is more remembered there in history books than in public statuary.

One evening Johnston went with four other young officers to the intriguingly named Señorita Widow (an unmarried widow?) in Viña del Mar, but then many South Americans have names that reveal where their ancestors came from; names like O'Higgins, Grau, Stewart and, for that matter, Widow. They spent the evening drinking, first of all, *pisco sours* (made from the local potato brandy), and wondering if it was really a drinks party they had been invited to, having arrived around 8.00pm, since there was never any sign of a meal; not even a table with nibbles. By the time they were asking themselves if they should get a taxi back to the ship it was already ten o'clock, and they were all slightly tipsy and totally ravenous. At that point, Miss Widow clapped her hands and the folding doors at the end of the salon were opened to reveal a dining table set for a meal of several courses and more than one wine. Johnston drank the Chilean red and enjoyed it. The meal was excellent and was followed by delicious coffee and, later, dancing to records. There was a final farewell cognac and then they piled into their taxi and reached the ship long, long after midnight. Johnston was tired enough the following morning to do nothing more energetic than insert the latest amendments into his *Manual of Seamanship* before beginning twenty-four hours on duty and on call. The duty was largely running a boat service between ship and shore with the consequences mentioned above. Another consequence was that

Riches returning hospitality on board Warrior *(Rowsell)*

Johnston bought a bottle of pisco which he doled out in disgracefully mean amounts all the way from Valparaiso to the Straits of Magellan. Others had bought Chilean white wine but, as the Gunroom discovered, this did not travel as well as the pisco.

On the Sunday, after church, Riches was invited out by the Deputy Manager of Cable & Wireless and was served a very English lunch of 'roast beef and two veg' then went to watch a hockey match in which *Warrior* played Viña del Mar Sports Club, losing 1–2. Then it was back for hot buttered toast and, after carefully washing and drying his hands, a look at his host's stamp collection during which he kept dropping off to sleep. Then, next day, he was able to satisfy his wish to visit the Andes, which had been denied him in Peru. 'Three of us took the bus from Valparaiso to Santiago, some sixty-five miles distant. The journey takes three hours as negotiation of mountains by winding roads is a lengthy business. A better day climatically couldn't have been wished for, brilliant sunshine and morning mist greeting us as the bus climbed out of the city. As each successive range of mountains succeeded the last, small plains would appear in between with sparkling rivers and grazing cattle in their margins. After one

First sight of Santiago (Riches)

and a half hours of bone shaking, we stopped for a cup of coffee and then on again until finally, after a climb of 5,000 feet, a most awe-inspiring view lay before us. In the plain lay the sprawling city of Santiago, the whole being ringed by range upon range of the snowy mountains that constituted the main Andean chain. For my first ever sight of snow-capped mountains I couldn't have wished for a more magnificent spectacle.' The rest of the day turned out to be rather an anti-climax, so much so that, after some shopping, Riches and his colleagues immediately took the train back to Valparaiso.

The ship was open to visitors on both the Sunday and the Monday but, by comparison with Callao, visitors had to come out to *Warrior* in chartered boats, meaning that they arrived in manageable quantities and were reasonably subdued by their boat journey. *Warrior* finally sailed for Port Stanley at 0830 on 27 August.

In the Gunroom, there was considerable argument and controversy as to whether *Warrior* should, for the purposes of propaganda, sail round the Horn, or go for the achievement of being the first aircraft carrier to navigate the Straits of Magellan. Strong cross-winds in the sometimes narrow channels of the Straits were, for an aircraft carrier, a matter of concern. Finally, radar and weather conditions permitting, it was decided she should make the passage through the Straits. During the Middle watch on the 25th, with a Chilean Pilot on the bridge, the ship entered the waters

Warrior *in the Straits of Magellan (Rowsell)*

where Magellan, the world-renowned navigator, made his famous crossing from the Atlantic to the Pacific, in the opposite direction of course.

That same morning they came to the first of the narrows. The Midshipman of the Watch was given the responsible but deadly boring job of watching the echo-sounder – sounding the passage – for four hours. During the transit they took continuous readings in order to compile a detailed record for the Hydrographers at Creechbarrow House. However, when off watch, they were able to admire the glorious rugged scenery and enjoy the bracing air. The rocky cliffs seen all the way down the south-west coast were lower and less sheer now and the snow, which had before nestled coyly on the distant mountain tops, now came down almost to the water's edge and frequently swirled about everyone's ears in short flurries. It was extremely cold, and the stillness and barrenness of the land close on either side gave an eerie impression of solitude. In *Warrior*'s wake huge albatrosses swooped and hung; brilliantly effortless 'aerobats' who had followed the ship since Valparaiso. While the *Rhyme of the Ancient Mariner* tells of disasters flowing from the shooting of an albatross, the Chilean Navy were under orders to do just that. Apparently, albatross would attack shipwrecked mariners and peck them to death![4]

That afternoon, *Warrior* came out of the second set of narrows and, as the coastline flattened out, the town of Punta Arenas appeared over to port on the mainland. It is a large town of some 30,000 inhabitants, and seems absurdly out of place in that vast and practically uninhabited land of scrub and sheep.

Johnston, with his textile background, knew about the sheep; but he also remembered a book he had read some years before which had made him keen to see this part of the world. The first man ever to sail *alone* around the world had berthed at Sandy Point, as he called it; the English translation of Punta Arenas, and had been given a bit of sound advice. Captain Joshua Slocum was warned that when he anchored overnight the native Fuegans from Tierra del Fuego might well try to slip on board to rob him and maybe even kill him.

> 'The port captain, a Chilean naval officer, advised me to ship hands to fight Indians in the strait farther west, and spoke of my not stopping until a gunboat should be going through, which would give me a tow. After canvassing the place, however, I found only one man willing to embark, and he on condition that I should ship another "mon and a doog". But as no one else was willing to come along, and as I drew the line at dogs, I said no more about the matter, but simply loaded my guns. At this point in my dilemma Captain Pedro Samblich, a good Austrian of large experience, coming along, gave me a bag of carpet-tacks, worth more than all the fighting men and dogs of Tierra del Fuego. I protested that I had no use for carpet-tacks on board. Samblich smiled at my want of experience, and maintained stoutly that I would have use for them. "You must use them with discretion," he said; "that is to say, don't step on them yourself." With this remote hint about the use of the tacks I got on all right, and saw the way to maintain clear decks at night without the care of watching.'[5]

In Slocum's time, before the construc-tion of the Panama Canal, the Straits were busy with traffic to and from Europe and the west coast of the Americas. Even in 1957, *Warrior* 'spoke', by Aldis lamp and radio, to several ships that were making the transit in the opposite direction.

Ship's wake as Warrior *turned for home! (Riches)*

239

Johnston was not the only one who had read Slocum's book *Sailing Alone Around the World*, and he and Cooper were able to exchange a grin and a reference to tin tacks to confirm, each to the other, they had noted the point. The Navy in 1957 in an aircraft carrier had no need of tin tacks but did keep a vigilant watch. The watch was 'enhanced' by the presence of a Chilean Pilot. Hutchinson observed that, '[This was much] to the chagrin of our navigator, [who felt himself entirely competent] to lead us through the Magellan Straits.' Riches talked with the Pilot who knew his part of the world in great detail. 'He told me that until about twenty-five years before there had been many wild natives in Tierra del Fuego who would attack anyone who landed. Despite the cold, they wore only a few skins, were very hairy and smothered themselves in animal fat to keep out the cold. Now in 1957 there were only a few left.'

Warrior had rounded the southernmost tip of the continental landmass, Cape Froward – almost 54°S, as far south as Manchester is north but much colder – and Riches marked the moment by photographing the ship's wake as it turned to port and towards home (see photo on opposite page).

Johnston had his photograph taken wearing his very smart charcoal grey duffel coat. He had been offered a camel coloured one from 'slops' but spotted the charcoal

Johnston (in duffel coat), Hutchinson and Cooper off Cape Froward (Hutchinson)

one. His greatest regret of the whole trip was that he was so broke when *Warrior* reached Portsmouth that he couldn't afford to buy it from the Navy and was obliged to hand it back in.

After dropping the Pilot and flying ashore some mail, *Warrior* eased herself through the third set of narrows and headed towards the open sea. The last point of the continent, to the north, where Chile's and Argentina's frontiers meet in a point, was passed at 2300 on the 25th. That point is known, interestingly, as Cape Dungeness! Then the Navigator set a course for Port Stanley, where *Warrior* arrived 0930 on 27 August in driving sleet and a temperature of 38°F. *Warrior* anchored in an outer bay near Cape Pembroke.

At Port Stanley, CINCSASA went ashore to call on the Governor. Robertson recalls this in some detail. 'My own first excitement was when I was bringing CINCSASA into Port Stanley to be greeted by the Governor, the latter in full ceremonial rig complete with plumed cocked hat, and by a band and a large crowd. The motor

Governor in full ceremonial dress (Rowsell)

boat's throttle chose to jam, fully open, as we creamed towards the jetty to make an impressively dashing "alongside" while the band played *Rule Britannia*. Red-faced and sweating despite the bitter cold of an icy south Atlantic winter wind, I struggled desperately to unjam the throttle as we swooped round in tight circles not far from the jetty. The band played bravely on. Finally, I had no choice but to cut the engine completely. To my huge relief I picked the right moment for this and we managed to glide alongside smoothly, avoiding a major incident. We came to a halt at exactly the right spot and my bowman and sternsman hooked us neatly to the bollards.' The Governor came on board *Warrior* later in the morning to the accompaniment of a seventeen-gun salute.

Despite the cold and occasional sleet and snow, members of the Gunroom went ashore to explore. Riches recorded that, 'A more desolate place would be hard to find. Amenities were few and life centred on the sheep farms in the "camp" where most of the work was carried out on horseback. While hiking, we met the Islands' Governor and our Admiral. The following two days involved the usual round of entertaining including a drinks party on board where I was expected to entertain the Governor's daughter (very sweet). Ashore there was a Colony Club cocktail party and Ball on the first evening – the former great, the latter ghastly.' As for Port Stanley, opinions were generally unfavourable: the Gunroom having been spoiled by earlier visits in warmer climes. Cooper commented, 'The town itself is pretty awful. It is on a fairly steep hill and one rather expects to find a coal mine at the top of the rows of red brick houses, but instead there is a snow-covered mountain of some 1,600 feet.'

Johnston had a stroll on shore and had a look at Port Stanley and 'what with the crispness in the air and the stacks of peat all around it could have been some Hebridean village, although the scenery was more reminiscent of the Scottish Borders.'

Pursuing his second career as a broadcaster, Johnston devised a programme for Falklands Islands Radio in which he and Lt Calcutt, a performer of consummate skill, recorded a tour of the entire ship. They

Stacks of peat (Riches)

would appear to have visited various parts of the ship which 'Harpic' described with loving detail. No one listening would have known that they did it all sitting in the SRE compartment with Johnston indicating the pauses by hand signals and then feeding 'Harpic' questions like, 'And where are we now, Lieutenant Calcutt?'

'Great fun,' wrote Cooper about the Ball. 'I was in the C-in-C's party and got on with Susan, the Governor's daughter like a house on fire. Ian Hume was also in the party, and we were made, by the Admiral, to give, with our respective partners, an exhibition of rock 'n' roll!' (One can but speculate whether Riches's relative disenchantment with the ball, as reported above, related to the 'very sweet' Governor's daughter having turned her attention from him towards Cooper!)

As well as the Ball for officers, there was a Dance (subtle distinction!) for the sailors at which some managed to behave badly under the eye of the C-in-C who gave the Commodore a blast that he, in turn, passed on, and so *ad infinitum*. In the men's defence, Robertson commented that there was little or nothing for the men to do ashore and that he had been told that the Falklands at that time held the world records for the *per capita* consumption of both alcohol and aspirin.

The following day, one of the principal activities was a children's party in the ship's hangar, and probably every child on the Islands, and not a few adults, turned up.

Johnston and Riches made themselves the targets in the Aunt Sally but managed to escape more or less unscathed. The more outdoors oriented members of the Gunroom took part in a hare shoot. Cooper, ever positive and forgetting his earlier criticisms, provides the best account.

Teatime at the ship's party with Anson as host (Rowsell)

'I quickly recovered from my Asiatic 'flu and was soon as well as ever. Port Stanley is the most magnificent place. Freezing cold, snow, mist and rain are the normal daily routine, but there is plenty to make up for it: (a) Governor's daughter, (b) Shooting. On Wednesday at 0730, six officers, myself included, and fifty-eight ratings to act as beaters, boarded a local trawler towing a ship's whaler and were taken ten miles round the Island to land in a rocky cove. It was a hare shoot organised by some locals. The whaler unfortunately hit a submerged rock on its second journey inshore with twenty passengers. I was one of them and had to wade up to my waist in the icy water when the boat sank some ten yards from the beach. However, not to be deterred, while we hauled the boat clear of the water the rest of the party transferred from the trawler by a small pulling boat. A message from the Commander was sent to the ship demanding shipwrights to be sent by helicopter whilst [soaked to the waist!] we unconcernedly started the shoot. The six guns from the ship were backed up by another six from the shore, to make a round dozen guns. Never have I seen a shoot organised on such a vast scale. We had a total of sixty-seven beaters. An enormous line was formed one and a quarter miles long, and we started to drive a headland to seaward. Thirty-seven hares were shot in an extremely amusing and dangerous two hours. Once, the gun next to me – a local – drew a bead on a hare running back and shot straight down the line, spraying us all. Nobody was hurt. I shot three hares.

After watching 300 penguins waddling down to the beach we had an excellent lunch of unlimited beer and sandwiches provided by our hosts. The whaler was by this time repaired and we re-joined the trawler and returned, tired but happy, to *Warrior*.'

Reed's account of his experiences, despite its measured and factual tone, makes distinctly more dramatic reading.

'Daylight was fading as we set off in the pinnace and there were snow flurries in the air. I had two crewmen with me. At Stanley there was a considerable crowd waiting at the jetty, among whom I found the officers I had been sent to collect. On the way back, we passed through the narrow channel and as we entered the outer bay, a local harbour vessel taking libertymen ashore for the evening, suddenly appeared in the dark. She was coming straight towards us and moments later struck us amidships on our starboard side. Some of my passengers managed to scramble onto the harbour vessel which was undamaged but we were badly holed and water was coming in fast. With the aim of saving the boat, I and my crew headed for land some 400 yards away. The engine sounded as if it might cut out but we made it and waded ashore in knee-high water. One of my crew made a fire without matches so we had some warmth and a beacon to guide rescuers.

On return to *Warrior* I saw that my crew were all right and went to the Gunroom where my fellow Midshipmen urged me to set down there and give my account of what had happened. The pinnace was not a complete write-off. The following day it was recovered, hoisted on board for later repairs in Portsmouth Dockyard. An Inquiry was held. I gave my version of events and listened to what other witnesses had to say. It transpired that when the harbour vessel got back to Stanley, her skipper had ordered a new set of lights.[6] I suggested that he might have seen me in time to take avoiding action if a dozen or so libertymen had not been standing on his deck in front of the wheelhouse obscuring his view. The Inquiry cleared me of blame and people were very thankful that there had been no loss of life; as there could so easily have been in the cold and the dark.'

Robertson was a member of the ship's squash team returning on board after a match with the locals which he thinks *Warrior* won, and was one of the officers collected from the jetty by Reed. He got a ducking, and his account is less calm than Reed's:

'Some of the passengers including myself were spilled into the icy waters before being spotted and hauled aboard the harbour vessel. I doubt I shall ever come closer to death than that brief immersion in the water; nor indeed closer to having a sex change than when I looked down in the hot shower into which we were pushed on our return to *Warrior* and saw that my "equipment" had all but disappeared inside my body. Ever since then I have enjoyed telling other Navy contacts that I was sunk in the Falklands, and seeing them puzzling over this claim by someone who was far too young for the great WWI naval battle but also far too old for the more recent "unpleasantness". There were incidentally four huge whale jawbones [at Port Stanley] forming a monument to the great WWI victory.'

Hutchinson recalls that, 'Lots of folk had a rough time in the cold water. Midshipman Robertson thought he had been saved from drowning by a large stoker, who asserted that, on the contrary, Robertson had saved him. This latter opinion prevailed, and the

The hulk of the
SS Great Britain
(Riches)

matter was not discussed at the Court of Inquiry conducted by three Lieutenant-Commanders who avoided judgements on the causes of the disaster.' Cdr Begg commented on the sinking of the ship's pinnace. He says he personally dived down to attach the slings to the boat so that it could be recovered. It sat on the flight deck for the rest of the journey home and was then immediately condemned by the Examiner so, as he notes, it might as well have been left there.[7]

There were other historic relics in Port Stanley. Riches noted the hulk of the once famous SS *Great Britain*, designed by Isambard Kingdom Brunel, which had finished up in the Falklands.

The story of her career in the Falklands is excellently summarised by Wikipedia.

> In 1882 *Great Britain* was converted into a sailing ship to transport bulk coal, but after a fire on board in 1886 she was found on arrival at Port Stanley in the Falkland Islands to be damaged beyond repair. She was sold to the Falkland Islands Company and used, afloat, as a storage hulk (coal bunker) until 1937, when she was towed to Sparrow Cove, 3.5 miles from Port Stanley, scuttled and abandoned. As a bunker, she coaled the South Atlantic fleet that defeated Admiral Graf Maximilian von Spee's fleet in the First World War Battle of the Falkland Islands. In the Second World War, some of her iron was scavenged to repair HMS *Exeter*, one of the Royal Navy ships that fought the *Graf Spee* and was badly damaged during the Battle of the River Plate.[8]

As we know now, a rescue expedition was organised in 1970, thanks to substantial donations from Sir Jack Hayward and Sir Paul Getty, and the restored ship is now a museum well worth visiting in Bristol.

Warrior finally sailed from Port Stanley on 30 August in a blinding snow storm. Special Sea Duties were no fun for many of those involved in weighing anchor. Once clear of the bay, *Warrior* set course for Puerto Belgrano, Argentina's main naval base in Bahia Blanca; almost certainly the last British warship to make such a journey. The following day, at sea, hands made all the preparations for replenishing the two frigates, HMS *Mounts Bay* and HMS *Lynx*, which were to join *Warrior* the following day and thus create a small but not unimpressive South Atlantic Squadron for CINCSASA's remaining visits, rather than the solitary aircraft carrier which had so far been the only ship in his squadron.

As a footnote to *Warrior*'s visit, this is what Wikipedia has to say about the Falkland Islands and, in particular, their name, in not two but *three* languages.

'The Falkland Islands take their name from the Falkland Sound, a strait separating the archipelago's two main islands. The name "Falkland" was applied to the channel by John Strong, captain of an English expedition, which landed on the islands in 1690. Strong named the strait in honour of Anthony Cary, 5th Viscount of Falkland, and the Treasurer of the Navy, who sponsored their journey. The Viscount's title originates from the town of Falkland, in Scotland, whose name comes from "folkland" (land held by folk-right). The name was not applied to the islands until 1765, when British captain John Byron of the Royal Navy, claimed them for King George III as "Falkland's Islands". The term "Falklands" is a standard abbreviation used to refer to the islands.

The Spanish name for the archipelago, *Islas Malvinas*, derives from the French *Îles Malouines* – the name given to the islands by French explorer Louis-Antoine de Bougainville in 1764 [N.B. seventy-five years *later* than John Strong.] Bougainville, who founded the islands' first settlement, named the area after the port of Saint-Malo, the point of departure for his ships and colonists. The port, located in the Brittany region of western France, was in turn named after St. Malo (or Maclou), the Christian evangelist who founded the city.'[9]

---

1 Or so it was noted in Journals at the time but, incredibly, one can now, thanks to Google, take a virtual walk round the narrow, sandy beach that runs all the way round Henderson Island.

2 See Thomas, Donald, *Cochrane: Britannia's Sea Wolf,* London: Cassell, 2001, pp.250/1

3 (1902–1989) Educated at the Royal Naval College, Osborne and the Royal Naval College, Dartmouth, Robson joined the Royal Navy as a cadet in 1915 during World War I and served as a Midshipman on the battleship HMS *Malaya*. He commanded the destroyers HMS *Rowena* from 1934 and HMS *Wren* from 1935. He also served in World War II initially as Commander of the destroyer HMS *Kandahar* and then with combined operations from 1943 before commanding the 26th Destroyer Flotilla in 1944 and then Captain of Coastal Forces for The Nore in 1945.

After the War he was given command of the cruiser HMS *Superb* and then, from 1948, of the Royal Navy Training Establishment HMS *Ganges*. He was appointed President of the Admiralty Interview Board in 1950, Flag Officer (Flotillas) for the Home Fleet in 1951 and Flag Officer, Scotland and Northern Ireland in 1953. He went on to be Commander-in-Chief, South Atlantic Station in 1956 and then retired in 1958. In retirement he served as Lieutenant Governor and Commander-in-Chief of Guernsey from 1958 to 1964. Source: Wikipedia accessed 6/8/2014

4 Begg, p.159

5 Captain Joshua Slocum *Sailing Alone Around the World,* Chapter VII

6 Reed says the harbour vessel suffered only minor damage and he doubts the harbour boat ever admitted liability.

7 Begg, p.159

8 http://en.wikipedia.org/wiki/SS_Great_Britain accessed 22/8/2014

9 http://en.wikipedia.org/wiki/Falkland_Islands accessed 6/11/2014

SEPTEMBER

From Puerto Belgrano to Rio de Janeiro

On the first day of September, by virtue of that particular naval skill in pinpoint navigation, *Warrior* made her appointed rendezvous with the two frigates HMS *Mounts Bay* and HMS *Lynx*.

Arrival of HMS
Lynx *(Rowsell)*

Lynx was almost brand new, completed only a few months before. Much later in 1982 she was sold to Bangladesh and became the *Abu Bakar*. *Mounts Bay* had been completed in 1949 after a period of being mothballed during construction. She was finally sold to Portugal and renamed *Vasco da Gama*. Once more there was the protocol of the *Lynx*, senior of the two ships (as measured by the Captain's seniority), firing a fifteen-gun salute to CINCSASA, followed by the same from *Mounts Bay*. Then there was a classic demonstration of seamanship as each frigate took station alongside and was hooked up to fuel lines, bosun's chairs plus other blocks and tackles for the process of replenishing them after their voyages from Salvador and Simonstown respectively.

Preparing to refuel HMS Lynx (Rowsell)

When it was the turn of *Mounts Bay*, seventeen Royal Marine musicians (and, separately, their instruments) came over by bosun's chair to join forces with, and add some extra professional polish to, the *Warrior* ship's band.

Early on 2 September, *Warrior* entered the muddy channel up river to Puerto Belgrano, near to Bahia Blanca. The pilot was embarked at 0730 by helicopter together with an Argentine Navy liaison officer, and by 0920 the ships had exchanged national salutes and were at the harbour entrance. As elsewhere *Warrior* had to turn round inside the basin in order to come alongside starboard side to. Three tugs were used, two for'ard and one aft, and she slipped her bows gently in past the sterns of the two cruisers, the *9 de Julio* and [although the name signified nothing to us at that time] the *General Belgrano*. One interesting fact about them is that these cruisers can carry up to six aircraft in a hangar right aft and they have two catapults for launching them. The other cruisers in port were the *Almirante Brown*, the *25 de Mayo* and *La Argentina*.

9 de Julio *(left)*
and General
Belgrano *seen*
from Warrior's
flight deck
(Rowsell)

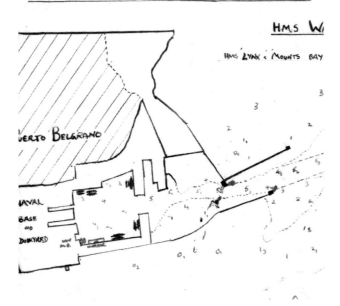

Chart of Puerto
Belgrano Naval
Base drawn by
Hume showing
Warrior *astern*
of General
Belgrano
(Hume)

251

The Warriors were told with pride that *General Belgrano* was named after one of the Argentine's founding fathers, Manuel José Joaquín del Corazón de Jesús Belgrano (1770–1820). She was the flagship of Vice-Admiral Rojas at the time of the successful coup against Peron in 1955. (What they were *not* told was that the *General Belgrano* had accidentally rammed her sister *9 de Julio* on exercises in 1956, which resulted in damage to both cruisers.) When the Admiral died in 1992, he asked that his ashes be scattered at the site where the *General Belgrano* went down in 1982. Reed's diligent research has recently uncovered the story that during *Warrior*'s visit to Buenos Aires, Rojas presented the ship with a handsome silver tray. When *Warrior* was subsequently sold to the Armada Republica Argentina (ARA), the contract of sale did not include the tray. Reed discovered that in April 1960 the Captain of HMS *Leopard*, acting on behalf of the Admiralty, presented the tray to the now-rechristened ARA *Independencia* in a ceremony held at Puerto Belgrano. The gesture was greatly appreciated at the time. Luckily for Britain, the carrier had been sold for scrap long before 1982. At the time of writing, Puerto Belgrano is in the process of becoming a launch site for the new Argentine Space Agency.

Hume formed a good impression of the Argentine Navy from the fact that every ship *Warrior* passed paraded a guard and bugler on the quarter deck to salute the visiting squadron of ships. Once *Warrior* was secured, four deserters from Valparaiso, their tails very obviously between their legs, were marched on board the starboard for'ard gangway. There was soon a queue of top brass visitors coming up the after gangway to the accompaniment of bugles, bosun's pipes and smart salutes, starting with the C-in-C of the Argentine Navy, followed by Rear-Admiral Vargo and Rear-Admiral Estevez.

The following day, there was *Warrior*'s well-practised helicopter display, and in the afternoon the ship was open to the public. The Officer of the Day was instructed to take precautions in case numbers proved too many.

Anson participated in the 'selling campaign', showing a party of officers around. 'Some had never been on a carrier before and could not quite grasp why we had no guns and only four helicopters.' Immediately on arrival, Johnston also had official 'duties' to perform. 'There being no volunteers, I was one of a group of officers who were sent on a bus tour of the naval base which consisted of little more than driving past various buildings and having the repair shops pointed out to us. I was lucky in having an English-speaking officer to point things out to me, because the

Top brass being entertained (Rowsell)

other Argentinian officers sat apart and did not speak to the rest of us.' That evening, however, the Argentine Navy hosted a *Viño de Honor* at the Officers' Hotel where everyone drank champagne and ate turkey. Riches confided in his diary, 'Panic again today as usual – with the addition of the Admirals' Flag Officer and SOO; everyone is trying to run everything. My goodness I'll be glad when Hicks is back in command!' In his Journal, he made a more political note. 'The armed forces are ruling the country and [are] consequently wealthy. Whereas two years ago they were greeted as the saviours of Argentina, today they are hated by the people primarily because of their wealth and also because whenever there is a strike troops immediately walk in and take over so it isn't worth anyone's while to strike.'

Everyone in the Gunroom had a series of social engagements to fulfil. 'The highlight,' for Hume 'was the visit to an estancia south of the Rio Colorado. The Commander led a party of eight and a luxurious coach took us to the Naval Air Station where we were to board a VIP Dakota. Once airborne, the endless *pampas* stretched from

253

horizon to horizon, only broken by a small group of hills and the occasional forest. Below us, the huge delta presented fantastic patterns as hundreds of small tributaries twisted and turned in amazing meanders as the waters made their leisurely way to the main estuary. We passed over a sea of mud flats, then came on small estancias clustered under tall poplar trees and then, once more, the endless plain. We circled over *Las Isletas*, the pilot giving us an excellent view of the buildings, and then we landed on an incredibly short runway which was basically nothing more elaborate than one of the fields. Our arrival was watched by the community and after staring at us they stared at the aircraft since it is rare that one of such a size lands at this remote spot.

'After a splendid "tea" in the main house, we walked over to the paddock where horses were selected for each one of us including our two pilots who by now had been fully integrated into the party. Although most of us had not ridden for some years, we soon found our "feet", the only difficulty being the "steering". Horses in the Argentine are guided by the feel of the rein on the neck, rather than the pull on the mouth. They are very soft-mouthed animals, capable of taking a single bit and no more. Those who were mounted in Argentinian saddles, like myself, had the comfort of two fleeces but it took some time to get used to the extreme breadth of the saddle.

'Before long we were on the trail, making for the sheep-shearing farm. Here, we saw piles of cow hides, stiff as cardboard, boar skins, fox furs and armadillo hides; all drying in a large shed. The fox and armadillo are the real pests and a financial reward is offered on the same basis as "the shilling per squirrel's tail" back home.

'Mr Rogers, our host, who manages *Las Isletas* for Argentinian owners, gave us some idea of the size of the place: all told there are 100,000 acres supporting 40,000 sheep, 12,000 head of cattle and a thousand horses, and that, he explained, was a medium-large estancia for the Argentine. The ride home was very enjoyable, as riding in wide open country always is, and by this time we had all mastered the art of staying on! An early rise the following day heralded our departure for a pig shoot. At 0700 we set off in a cavalcade of some fifteen persons, accompanied by some of the gauchos in their typical hats, high boots and baggy trousers. They all had lassos and knives, and wherever they went they were followed by numerous dogs, many resembling the collie breed. The Commander did not accompany us as he was convalescing from a severe attack of *la gripe*, no doubt brought on by long periods in the cold at Port Stanley directing salvage operations of the pinnace.

'Amongst us there were some ten firearms ranging from .22 and .303 to 12 bore. The 10-mile ride across the green country on the most perfect morning was really invigorating, and feeling somewhat tired we arrived at the Rio Colorado. The plan was in two parts. Firstly, some twenty-five gauchos with forty dogs were to comb the thick woods on the other side of the river, driving the pigs into the water. Then we, stationed on the right bank at suitable intervals, would fire once the pigs were in the river. Unfortunately, we had no luck and although the hoof marks could be seen quite clearly in the sand, we did not see a single pig. [Eventually] we set off for *Las Isletas* by a different route and at a steady canter as Argentine horses do not trot. After a while the column became spread out and we arrived one by one at the finishing point, glad to dismount. The ten-mile canter without stopping proved to be something of a trial and we suffered for it later!

'Although lunch was ready for us, there was no sign of the Surgeon Commander and an officer from *Lynx*. Eventually, a phone call came through from a distant farm and the only way to get them home was by plane. At once, Mr Rogers's friend took off in his private two-seater and rounded up the stragglers who explained they had headed for the "wrong clump of poplars". At that moment, news came in of a 'kill'. Apparently only a few minutes after we had all set off for home, the gauchos ran into five wild boar. Having no gun, the gauchos lassoed one and held it until a gun arrived – and that was how "roast wild boar" appeared on *Warrior*'s Wardroom menu later in the week. After an *asado* on the lawn, involving eating plenty of roast lamb and drinking substantial quantities of white wine, we returned to our Dakota and flew back to the air base, arriving back on board with barely enough time to present the surprised Officers' Cook with the boar and, suitably washed, brushed and changed, to present ourselves at the reception being given on board.'

At least half the Gunroom managed to get on horseback while in the Argentine. In their equestrian absences, the ship was open to the public and several returned to find riotous scenes similar to Callao with far more people trying to get on board than could possibly be handled. The chance to visit the ship proved so popular that the Officer of the Day had to call on the Army to control the crowd of around 3,000 which was packed round the foot of the gangway which allows only single-file traffic. They managed the problem with gusto, hospitalising at least twenty, and only refraining from using fire hoses at the OOD's particular request. After that, it was a relief to see the jetty slip away as *Warrior* left for Buenos Aires.

The hard-working Robertson commented in his journal about the probable underlying reason for *Warrior*'s visit to Argentina and, in particular, her visit to Puerto Belgrano, the Portsmouth of Argentina and headquarters of the Argentine Navy. 'Our two-day stay was taken up almost entirely by showing off the ship to the Argentinians (see Appendix A). It is rumoured of course that, loath to be outdone by Brazil, they are thinking of purchasing a carrier to counteract the swing in the balance of naval power caused by [Brazil's recent purchase of HMS *Vengeance*.] Many officers and men saw round the ship, and the usual helicopter display, possibly slightly gingered up for the occasion, was very well received.' The only time I managed to get ashore was to watch a football match between the squadron and a local command team, in which we were well beaten by a vastly superior side. The base 'town' [Punta Alta] as far as it went was dull and rather dirty. I was surprised to see pavement trees bearing the notice '*Prohibido pisar*'. [Only later did Robertson learn enough Spanish to understand that this simply meant 'Don't walk' (on the grass).] Libertymen found the adjacent Bahia Blanca more alive, to the tune of smashing up one of the local nightclubs. The only other incidents of note during our stay were the visit of the C-in-C Argentine Navy, and yet another very successful cocktail party on board.

Cocktail party guests (Rowsell)

Hutchinson recalls how some of the crew returning from shore leave used their initiative. 'Two *Warrior* seamen hitched a lift back to the ship, joining some friends getting into the back of a van, a police van as it turned out which took them to gaol. That was their story to the Commander. Many people believed them.'

The visits completed and the stragglers rounded up, *Warrior* sailed on 4 September, not a few of the saddle-sore officers bagging the comfortable chairs in Wardroom and Gunroom. The Squadron steamed north in line ahead towards Rio de la Plata and what would be ten days of concentrated enjoyment. Riches's diary for 5 September summed up the Gunroom's feelings. 'Recuperating and preparing for a hectic ten days ahead. I wonder if we'll all live to tell the tale – doubt it, looking at the programme!' The 'selling' of the ship continued. Ten technical specialist officers took passage with *Warrior*, and apart from intensive tours of inspection, on 5 September they were all transferred by jackstay to *Lynx* which then carried out firing trials before returning them to *Warrior*. Reed continues the story. 'We reached the River Plate on 6 September and passed and saluted the Argentine Minesweeper Squadron. Two hours later tugs took us up the channel to Buenos Aires.'

Warrior *under tow with* Lynx *and* Mounts Bay *in line astern (Rowsell)*

Robertson was on the bridge. 'I had my 20th birthday as we entered the River Plate. I hardly had time to notice. We steamed slowly and cautiously up the dredged channel in thick fog, with only two or three feet between our keel and the muddy bottom. Our Argentine river pilot, Captain Granelli, joked that the channel was effectively kept dredged by the screws of the tankers heading fully laden for the refineries up the river. He also scorned our short-distance inshore radar equipment, claiming to 'sniff' his way up the river in the fog by recognising the different smells of various factories along the banks, adjusting for wind-speed and direction as he went along. An unlikely story – but we made it safely to BA,' where the British Naval Attaché was waiting on the quay. Talking of smells and tastes, the pilot did not seem to appreciate the ship's coffee handed to him in a large mug which he left, barely touched when he disembarked. Robertson's Journal continues, 'Late in the afternoon, the fog thinned out and as we steamed on with the muddy brown 'fresh' water of La Plata swirling past our bows, a reception committee from the Argentine Navy came out to greet us. Destroyers, frigates and torpedo boats surrounded us on all sides and the ship's company was hastily fallen in on the flight deck to return the many salutes as well as possible. Later, all except one destroyer, the *Mendoza*, then left us to continue on up the channel at reduced speed towards the city. Tugs took us into the basin and alongside Darsena A at Puerto Nuevo, the "new port" of BA.'

Hutchinson wonders still what he might have been expected to do with the side arms he was given as he recalls part of his visit to Buenos Aires. 'From Puerto Belgrano we sailed to Buenos Aires up the River Plate. [...] Ashore I was given a pistol for my protection and a sealed package to take to a distant dockyard office. Still ashore I had an introduction to a game of squash and dinner at the Hurlingham Club. I was also lucky to be with Midshipman Anson at a private dinner party. He invited the daughter of our hosts out the next night. The parents gave permission as long as I went with them. They would invite any other girl at the party to keep me company. Naturally I chose the lady sitting on my right, who was unusually attractive. We had a very good evening. We could all speak English.'

Reed records that, '[the city] had fine buildings, wide boulevards, a Harrods department store and a large British community. Johnston, Robertson and I visited the English school called St George's at Quilmes. We were the guests of one of the housemasters there.' Johnston wrote home about that visit, telling his parents that the three officers had talked about *Warrior* to several classes of ten-year-olds and were then taken to lunch at his home by the housemaster, Mr Burke-Gills, and his wife.

'Her almost continuous monologue was about her friends and acquaintances who seemed to lead and/or no longer lead tragic lives – "She's dead now!"; "She lost her husband last month"; "Her mother is dying"; "They were all killed in the war!" – and she would pick up and leave off her narrative as and when there was a gap in other conversations. The Housemaster was a chain-smoker; the most addicted I had ever seen. He was smoking as he showed us round the school, not putting his fag out even in the classrooms. He tended to keep his cigarette between his lips most of the time and the ash grew steadily longer and the tension about when it would fall off was palpable. Then he invited us to join him and his family for lunch where there was a huge hunk of roast beef on the table ready to carve; he picked up his utensils and began to carve the meat with the fag still in his mouth. I was fearful that the ash would drop onto one of our plates, or even worse, onto *my* plate, but it didn't happen. I remember his fingers and moustache were every shade of orange from pale to burnt umber and he had a racking cough. No doubt he is pushing up the pampas grass now after all these years, but there seems to me little doubt what he must have died of. If he predeceased her, at least she would have another anecdote to relate.'

Robertson and Cooper had an excursion that aroused their compatriots' envy.

'Cooper and I were literally ordered to accept an offer, one of so many of hospitality which flowed in as soon as we arrived or even before, from an expatriate couple living in the mountains near Cordoba to have us fly up for a long weekend's visit. It didn't sound like much fun at first (which is why we had to be ordered) but for me it was the

most memorable "run ashore" of the entire *Warrior* cruise, starting with the pilot of the Aerolinas Argentinas Convair Metropolitan which flew us up to Cordoba and heard that we were officers from the *porta-aviones* in the harbour.

LEFT: *Convair Metropolitan*

After the giggling air hostesses had plied us with wine, he insisted that we come up to the cockpit and show him some real flying skills. We did try, after quickly letting on we were deck officers and not flyboys.'

Cooper's account in his Journal was even more alarming. 'I found myself flying the plane and in a steep dive at that. However, the pilot thought I was just fooling and insisted that I flew for another quarter of an hour.' Robertson's account continues:

'In passing, we had been amused while waiting at the airport by the enormous number of private planes standing about, taking off and coming in to land. A tiny Piper would touch down smoothly and taxi to a standstill: then out would step its owner, dressed in "city gent" suit and complete with hat and briefcase, just as if he had parked his car outside the office. The road from Puerto Nuevo to the passenger airfield ran along the water's edge and we passed a trot of eight or nine buoys with a Sunderland flying boat at each. In the port itself, we also passed the American cargo ship *Mormacsurf* having a large patch put on her bow. She was very recently in collision with the Buenos Aires-Montevideo ferry which sank rapidly and drowned one hundred people. The collision took place on a foggy night; but apparently it was entirely the ferry captain's fault, as he more or less admitted by killing himself.'

Later, on her own passage down river to Montevideo, *Warrior* would cast a wreath onto the waters at the spot where the ferry went down.

Dropping a wreath where the ferry went down (Rowsell)

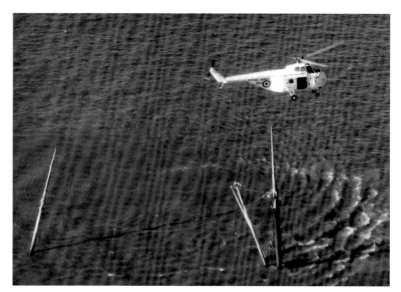

'Our host in the mountains, Colonel Pearson, blue-eyed, ruddy-faced, white-moustachioed, greeted us with a blast of gin-infused breath and, a revolver on his hip, drove us at terrifying speeds round hair-raising bends in his ancient Hotchkiss car *en route* to his estancia. "We should be home just in time for tea," he said. "I know you chaps would prefer Sea You Enn Tea, but that will have to wait till a bit later." And he added, "The gun's just in case of trouble with the locals, by the way." Motherly Mrs Pearson was both as tough as old boots and a real sweetheart. Soon after our arrival the old couple sent us off across the hills on horseback with a group of *gauchos* from their farm and some other young people including two extremely lovely young women, one of whom, called Beatrice Roulet, was the daughter of a Franco-Argentinian neighbour. We were to have an *asado* – Argentina's version of an open-air barbecue, preceded by *empanadas* and washed down with copious quantities of *vino tinto* and accompanied by guitar-playing and sweet-voiced *gauchos*.

Before long I found myself apart from the main group, quoting to Beatrice from Ronsard's famous love poem, "*Quand vous serez bien vieille, au soir, à la chandelle* ..." Yes, the age-old voice of the impatient young man urging his reluctant girl to "gather rosebuds while she may." [Perhaps it should be noted that in a letter home from Montevideo Cooper said that on that same evening "I got off with a honey of a French girl." Some might think "Busy girl!" but Robertson insists that Cooper must be referring to the *other* of the two beauties, and certainly not *his* Beatrice.] Our stay in Cordoba was blissful.'

But they did have official duties in Buenos Aires to return to, of which the visit on board of Vice-Admiral Isaac Rojas, reputed strongman of the junta, was a highlight. That was on 9 September which began with the order to 'dress ship'. *Warrior* limbered up for the most important visitor by first welcoming the National Maritime Prefect, the Chief of the Naval General Staff and the Lord Mayor of Buenos Aires. Then all hands were piped to Divisions on the flight deck and the guard of honour and the augmented ship's band paraded to welcome Admiral Rojas who inspected the divisions. Rojas was representing the provisional president, General Aramburú (yet another victim of *la gripe*). Rojas had played a key role in the coup which toppled Perón by threatening to shell the La Plata Oil Refinery with the guns of his flagship, the *General Belgrano*.

*Guard of
Honour for
Admiral Rojas
(Rowsell)*

*Admiral
Rojas meeting
senior officers
(Rowsell)*

Meanwhile, other Midshipmen were unselfishly taking their share of drinking cocktails and riding horses. Hume and others went to a cocktail 'scrum' at the English Club from where, together with three girls, they were taken to dinner at the American Club, a far more luxurious establishment than the English, and thence to their hosts' apartment for yet another meal and dancing.

Riches wrote home about his journey into the interior.

'Then, on 9 September, Johnston, Lt Rowsell the ship's photographer, and I set off by road for a three-day visit to the Estancia San Juan, near Nueve de Julio, at the invitation of Mr Van Deurs, one of the richest landowners in the Argentine. He owned six estancias; the one we were to visit was the smallest but still comprising several thousand acres. The Reynolds family, Anglo Argentinians from Tierra del Fuego, joined us on the all-day journey across mile upon mile of flat cattle country.'

Johnston recalls stopping for a picnic halfway there and being suddenly confronted by an army road-block which was rather unnerving until the heavily armed soldiers waved the car through. Riches's account continues:

'The plus-four wearing farm manager, Mr Forrester, met us at "The Homestead", a luxurious wooden farmhouse with oak floors and panelling, big airy rooms all opening onto a verandah which surrounded the house, log fires in all the bedrooms and an array of servants including a butler and maids. It was early spring with the trees just budding, beautiful sunny days with crystal clear air and frosty nights.

Johnston and Riches on horseback (Riches)

During our visit we went out hare shooting at night, and for *chimangos* (a type of crow) in the daytime, and in between we went riding with the farm manager visiting several herds of cattle on the estancia. I especially remember breakfasting on three fried eggs and several mugs of delicious tea. Over the three days we spent several hours in the saddle and I realised the practise I had in Puerto Belgrano was time well spent.

263

On Sunday, we enjoyed an *asado* where a whole sheep was roasted on a tripod above the fire and guests cut off whatever meat they wanted: all this accompanied by spiced meat rolls in batter, bowls of fruit salad and clotted cream, washed down with copious quantities of wine. We all slept the afternoon away in the sunshine. Before we returned to BA on the Tuesday, eighteen-year-old George Reynolds and I shot, skinned and cleaned hares and my diary records that I took the skins back to the ship to dry them, but there is no reference to them thereafter!'

Riches inspecting the asado (Riches)

Johnston wrote home to pass on a grimly funny story related to the party by Mr Reynolds. 'He was on another estancia when he saw a fat and very jovial man cooking for the men. He remarked on this and was told the cook was only just out of jail. It appears that he and a friend went out to shoot ostriches, each taking with them a bottle of *caña* (sugar-cane brandy). Having hunted high and low without success and consumed all the *caña*, the cook turned to his friend and said, "Pretend you're an ostrich." The friend who was just as drunk, got up and ran around flapping his arms. To make it seem more like the real thing, and so that the illusion of an ostrich hunt should be preserved, the cook levelled his rifle and shot the man dead!'

For all of these officer-tourists, the stay in Buenos Aires had been a brief chance to forget all about the Navy. But duties resumed on return to the ship with a final on-board cocktail party. While they had been away, *Warrior* had paraded a guard and band and laid a wreath at the appropriate memorial, that of Almirante Brown, another liberation hero of Irish descent, like O'Higgins in Chile.

Saluting Almirante Brown (Rowsell)

With all the trips away to estancias, there was not a great deal of leave time for sightseeing in one of the most interesting cities of South America. Anson managed to make time.

'From where we were berthed quite near the city centre, the skyline was filled with the outlines of tall buildings, symbols of a young and thriving capital. Like most other South American cities, it is built round its wide avenues and great plazas, filled with historical monuments and statues. The most spectacular sight is the Avenida 9 de Julio, reportedly the widest road in the world, which runs for about a mile through the centre of the city. From there, it is a short distance to the Plaza de Mayo, the principal square. On one side is the Casa Rosada, a magnificent pink building and seat of the government. Its walls still bear the marks of the fighting which raged outside during the revolt against Peron only two years earlier. In the same square are the old "Catildo", or "meeting house", and the Metropolitan Cathedral with its Greek-styled architecture.

The railway station is a massive building, called Retiro. Situated near the docks it is a hive of activity all day long as people move between city and suburbs. Not far away is the "Tower of the English Nation" surmounted by a clock, which was presented by Britain as a gesture of goodwill. Some people think that the clock has a deeper meaning (i.e. the importance of *la hora ingles*) as the Argentinians are notoriously unpunctual. Leading off from the square is the "Bond Street" of Buenos Aires. It is a narrow road known as "Florida" and it is always so packed with pedestrians that no traffic is allowed to pass through.

A thing one I will never forget after visiting BA is the traffic. There are practically no traffic lights or other controls and the only law seems to be that the fastest man in the biggest car always gets through first. It is an experience to be driven round some of the busier streets for, as well as the darting, weaving cars, there are ponderous, clanking trams to be contended with. And, despite this seeming chaos, there are relatively few accidents; a fact ascribed to a combination of the high cost of cars and the difficulty of getting spares for repairs being sufficient of a deterrent to pushing one's claims of priority to the point of collision.

We found Argentina as a whole still recovering from the tyranny and oppression of Perón. While there is no doubt that he did a tremendous amount in social reforms, his great mistake was the unscrupulous suppression of the middle and upper classes. Even now, he still has supporters among the poorer people as he managed to buy their loyalty by gifts of unearned money. He nationalised the railways, trams and many other concerns which before had been under the management of foreign (often British) companies. Not only did these enterprises cease to pay but the infrastructure fell into a state of terrible disrepair which has now only partially been remedied. The people now are happier in their new "democracy" but they experience the same trouble as France as there are too many political parties and the ordinary voter finds it hard to pick intelligently between them. … Buenos Aires was the only port I have left so far with any real regret.'

Anson's regrets might be coloured by recollections of an encounter. It was his turn, after all; indeed, as we will learn later, he took at least two turns.

'I've found a girl here, or you might say we found each other. The one thing I thought I might be spared on this trip was a bit of heartbreak but I can see the sweet sorrow of our parting looming up ominously. On the second evening, we were invited to dinner by a very rich and charming couple called Majdelany. Four of us went to their house and had a wonderful meal in modern surroundings. Afterwards, their daughter Anne came back from the British Hospital where she works as a nurse so we rolled back the carpet and danced until the not-so-small hours.

The next day was the Ball given by the Chargé d'Affaires at the British Embassy. We had dinner beforehand with the Assistant Secretary in a very lavish flat. Marvellous food and butlers all over the place. Once more there were four of the most attractive girls at the table (he's a bachelor and has good taste, I think!) The Embassy is a small place in one of the finest districts in the City. All the top brass were there and I was very lucky to be able to go. Anyway, who should be there but Anne, looking quite divine in a long pink and white dress! It was a lovely party and ended just in time for us to get back on board for breakfast.

The ships have been making big headlines in the local news and there are huge crowds round the three ships all day long. We are berthed near the centre of the city and not in a dockyard so the public do not have far to come. Without doubt it is the finest place we have been to yet and no effort has been spared to make us welcome here. On Sunday, the ship was open to visitors and you should have seen the crowd – it was far worse than Callao! There was a complete riot at the bottom

Patient visitors waiting to board in Buenos Aires (Rowsell)

of the gangway as the people fought each other to get on board. The local police drew their swords and charged into them whenever things got too bad. All these South Americans just love being in a big noisy crowd, and if they can start a fight, so much the better. They bring all their women and babes in arms and shout and scream at each other in violent Spanish. The ones that did get up the gangway beamed at us and proudly showed off their torn and tattered clothes as evidence of extreme goodwill towards the British. They then went up onto the flight deck, forgot all about the ship, and leaned over the rails to watch the fight below and yell encouragement to many of their brothers and cousins. … Must stop and get a bit of sleep.

I'm afraid this letter may not make complete sense as I'm feeling a bit light-headed (or perhaps –hearted, I don't know!)'

His next letter told more about his social life in Buenos Aires.

> 'Since I last wrote to you things have been moving fast. On Wednesday evening we held our cocktail party on board for 700 people. Anne turned up, plus parents, and afterwards I took her out in a Gunroom party and we explored some of BA's more famous nightclubs. A splendid evening without too much heartbreak at the end of it! We crawled back on board in time for breakfast on Thursday morning.'

It was expected of Midshipmen that their Journals were more than a diary in which the cocktail parties and horse-riding were recorded. Some serious reflection on the countries visited was expected, as well as descriptions of nautical matters such as an understanding of the clump cathead.[1] Hume reflected on the heritage of the former rulers of Argentina, Juan and, of course, Eva Perón.

> 'BA's magnificent skyscrapers stand as witness to the greatness of Perón and yet, at the same time, represent misspent money. The excellent shopping centres,

echoing Regent Street and Bond Street, declare the prosperity of some, and yet the multitude of horse-drawn vehicles, antiquated cars and the absence of many new models in these streets remind one of the plight that the country is in. The people are not lively like the Chileans, or ambitious like the Peruvians; the melancholy Tango is the embodiment of their feelings. The city has many beautiful parts; great parks, unfenced, roads with dual carriageways, luxurious houses in residential areas and the model villages of Perón; but the general public benefits little from these manifestations of wealth and progress. It is only necessary to drive through the poorer parts of the town to see the shacks, the tin-plate houses; or to drive up to the refuse dumping area where a car is almost unknown and hundreds of people live the life of the gipsy, driving their horse-drawn refuse carts to the city and back and knowing no other existence. But it must be admitted that nearly everybody has a roof over his head and is well clothed. A fact which could hardly be stated about Lima or, even less so, Callao.'

It was to the credit of their expatriate and Argentinian hosts that Midshipmen were shown the less attractive side of life. Hume continues:

'I had the opportunity to visit the Anglo Frigorifico meat factory and what I saw there revealed some of the answers to the country's problems. This concern, the biggest of its kind in the country, if not the world, is owned by Lord Vestey, and the manager and chief supervisors are all British. The plant has its own docks and is served by ships from three different lines, all owned by Lord Vestey. Hundreds of processes are housed under one roof and, apart from its inaccessibility, the buildings are well laid out. Although completed in 1928, the machinery looks modern enough though it is soon due for modernisation on a large scale. I was told that the replacement of machinery was long overdue but the former regime had hindered the process to a great extent. […] When working at full load over 8,000 people are employed in this one factory. I followed the fate of one particular steer from the moment it left the cattle pen to the moment it arrived in the corned beef tin, the whole process taking only forty minutes.'

Warrior sailed from Buenos Aires at 0700 on 12 September with a fair crowd on the jetty waving farewell, and most of those not on watch at their Special Sea Duty stations were fast asleep, resting in anticipation of another round of entertaining due to begin that same evening in Montevideo. Hume had been transferred temporarily to *Lynx* and was enjoying his first experience of a ship smaller than an aircraft carrier. Instead of resting, he used his time productively and wrote an extensive appreciation of the ship in his next Journal entry.

 From the sea in the evening sunlight, Montevideo is a majestic sight. The centre portion is taken up by clean-cut, modern skyscrapers mixing evenly with the Victorian spires of a few older buildings. From this solid beginning the city rambles on along the coastline in what is a series of summer resorts that have sprung up and gradually been included in the framework. The harbour where *Warrior* secured is behind the peninsulas of land on which the old city is built, so we were right in the middle of things. She sailed in through the harbour, watched by vast crowds cheering and clapping, some of whom, or their parents, would have stood on the same breakwater watching the doomed *Graf Spee* in December 1939. As *Warrior* approached the site of the *Graf Spee's* scuttling, the crew were called to attention and a wreath was cast on the waters. At 1800 hours the ship was secured and at 1830 many officers were off to the first official party. This one was cocktails at the Embassy, a much less impressive place than the one in BA. A bit dull this one, the Midshipmen felt, as very few of the daughters attended, in fact there was quite a shortage of young English people. The British Community is small, they learned, because all the children are going back to the UK to find work.

There was no rest for Robertson, however.

'Once more the wide river was covered in patches of fog. *Lynx* followed us out but *Mounts Bay* went off on her own to visit Fray Bentos, in Uruguay, where the tinned steak and kidney pies come from. She is due to rejoin us on our way north to Brazil. Our friend Granelli, the river pilot, was with us again as we made the fairly simple entry into the breakwater-protected harbour after firing the national salute. Two tugs seemed to take quite a long time to manoeuvre us alongside the jetty, where a large crowd was watching our arrival. I think they would have done better to push us in rather than pull us: as it was, *Lynx* was alongside and secured long before our first wires were out.'

Johnston too was working. 'We were at Special Sea Duty stations all day. We had been enjoying a hectic six days of party-going and tourism and now, in the early morning of the 12th, we had to pretend to be sailors for a short time in order to sail down the Rio de la Plata to our next destination, Montevideo in Uruguay. As part of my "seamanship" I had looked up the tide range in Montevideo and so was well-informed when the mooring party called the bridge and asked about the tide range.' One must, of course, make allowances for the amount the tide will rise and fall or the ship might pull the jetty from its piles as the tide rose. 'What's the tide range,' he was asked. 'Doesn't matter,' he rather hastily replied. 'I'll be the judge of that Johnston, not you. What's the bloody tide range?' 'Eighteen inches, Sir!'

Robertson behaved himself much better.

'In spite of the very small size of their fleet, which only numbers some half-dozen ships manned by 1,500 officers and men, the Uruguayans visited us in force. Two helicopter displays were given, one off a beach some way down the coast and the other just off the ship. Unfortunately, the port forward motor-cutter could not be lowered, because of a very large fuel lighter secured underneath, so a boat was borrowed to act as the crash boat for the display near the ship. For interest's sake I went away in the boat, a splendid fire-tender bought very recently from America, with two General Motors engines giving a speed of 16-plus knots, and coxed by a Chief Petty Officer. We cruised around, dropping bodies into the water now and then, and watching the various different kinds of rescue operations. The boat was superbly easy to manoeuvre, and without all her heavy pumping equipment would no doubt be impressively speedy. However, the interpreter in the boat told us that Uruguayan maintenance was extraordinarily haphazard, and the engines would have to stand up to a great deal.'

Riches recalled the pomp and ceremonial provided by the ship's band and its well-drilled guard.

'By 1600 the same day we were receiving an even greater reception on the other bank of the River Plate as we sailed into Montevideo Harbour with the now supplemented Royal Marine band playing and large crowds lining the breakwater, cheering and clapping. The following day the Guard and Band, totalling 140, beat the retreat in Plaza Indepencia in front of the presidential palace. After the ceremony the guard and band marched through the main streets of the city and finally up the Avendida Diez y Ocho de Julio, by which time, according to the local newspapers, 20,000 people were lining the streets shouting "viva Inglaterra". They proceeded to sweep aside the police and their horses and engulfed the contingent. In 1957 there was no doubt that along the eastern seaboard of South America it was to Britain that the countries looked for guidance; and time and again we were assailed with complaints from the British communities that our government was failing to take advantage of these sentiments.'

Those who went to see Fray Bentos (which turned out to be the name of the city), a plant making corned beef and steak and kidney pies, reported back that the whole cow went in at one end and the whole cow came out of the other but separated into many different bits, and with quite a great deal of recycling into hides, bone meal, glue and fertiliser, as well as the millions of tins of corned beef which were still warm as they came rolling off the conveyor belt.

Johnston recalls his experiences of a day and date sailors mistrust; Friday the Thirteenth.

'I went with others from the Gunroom and a bevy of British expatriate beauties to the Park Hotel where I saw a roulette wheel for the first time, apart from in the movies. I seemed to be on a winning streak, betting on 10 and 13 by placing my chips on the line between and getting odds of 17 to one. I was up a whole £4 by the end of that session, despite having given away about 30 shillings to my less fortunate friends. To celebrate my success or maybe because it just happened to be next on the itinerary, we went on to the Pygmalion nightclub where Spanish dancers, a man and a woman, entertained. *She* entertained more than she intended because her left breast kept popping out of her dress despite her flustered attempts to shove it back in again. At the end of their show, she fled from the stage while we coarse men cheered, clapped and called for an encore. As the wealthy roulette winner, I had said I would buy the first round of drinks, and only three or four of us had anything alcoholic. It was just as well I was flush with cash as that first and, as it turned out, only round came to well over £3 – something like £60 in today's money!'

Anson, it appears, was to be a victim of serial infatuation. He wrote home that:

'The next day we went to a luncheon party at quite a very cheery house and spent most of the day there. It was here I met one June Castleton, without a doubt the prettiest and most charming girl so far sighted in South America and the daughter of the Vice-President of Hoover (South America) Ltd. The Gunroom went after her as one man, but honesty compels me to admit that I won through in the end and friendly relations were soon established. I can see you shaking your head and muttering that no good will come of this but actually she is leaving for a finishing school in Lausanne and will be coming to England next summer!

The following day we were invited to an *asado*. It takes about six hours to prepare and tastes quite splendid. We had the choice of about six different types of meat and there was just no limit to how long you could go on eating. This one lasted all afternoon!

On Sunday I was on duty and we had the customary visitors' day when the ship was open to the public in the afternoon. We had expected the usual crowds and riots but all was very quiet and orderly until just before closing time when those at the end of the queue realised they weren't going to make it. A few slipped through the police barrier and rushed up to the gangway and that did it. In a moment the queue had vanished and we had another heaving mass of humanity fighting to get on the ship. There was nothing we could do about it so we just shut the ship and the police brought on a dozen horses which broke up the crowd wonderfully well. Even so, we actually had more people on board than at BA where they were rioting the whole time.

In the evening we held our usual cocktail party in the hangar deck and the Castleton family turned up in force. June had remembered my saying how wonderful the meat was out here and she arrived with a huge chunk of prime Uruguayan steak. "It has been put in the deep freeze on board until I can get it back to you. I don't think I told you that, with a mind to the family larder, I have also bought you a leg of ham from BA and a sheep in the Falklands (a whole one selected from the fields by me and arriving in the UK in a special meat ship, total cost: 10 shillings.)"

After the party, I went out with June and some others and was lost to the world for a few beautiful hours! However, Rio is not far distant and we are looking forward to it. I've been getting all your letters and it's been very nice to have one waiting for me in every port.'

One wonders if there will also be a girl waiting for Anson in every port! It turns out from his next letter, however, that things were subtly different in Rio de Janeiro.

'We have had a very hectic four days in Rio. It is a very beautiful place to look at and is, of course, quite huge. Here, though, we have had an excess of formal parties and have run up against a set of the most jealously chaperoned girls in the world. Even the older ones are never allowed out alone – even to come home from a dance. Father's word seems to be absolute law, but I suppose they know what they are doing as Brazilian women are … wow!' But we must first return to Montevideo and then sail *Warrior* to Rio before continuing Anson's Brazilian reminiscences.

Cooper's Journal entry for 16 September sighs with relief. 'Slipped at 1000 hours this morning and sailed for Rio. A make-and-mend [Naval slang for a day off] was given this afternoon and all but a few slept for the first time in several days.' As *Warrior* sailed past the eerie tip of the *Graf Spee* poking just above the surface, the ship cast another wreath on the waters of the River Plate. Hume recorded in his Journal some of the formality and one of the unintended consequences of the squadron's departure. 'About an hour before we sailed, the Uruguayan destroyers *Uruguay* and *Artigas* put to sea for exercises. Both these ships were former US Navy destroyers and they are the largest units in their Navy. As we headed for the breakwater we were saluted by the training frigate *Montevideo*. HMS *Lynx* followed on astern but she appeared to have some difficulty in getting her head round, passing very near to the breakwater; it was later reported, after an inspection by divers, that she damaged the blades of one screw which will necessitate a short period in dry dock at Simonstown.' Cooper continues, '*Lynx* remained in company, three cables astern, joined this evening by *Mounts Bay*. Some amusement was caused by mistaking a radar contact of a tanker for *Mounts Bay*. I understand the tanker was a trifle surprised when we called her up with our 20' Aldis signalling lamp at fourteen miles, addressing her as *Mounts Bay*.'

During the forenoon of the second day, *Warrior* and *Lynx* took part in radar trials during which the latter took station at different distances from the carrier and the effects were noted on *Warrior*'s radar screens. Similar trials were apparently planned with HMS *Girdle Ness* during the passage from Gibraltar to Portsmouth. A few hours after *Mounts Bay*, the squadron was joined by HMS *Burghead Bay*, another Bay Class frigate. She fired the customary fifteen-gun salute and then came alongside *Warrior* to carry out a light jackstay transfer of some stores and official mail before taking station as part of the squadron. As one of the main functions of frigates accompanying aircraft carriers is to provide their protection, the three frigates formed a bent screen with *Lynx* in the lead and the other two on the port and starboard beams. And thus *Warrior* proceeded towards her final call in South America, the fabled Rio de Janeiro (literally, 'January River'). Until the order was issued to switch to whites again, dress had been optional and there was the slightly incongruous sight of about half the ship's company being in blues and the rest in whites. Consistency was restored the next day.

18 September was, it turned out, Chilean National Day and this was marked on board *Warrior* in honour of Teniente (Lieut.) Alberto Alarçón, known to everyone as 'Al'. He was an electronics officer from the Chilean Navy, taking passage with *Warrior* to England to take a course at Marconi. The Chilean flag was flown at the masthead and the Admiral asked Al to a lunch party which Midshipman Hutchinson was also invited to attend. In accordance with protocol, CINCSASA proposed the health of the President of Chile while Al proposed a toast to the Queen. Al returned the hospitality by giving a *Viño de Honor* in the Wardroom that evening.

Warrior sighted the light high on the Corcovado, the high mountain among the many peaks surrounding the Bay, early in the morning of 19 September. At 0645 the squadron took up Formation One, and as the squadron entered the outer confines of the bay *Warrior* lowered both motor boats and a cutter. Robertson coxswained the second motor boat and, for once, had a perfect view entering harbour. Although it was a dull morning this scarcely detracted from the impression that Rio has the most beautiful harbour of any city in the world. Against a background of towering green mountains, a gleaming white semi-circle of great buildings surrounds the famous beach of Copacabana.

Over to port the aptly named Sugarloaf mountain and the towering Corcovado with its huge white marble statue of Christ the Redeemer dominate the harbour. There are many little bays and inlets, with great ships from every country in the world riding gracefully at their buoys. At one end of the city's seafront, aeroplanes were landing and taking off in a never-ending stream against the dark green mass behind. One of *Warrior*'s helicopters took off to photograph the squadron's entry into the bay including a ciné film made by the Admiral's Flag Lieutenant.

The motorboats followed *Warrior* in, with the first motor boat under full power producing 2,200 revs compared to the second's meagre 1,800, planing gloriously and leaving the Admiral's Barge standing. A bevy of tugs came out to meet the ship,

Warrior *against the backdrop of the Sugarloaf (Rowsell)*

among them, amusingly enough, being one marked R31, *Warrior*'s own pennant number. This was a relatively easy coming alongside, necessitating nothing more than a gentle swing to port and a nudge here and there. *Warrior* was starboard side to on the main seafront, with *Lynx* secured to a jetty running out at right angles, and the two Bays alongside one another just astern of *Lynx*. Spring hawsers were put out as well as the normal berthing wires to counteract the appreciable swell which gave the ship a noticeable motion throughout the stay.

Then, Robertson was given a fright. 'Lying off in the boats while waiting for *Warrior* to come alongside, we were intrigued by a neat display of formation flying by two yellow aeroplanes circling overhead. Our interest turned suddenly to dismay as they went into a steep dive, heading straight for us, but at the very last moment they pulled up a matter of feet over our heads and roared away through a narrow gap between two buildings. For some minutes they continued to beat up the harbour in a most hair-raising manner, skimming the water near us and making a hideous noise.

Warrior *coming alongside in Rio (Rowsell)*

Whether this was an official or an unofficial welcome is anybody's guess.'

Warrior had been met and saluted by the Brazilian destroyer *Greenhalgh* and escorted to Cais Comercial where she was secured at 0905 on the 19th. Another round of entertainment, given and received, was about to begin. On the formal side, the next day *Warrior* dressed ship and a guard of honour plus the band paraded on deck to greet the President of Brazil, Juscelino Kubitschek de Oliveira. Kubitschek, known in Brazil simply as JK, was the Brazilian leader who commissioned the creation of the new ultra-modern capital of the country, Brasilia, which became the huge country's seat of government.

Before receiving the President, *Warrior*'s guard and band carried out their customary ceremonial. This was the ship's last wreath-laying in South America. Anson had not been able to see one of these so far so he went with the party of twenty or so officers from *Warrior* and the three frigates. The Brazilians provided a

Royal Navy and Marines Band (Rowsell)

Brazilian Navy brass band (Rowsell)

Royal Navy Guard firing a salute (Rowsell)

Warrior's helicopters above Copacabana beach (Rowsell)

large guard and three separate bands: one brass, one bugle and one made up entirely of drummers. They had rather a quaint way of doing drill as all their orders are given by bugle call. At 1015, *Warrior*'s guard and band marched into the square. The event cannot have been very well publicised as there were very few spectators. CINCSASA arrived at 1030 accompanied by the Commodore and the three frigates' captains. The wreath was laid at Admiral Tamandaré's statue at 1035. His long military career extended from the Brazilian War of Independence (1822–24) to the Paraguayan War (1864–70) and, for being the very first Brazilian native Admiral, he is the Brazilian Navy's patron. It was a short ceremony but an impressive one which Anson was glad that he had been able to attend.

Monument to Admiral Tamandaré (Rowsell)

The anticipation the Gunroom had felt in approaching Brazil and Rio was only exceeded by the reality. Most of the ships officers and men concentrated on the purchase of coffee and aquamarines. Hume managed to have a good look at the city, being taken out to lunch followed by a tour. He wrote home:

'Rio far surpasses all the other ports we have visited for beauty. The scenery is breathtaking and the postcards I have sent give you some idea of the place. The magnificent harbour surrounded by hills with the city at the water's edge and the Sugarloaf, with the statue of Christ on the Corcovado high up in the background makes this a place hard to forget. As a city, it is much more alive than BA and as far as the traffic goes is fully modernised though there are restrictions on cars. Here there are no horse-drawn vehicles and the trams are out of this world in their antiquity. They are open on both sides and you can stand on the running boards if it is full. Most of the cars are American, unlike Montevideo where a large proportion were British. […] Three of us went out to lunch accepting an invitation that meant we left the ship only one hour after we had secured alongside. As it turned out it was very enjoyable and we saw a large amount of the city by car. There are a great many people of Negro descent and, sadly, for the most part they live in the most frightful slums that I have ever seen. Shacks surrounded by mud and filth, crawling up the hillsides. It was a patchwork with here a very modern block of flats and just round the corner the worst slums. I wanted to take a photograph but our host would not stop the car for fear of getting it stoned! The Copacabana beach of great fame left me disappointed, for although it looks magnificent when seen earlier that day from the sea with a backdrop of tall modern-looking buildings, on closer inspection the buildings are of the immediate pre-war era, heavy in style. However, all the pavements are done in a mosaic as are many of the walls. [Later] I found it very pleasant to stroll through the streets, tasting the coffee here and there, and to take a ride on the quaint but very practical trams. The Portuguese language offered some difficulty but we found that by speaking Spanish very slowly the people understood what we were saying and were very obliging.'

Robertson was good on summing up the mood of the Gunroom.

'As far as entertainment went, most of us were on the fringe of being worn out.

However, one superb evening at the Embassy Ball cannot go undescribed. The ball was quite an admirable diplomatic occasion, held in fantastic surroundings. The British Embassy, built by the previous Labour government in the UK at a cost of over two million pounds, must be the finest embassy in the world – certainly the finest British one. Complete with carriage sweep, lawns and shrubberies, swimming pool and other luxuries; the building itself was floodlit that night. Built in the style of Robert Adam and lavishly furnished, it takes one straight back to the days of Imperial Greatness. We only saw the huge reception hall, the dining and withdrawing rooms and the ballroom itself – and although I do not take to Robert Adam style myself this was grand. The only jarring note (for me) was struck by some very ugly John Piper paintings on the walls of the small dining room, allegedly scenes in Bath and Cheltenham, and supposed to be typically English. Never do I hope to hear such a monstrous allegation again!!' (Robertson admits that his taste has 'moved on a bit' over the intervening years!)

Riches was another one of the Midshipmen lucky enough to be invited to the Embassy Ball.

'One thousand guests were invited. Being back in the Tropics, we were in whites, and so stiff shirts, white mess jackets, and white tie and tails for the civilians. On arrival, each party moved up the grand staircase to be greeted by the Ambassador, Sir Geoffrey Harrison and his wife, and by our Commander-in-Chief. Behind the receiving party was the central hall lined with paintings and on either side were large reception rooms with many crystal chandeliers, one becoming the ballroom, while the other had an enormous buffet supper laid out. Large French windows on the outside of the rooms opened onto verandahs which ran all round the building, and on the inside of each room similar windows opened onto a courtyard with floodlit fountains, tropical trees and, nearby, there was a swimming pool. To a relatively innocent nineteen-year-old it was breathtaking; something you read about but never expect to experience. I remember the champagne flowing, the caviar and the unlimited 'supply' of ravishing girls. The ban played until 4.00am when we adjourned to somebody's flat and started all over again. The whole diplomatic corps in Rio was invited to the Ball and I recollect meeting the American and Italian Ambassadors – and an Indian Princess!'

Reed also met this princess, the daughter of her country's Ambassador, who was nominated as his partner for the whole evening and it was generally believed that he fell head over heels in love with her. He has, so far, chosen not to confirm or deny the rumour.

On the Friday, Hume had to work for his living.

'Most of the day was taken up with boat running. During the forenoon I took the first motor boat over to the Rio Yacht Club with Lt Harland and Midshipman Cooper. The Club lay at the far end of the bay opposite the Sugarloaf, the object of the visit being to spy out the land since *Warrior*'s Children's Party would have some forty guests to be collected from this particular place in the afternoon. From the Yacht Club we went across to the Yacht Club at Urca. On the way, we ran with a very heavy swell and attained a speed very near to 20 knots, the motor boat doing a consistent 2,000 revs; the best it has ever done since leaving England. From this Yacht Club whose jetty was open to the incoming swell we proceeded across the harbour to the Niteroi ferry and thence back to the ship; the round trip taking about two hours. In the afternoon, the second motor boat accompanied us to collect the children. They thoroughly enjoyed their trip over to the ship and back again in the evening.'

Riches records that:

'The following afternoon, Saturday, four of us hired a car and, having beaten the driver down by 400 cruzeiros, told him to drive us to the Corcovado on which at a height of 2,300 feet stands the statue of Christ the Redeemer. On the Thursday and the Friday and, as it turned out, the Sunday too, the mountain was shrouded in low cloud. The afternoon we went, however, the sun came out, the wind increased and the visibility was moderate. We were all prepared for a magnificent view but the panorama which greeted us was altogether breathtaking. Down below were planes flying nearly 1,000 feet under where we were standing, in a steady procession landing and taking off from the airport in the bay. To the right was Copacabana beach and straight ahead was Niteroi where the sports team were playing cricket, and on the left in the mist was Metropolis, the wealthy summer resort in the mountains.'

Johnston was also kept busy helping to run the ship's boats which were, in a large bay like the harbour of Rio and not at all like a river, the ideal method of transport to the various destinations around the periphery. Since *Warrior*'s visit, there is now a bridge over the bay from Rio to Niteroi but that was not even a plan in 1957. Based on his outstanding performance in an impromptu cricket match on Malden Island, Hutchinson was selected to lead the team out for *Warrior* that day. 'I opened the batting for a brief while, for the Squadron against a Brazilian XI on a cricket ground across the bay. Later I attended a concert of piano concertos by Villa Lobos, Chopin, Rachmaninov and Liszt played by prize-winning young pianists at the Teatro Municipal. I went up to pay my respects to the Cristo de Corcavado. I walked around the streets and the beach.' Johnston had taken the cricketers over to the Club in Niteroi; a match on which Robertson commented sadly in his Journal. 'A cricket match on the last day resulting in a decidedly unfavourable draw was followed by a cocktail party on *Warrior*'s flight deck, rounded off by a very well done "Beating Retreat" by the combined Royal Marine and *Warrior* Volunteer band.

Beating Retreat (Rowsell)

'They have made a great contribution to the success of this "cruise" and deserve to be highly praised, especially the volunteers (including Midshipman Kirchem).' Kirchem had then to hang up his euphonium and climb back into his Midshipman's uniform for the remainder of the voyage. But just as Kirchem once more took up his full share of watch-keeping duties, sadly, *Warrior* was about to lose one member of the Gunroom.

Midshipman Reed was not, contrary to some idle speculation, planning to desert in order to carry off a princess, but instead, with the permission of the Admiralty, CINCSASA, the Commodore and the Commanding Officer of *Lynx*, he was transferring to the frigate and would be sailing with her over to South Africa for the rest of his National Service, which would have to be extended until *Lynx* returned to the UK. The Commodore wrote on his Form S.206 that he was 'A bright but intense young officer, high-spirited and quick tempered, and apt to make hasty decisions. He is, however, keen to learn and with maturity will overcome these present limitations. A good artist.' This last remark owed everything to his having largely designed the Crossing-the-Line certificate that everyone in *Warrior* had as a souvenir. His friends 'dined him out' and Anson noted the departure in his Journal. 'Midshipman Reed left *Warrior* today to join *Lynx*. He had travelled on board *Lynx* from Montevideo to Rio and his request for a transfer coincided with their need to ship Sub-Lt Scott RNVR back home to the UK to complete his National Service. A new guest in the Gunroom is John Harrison, the son of the British Ambassador who is taking passage with us to Gibraltar.' Robertson recalled that he had been with Reed 'since our first weeks in the Navy and I am as sorry as the rest of us to see him go and can only wish him the very best of everything.'

All the midshipmen recorded *Warrior*'s departure the next day, some of them reflecting on the circuit of South America. First Riches.

'The squadron sailed at 1000, leaving behind South America and some exhausted officials, not least among whom was the British Naval Attaché! Looking back over the last seven weeks since the Commander-in-Chief arrived, we can say that "the flag has been shown" to very good effect and this has been amply demonstrated by the interest shown in the Royal Navy in every port visited. It's difficult to pick out any one port in particular as being the most glamorous, or popular, as everyone on board has different tastes. But, if pressed, I'd say Buenos Aires takes the lead; prices were low, hospitality was overwhelming and it had all the bustle and night life of a big city. Of course, every country had something that stood out. Peru will be remembered for the uncontrolled enthusiasm of the people when the ship was open. Chile for the genuine warmth of feeling between the two navies and the beautiful countryside. Argentina for its *vastness* in every aspect and the overwhelming hospitality. Uruguay for the very pro-British feeling of her people and the tremendous reception accorded the contingent at the wreath-laying ceremony; and last but not least, Brazil for the quiet and unobtrusive way in which the police managed the crowds both when the ship was open and during the weekdays.'

Robertson's summing up, decidedly pretentious-sounding to him as it is in retrospect today, took a generally more negative look at the continent.

'Before I leave Rio, perhaps I should attempt some generalised summing-up of the Latin-American character as a whole, if such a generalisation is not too sweeping. I would not like to have created the impression that because of the excellent time we have had in all these South American ports, I think that everything is all butter and honey. Incredibly venal, addicted to spitting, idle, unstable – one could apply many of these description to countless individual people – and worse too! Countries riven by graft, apathy, lawlessness, greed – so many of them are in ways. But I still feel that, as well as having had the time of our lives, we have seen a continent with a future which is bound to be great in time. The Latin-Americans are an unstable people but among them are men with the knowledge, intelligence, money and strength to go a very long way indeed.'

As the squadron prepared to sail, the Royal Marine Band returned to *Mounts Bay*. The squadron then sailed out into the Atlantic in formation for the last time and, at 1615, *Lynx* came alongside *Warrior*. Vice-Admiral Robson, CINCSASA, was transferred by light jackstay, standing with one foot in the stirrup and waving jauntily back at *Warrior*. Fifteen gun salutes were exchanged and the Admiral's flag was struck in *Warrior* and hoisted in *Lynx*. The Commodore's broad pennant was then broken at the masthead and, having received permission from CINSASA, *Warrior* resumed her voyage home while the frigates set course for St. Helena. Perhaps the Admiral's stay with *Warrior* and her whole tour around South America is best summed up by one of his last signals which read, 'Christmas, what a cruise!'

And so, *Warrior* set off to tackle the Atlantic again, expecting a better crossing on the homeward leg. That said, the Atlantic is an unforgiving ocean. *Pamir*, a four-masted barque, was one of the famous Flying P-Liner sailing ships of the German shipping company Laeisz. She was the last commercial sailing ship to round Cape Horn in 1949. By 1957 she had been outmoded by modern bulk carriers and could not operate at a profit. Her shipping consortium's inability to finance much-needed repairs or to recruit sufficient sail-trained officers caused severe technical difficulties. On 21 September 1957 she was caught in Hurricane Carrie and sank off the Azores with only six survivors rescued after an extensive search.[2]

Anson and Hume had spent the last six weeks doing their spell in the Engine Room which both found fascinating but it did mean that they missed seeing the impressive sight of the squadron steaming in formation and, more of a sacrifice, they were not on deck to see each new port as *Warrior* arrived and departed. Anson's new Special Sea Duty was as assistant to the First Lieutenant on the cable deck from where, it must be said, the view is restricted. However, as he wrote, 'The routine on board has eased off a little now. It is hoped to give "make-and-mends" each day until we arrive at Gibraltar. This gives time to reacquire a layer of sun-tan before arriving in the UK and also to starting up deck hockey and similar sports which had to be dropped while we were in harbour. We crossed the Equator for the last [and 14th] time on the night of Friday/Saturday and, once more, are experiencing "Christmas Island" temperatures.'

The Navigator called in all the Midshipmen's Journals and wrote his final comments. He especially liked both Anson's and Robertson's. In Anson's Journal he wrote, 'This is the first and, I regret, last time I shall see your Journal. It is well up to standard – the sketches being particularly good, which is a *very* refreshing change from the normal.' And to Robertson he said, 'It is with the sincerest regret that I have to admit that I have not found time to read your Journal thoroughly – one of the most amusing; albeit in a dry, aloof vein! – I have seen. This makes up in large measure for the continued lack of sketches. However, I suppose one can't have everything. D T Watts, Lt-Cdr RN.' Hume's final Journal entry for September was also in reminiscent mood. 'Now that we are a week out from Rio de Janeiro, most people have had the opportunity to recover from the rigours of the South American cruise. Everyone had to play his part to fulfil the obligations imposed on us; more often than not every night would be a very late one and sleep was a prized thing.

Now, our attentions have been diverted to recovering our Christmas Island tan, but yesterday, as we encountered for the last time the famous inter-tropical convergence, we witnessed a solid downpour lasting most of the day. Today, Monday, we are in the NE Trades and should encounter some fine weather ahead.' The Royal Navy's last Gunroom afloat had only one more port of call, Gibraltar, and then everyone would go their separate ways.

---

1 For those sufficiently interested, there is a stimulating paragraph on the subject on page 383 of *Manual of Seamanship*, Vol. II B.R. 67 (2/51), Her Majesty's Stationery Office, 1952

2 Source: Wikipedia http://en.wikipedia.org/wiki/Pamir_%28ship%29 accessed 3/10/2014

OCTOBER

Home is the sailor

Warrior was sailing across the Atlantic towards Gibraltar. Tropical tans which had faded somewhat in the Falklands were being topped up, and most of the ship's complement, both officers and ratings, were taking an afternoon off; the so-called 'make and mend'. Not so Riches. 'The twelve days to Gibraltar were busy in our department, with all accounts being closed and audited and officers assessed on Form S.206, the so-called flimsy.' This is the form on which the Divisional has to write one of several phrases that sum up his view of how the officer in question has acquitted himself. The remarks range from the laudatory 'to my entire satisfaction', through 'to my satisfaction' or, worse, just 'satisfactorily', to the very unwelcome in terms of career prospects 'unsatisfactorily'. These are then countersigned by the Commodore and normally given to the officer by his Divisional Officer; in the case of almost all of the Gunroom this was the Navigator.

The exception was Robertson. He at least is the only one of the group who admits to remembering at least part of what was said then on his individual S.206. 'This Officer is more interested in having a good time ashore than in his divisional duties.' Robertson accepts there may be a smidgeon of truth in this statement, but also states that the superior officer who actually wrote it (neither Watts nor Hicks) was widely, and rightly, regarded as a very unpleasant person and a poor judge of others' characters. In support of his case he also recalls that Commodore Hicks – as required by Navy regulations in the case of any seriously negative element in a report, it was the ship's commanding officer who read the passage out loud to the 'offender' – winked unmistakably as he did so, and added that it was not to be taken too much to heart.

Riches recorded the fact that 'One evening we had our final Gunroom mess dinner when we dined seven guests including John Harrison, son of the Ambassador in Rio. After a week, the temperature started to drop and we saw several whales. Through the Cape Verde Islands, up the coast of Senegal, and then we finally sighted Casablanca in Morocco on the eleventh day.' Africa made its presence felt. Although

Hume, Cooper, Riches and Kirchem dressed for dinner (Riches)

twenty or more miles away, there were traces of sand on the flight deck and various strange smells wafted across the ship.

Then, on 4 October, Russia also made its presence felt. There was the sensational announcement that the USSR had stolen a march on its Cold War rivals and launched a satellite into low earth orbit, weighing nearly 184 lbs, many times more than the planned American orbiter. This Russian craft was *Sputnik-1*, a 23-inch diameter sphere, circumnavigating the earth every 96.2 minutes. That day dramatically changed the West's perception of the Soviet threat, flagging up as it did the future role of intercontinental ballistic missiles, armed in due course with thermonuclear warheads. It would also mean that the future of supersonic bombers, such as the Valiant, was now called into question. In the here and now of 1957 they would still have the task of carrying and, if needs be, delivering Britain's nuclear deterrent, *once the device was perfected and manufactured*; but the future would seem to lie with rockets, with Polaris and eventually Trident. The Cold War still had thirty years to run, although no one was aware of that in 1957, and no one was seriously predicting any post-Cold War scenarios arising from an economic and political implosion of the Soviet Union and of Communist governments across Eastern Europe and Central Asia.

While running a boat ashore to Fisherman's Jetty during *Warrior*'s twenty-four-hour visit to Gibraltar on 5 October, Johnston was lucky enough to gaze up into the starry sky at just the right moment and saw the 'shooting star' (in fact, of course, the Sputnik) that tracked across the heavens from south-west to north-east before disappearing over the horizon. If someone had not shouted 'Look out!' he would have rammed the jetty.

Warrior *in Gibraltar (Rowsell)*

One regular boat running hazard is bringing drunken libertymen back on board, as Hutchinson recalls.

'I was in charge of the last liberty boat back from a jetty in Gibraltar to *Warrior* around midnight just before she sailed to England. My passengers were quiet and dazed looking. They needed help and many began to smoke. I told them not to smoke. They carried on smoking. I turned the cutter round and went back to the jetty where they put out their cigarettes. We started off and they started to smoke again. We went on to *Warrior* where the Commander was standing at the gangway with the Officer of the Watch. I told the Commander that I wanted to charge some of them, petty officers, cooks, whomever. He agreed. I identified the recusants as they came on board. It was at least 0100 by now and we kept the process going for another two hours or so. I was furious with the petty officers. Under the quarterdeck lights many younger men were haggard with fatigue and drink, their make-up disintegrating and running down their faces. We kept them a long while, standing one after the other to deny the charges. I was the only witness for the prosecution. The Commander summoned them all to hear the "not guilty" verdicts and some carefully chosen additional remarks. I appreciated his support.'

While the seamen midshipmen all seemed to have stopped writing in the Journals after the Navigator had made his final comments, Riches found time to describe this part of the voyage.

'On Friday, land was sighted – French Morocco – and early on Saturday morning *Warrior* slipped into Gibraltar where she anchored half-a-mile from the southern entrance to the inner harbour. With the Mediterranean Fleet at Malta, Gibraltar looked deserted, a relic of better days, but the town was very much alive – all the shops having had prior notice of our arrival.

On the Saturday, three of us from the Gunroom went ashore with the sole idea of "conquering the Rock". However, we hadn't reckoned with the heat, reflected from the white buildings, which was so intense that, very shortly after stepping ashore, it was agreed to "settle for the Apes".'

Johnston bought a 'fourteen-day clock' for his sister – which only went for two days and, on later examination, only had a two-day spring! To reacclimatise himself to British life and food, he ate fish and chips. Robertson went sailing and managed (for the umpteenth time) to capsize a 14-foot dinghy. Also, the effects of Latin America had not entirely worn off. He managed to meet and fall for a charming lady lawyer, who later moved to England and became a distinguished QC.

And at last, as *Warrior* sailed from Gibraltar after only twenty-four hours, she was on the final, final leg of her journey home. Robertson recalls that 'on 7 October we sighted the lights of Lisbon, then on 9 and 10 October we carried out sea trials and radar interference trials with HMS *Girdleness* off the entrance to the English Channel.' Signals passed between *Warrior* and the C-in-C at Portsmouth. It seemed to the Commodore and his senior officers that, after a voyage of eight months and nine days and participation in the most significant scientific and strategic experiments since the war, the ship ought to be allowed to enter harbour at a time which would allow the Fleet, as well as friends and relatives, to watch, wave and cheer. However, a NATO exercise was taking place, and *Warrior* had been told to enter harbour at 0600, much to the dismay of all. Thus it was that after a journey of 39,985 nautical miles, *Warrior* finally berthed in Portsmouth Harbour at 0720, with the ship's company lining the decks and the ship's band playing together for the very last time. Despite the hour, the ship did in the end receive an enthusiastic welcome.

While we had been away, the Government had announced the end of National Service. Riches's reflections convey the sentiment every one of the Gunroom felt then, and now.

'I do not regret one moment of my National Service, and am only sorry that subsequent generations have not had the opportunities of service that I enjoyed.' Yes, 'enjoyed' is the operative word! Hutchinson later wrote, 'We saw great natural wonders, the Atlantic in full fury, the Pacific in full sunshine and the Andes mountain range, extraordinary human achievements, the ingenuity and toughness of the makers of the Panama Canal, the frightful power of the nuclear bomb. We met very different, interesting and charming people, Caribbean and Pacific islanders, Americans so apparently like us in language and culture, but strangers, I found, and the Spaniards, elegant and vital; not least the officers of *Warrior* who seemed to me to be very proficient in their work, conscientious, responsible and careful for their subordinates; and above all our friendships in the Gunroom still celebrated nearly six decades later.'

By early afternoon, the nine RNVR members of the Gunroom who had remained in *Warrior* after Midshipman Reed's earlier departure in Rio had all dispersed, heading home to, or with, their families. They were not to reassemble as one group for another twenty years.

APPENDICES

Appendix A
THE SALE OF HMS *WARRIOR*

Much of the material in the National Archives about HMS *Warrior* and Operation Grapple is labelled Secret, Top Secret and even Top Secret – Atomic. It was covered by the conventional thirty-year rule but that restriction has long since expired. Former Midshipmen who served in *Warrior* can see again where, long ago, they signed the daily muster of signal publications in the ship's log books, month by month. No doubt there are some files with details of Britain's nuclear weapons that are still under wraps somewhere but, for the purposes of this memoir, most is now in the public domain.

Pertinent to *Warrior*'s homeward passage round South America in 1957 was the rumour, current in the Wardroom and Gunroom, that the Navy wanted to sell their ship, and probably to the Argentine. No public announcement was ever made on board. No injunction was issued to be on one's best behaviour, especially in Puerto Belgrano, but one could not help noting the degree of interest being taken by officers of the Armada Republicana Argentina when they visited the ship and even sailed with her from Puerto Belgrano to Buenos Aires. As the files now reveal, by the time *Warrior* docked in Puerto Belgrano, the sale was almost a done deal.[1]

As early as a Cabinet meeting on 11 December 1956 there is a note to say that it had 'authorised the First Lord of the Admiralty to proceed with the sale of an aircraft carrier […] to the Argentine Navy.' The ARA had some time previously been offered HMS *Magnificent* (which was later sold to Brazil) but the government of Argentina would not fund that purchase. Now, it seems, interest had revived. The First Lord offered them *Warrior,* 'as lying', for what he considered a bargain price of £2.25 million. Unsurprisingly, the ARA responded with a lower offer, £1.75 million. The haggling continued with the Admiralty suggesting that they just might be able to get a price of *only* £2 million approved by the Treasury and that payment could be spread over five years at one per cent above the Bank Rate. The ARA then submitted a written offer of £1.75 million spread over five years, pleading that this was all their impoverished government would allow; and that the offer might not be open for much longer as public opinion was against such extravagance. There was oblique reference, in the correspondence between the Argentine Naval Attaché and the Admiralty, to the fact that in agreeing to buy a carrier for the ARA the Argentine government was honouring a debt of gratitude to its Navy for its support in the recent coup against Perón.

The Minute went the rounds of various civil servants who worried about selling a carrier to a government they were in dispute with over Antarctica and that Washington might not approve the sale of anything in *Warrior* that came from lend-lease. One mandarin wrote, 'I heartily dislike accepting from the Argentine, of all countries, a price that represents about 22½ per cent below what we would normally regard as the lowest price we should take. On the other hand, I realise there is some political advantage in getting the Argentine to turn her face towards the RN for naval equipment and, on the whole, I endorse the views which have been expressed in the foregoing Minutes.'

The Admiralty decided that, in the long run and with no other buyers in the offing, £1.75 million at 6½ % over five years would be a useful addition to the Navy Vote. The Admiralty did remove the prototype Type 963 radar that had guided the Valiants over Malden and the silver plate presented to the ship by Almirante Rojas in 1957 but, after a final bit of haggling over what was literally meant by 'as lying' and whether that should include the ship's boats, title was transferred to the Argentine Government on 24 July 1958 and *Warrior* became the ARA *Independencia*. The final instalment was duly paid in late 1962. The ship was decommissioned in 1970 and finally scrapped in 1971.

Appendix B

H-BOMB BLUFF?

....

In a final afterword which follows this Appendix, there is a short personal summary of how each of those Gunroom RNVR officers spent some or all of the next *sixty* years: but for the moment, let us run the calendar forward some *thirty-five* years, to the moment when particle physics professor Norman Dombey and naval historian Eric Grove wrote a paper, published in the *London Review of Books* in 1992 with the title, 'Britain's Thermonuclear Bluff'. It raised the possibility that *some* of the tests the Warriors witnessed were not really 'in the megaton range' and might not even have been *hydrogen* bombs.

Their original contention was that the British tests at Christmas Island in 1957 had not been H-bombs at all, but rather 'enhanced' atomic bombs. There had been odd rumours and press stories to this effect, but they had largely been dismissed by Whitehall. The authors later accepted that, in the light of the release of certain previously classified documents, the *first* and *third* tests (Short Granite and Purple Granite) *had*, in fact, been H-bombs, albeit of disappointingly low yield for the scientists. As Lorna Arnold says, 'They were disappointing in yield but were successful as proofs of principle.'[2] The *second* test, however, Orange Herald, the one which the press attended, had been beefed up to make a good show, but unlike the 'Granites' was *not* a 'two-stage fission-fusion' H-bomb. Yet the Whitehall story, maintained from the outset, was that all the Grapple tests were H-bombs and all 'in the megaton range'.

This turns out to have been a very successful public relations bluff, whether or not wholly or partly deliberate; certainly as far as the British public (and probably most of the rest of the world) was concerned, but – potentially of much greater importance – quite possibly for the Soviet Union in particular. Even the USA was not fully in the picture until 1958, after the US–UK agreement was signed.[3] This was something which it is possible that not even the then Prime Minister, Harold Macmillan, ever fully understood. Indeed, it might be construed from his ultra-detailed six volume autobiography [see Volume IV, *To Ride the Storm,* Chapter IX] that, in the absence of any direct reference to it, he may not have been told that Orange Herald, the second of the Malden Island tests, was a high-yield A-bomb rather than an H-bomb.

The significance of this 'bluff' meant that Britain had a claim to be involved 'as of right' in the up-coming international talks on arms limitation. Macmillan, it should be noted, believed strongly in the need to possess British H-bombs as a deterrent, not so much against their nuclear weapons as against the overwhelming numbers of Soviet conventional weapons and troops, were they ever to be pitted against Western Europe; in no sense a remote possibility in the 1950s. However, those ten young RNVR officers who served out in the Pacific in 1957 never had any reason to doubt, until *much* later when the elements of the truth began to reach public attention, what they had been told and what they had seen with their own eyes.

Right from the beginning of the first Grapple tests, it seems the British scientists had reservations and felt some disappointment about the first of the three tests. Short Granite had a yield of less than 300 kilotons as they recorded it, and also as assessed by an experienced US observer present simply from observing the volume of the fireball – very far short of the megaton target; while Purple Granite, at only 200 kilotons, would be referred to disparagingly by some as a 'damp squib'. Nonetheless that first explosion on 15 May 1957 was reported by the British authorities, and described by Macmillan, as 'in the megaton range,' and an erroneous public impression was allowed to gather and grow that it had been more or less the equivalent in explosive power of one million tons of TNT.

Since Orange Herald was to be a more 'public' test, Penney's team at AWRE had good reason for wanting to be certain that it was impressive, not least to the Soviet Union. It certainly *seemed* much bigger (and therefore 'better', in the simple rationale of non-technical observers) to those watching on the flight deck of *Warrior*. Dombey and Grove argued, however, with supporting evidence, that Orange Herald was actually a large fission (i.e. atomic) bomb, and it was intended as the basis for Yellow Sun Mark 1 which was operational from 1958 as Britain's first and only 'home-grown' *supposed* H-bomb. It was carried in a Vulcan aircraft. That said, with a yield of over 700 kilotons, Orange Herald is probably the largest *fission* weapon ever exploded. However, as the press spectators duly reported, by June 1957 Britain was now regarded as a *thermonuclear* power. The *Times* headline read, 'Second British Nuclear Test in the Pacific: Bigger Explosion than the First.' Dombey and Grove correctly adduced that all but one of the press descriptions, published in UK newspapers on 1 June, had been creatively written the night before the test and flown to Honolulu for swift cabling to London as soon as Orange Herald had been detonated, at 1941 GMT on 31 May, in time to make the first editions on 1 June. Only William Connor (Cassandra of the *Daily Mail*) filed his despatch *after* the event. Interestingly, 'all the correspondents gave the estimated yield as 5 megatons', relying on the data in their information packs and more than five times the actual yield.[4]

The Macmillan government persuaded the Eisenhower administration first to extend closer co-operation; then, very soon thereafter, to share information; and finally and most importantly, to provide Britain with the nuclear weapons which would have been cripplingly expensive to develop and produce independently. Thus, Britain could publicly retain her place as a 'great power,' according to the definition that greatness is the same thing as possession of the hydrogen bomb.

Dombey and Grove revealed that part of the persuasion that helped to convince the US authorities was the work of British scientist John Ward. Dr Ward had been head-hunted by Churchill's scientific adviser, Lord Cherwell, and appointed to AWRE at Aldermaston without any prior consultation with the Director, Sir William Penney, and the two men never hit it off. However, in the mere six months Ward was able to put up with working there, he came up with an independent working out of a breakthrough which the American émigré scientists, Teller and Ulam, had 'solved' some time earlier in 1951; a two-stage process in which the first fission stage would, by means of X-rays, instantly trigger a second fusion stage. The process is known as radiation implosion; and according to the normal US nomenclature, a 'hydrogen' or 'thermonuclear' bomb refers to a weapon which incorporates the Ulam-Teller concept of primary and secondary (or more) stages and radiation implosion. In the event, it was Keith Roberts and Bryan Taylor's 'spherical' secondary that was used in the Granites. So far as is known, Ward's 'cylindrical' secondary was never tested.

Penney, who led the British team at Los Alamos during the war, was an expert on instrumentation for measuring blast and radiant heating but with no special expertise in nuclear or plasma physics, and had still not taken kindly to Cherwell's appointing of Ward without his agreement. After only six months, Ward left AWRE and returned to work in America. However, William Cook, Aldermaston's Deputy Director, did arrange for Roberts and Taylor to follow up Ward's ideas. Thus, in the autumn of 1957, after the first three Grapple tests, and a degree of post-Suez rapprochement, it was this design that impressed the US scientists. AWRE had developed the concept of a two-stage implosion weapon, 'on a shoestring,' and incorporating what the US would continue to refer to as the Ulam-Teller concept.

This positive impression received by American scientists, as much as anything else, led advisers to President Eisenhower to urge amendment of the McMahon Act prohibiting the sharing of nuclear information in order to allow it to be passed on to allies who had, independently, made significant progress in the field. The amended legislation was signed into law in July 1958 and marked the real beginning of the post-war 'special [and very close] relationship' between the US and UK on nuclear weaponry. However, that relationship had the undoubted consequence that Britain never attained an entirely *independent* nuclear deterrent, since much of the UK's American-designed, though British-produced, weaponry remained – except where 'the life of the nation is at stake' – under the operational control of NATO and the Supreme Allied Commander Europe (SACEUR), and who is always an American General.

Another possible 'downside' of the close Anglo-American co-operation, and the obligation it placed on the UK to guard American secrets, was to emerge not too many years later. This was in 1963, when the French President, General de Gaulle, first vetoed the British application for membership of the European Community. He did this less than a month after the Kennedy-Macmillan Nassau agreement on Polaris, which in turn would lead to Trident. 'As it is,' wrote Dombey and Grove, now already some twenty-five years ago, 'the thermonuclear bluff achieved its purpose: it helped Britain to delay acknowledging its loss of power and to resist the European logic of the post-war settlement by clinging onto the skirts of its transatlantic protector for another forty years.'[5]

So it seems it might just be possible to argue that all those serving in Operation Grapple, including in particular *Warrior*'s ten young RNVR officers, had unwittingly witnessed a political and scientific bluff that *did* deceive the USSR – and which indeed led to political and strategic advantages and disadvantages, depending on one's point of view, over the next sixty years. In the end, the only safe conclusion is that the second British test off Malden in 1957 was not a *hydrogen* bomb but it did at least show what the British scientists could produce when the need arose. That those scientists could produce a genuine and powerful H-Bomb was proven at the later tests after *Warrior* had departed. Grapple-X, in November 1957, an air burst off Christmas Island, had a measured yield of 1.8 megatons, and Grapple-Y on 28 April 1958 yielded 3 megatons.

Appendix C

IN LATER LIFE

Warriors *at their HMS* Belfast *reunion (Johnston)*

Each of the ten young men went his separate way after *Warrior*. It was to be twenty years before they began meeting again as a group on a regular basis.

The first group reunion took the form of a dinner at London's Café Royal. In the interim, some had had occasional encounters, and some quite frequent contact, with one or more others among that group of Gunroom shipmates. However, given their geographic dispersal, at times over the years ranging from Scotland to Singapore and beyond, for many it was a first time. They enjoyed themselves so much at this initial reunion that after another ten years they did it again. By that stage in their lives they were becoming more conscious of the passage of time and of his wingèd chariot, and they decided to meet more frequently in future.

To begin with, reunions took place every five years. More recently, the interval has shrunk to every two. They have met at a pub by the Thames; on board HMS

Warrior 1860, the Navy's first iron-clad sailing ship in Portsmouth Harbour; and in the wardroom of HMS *Belfast* in the Pool of London. One recent November they marched as a group in the Remembrance Day Parade past the Cenotaph. Over the past few years, they have been convening regularly at the Royal Yacht Squadron at Cowes on the Isle of Wight, where Rupert Cooper is a member. When, *Deo volente*, they meet there for their sixtieth anniversary, it will be only three years since their previous meeting.

One of their number, Michael Kirchem, opted not to attend these reunions and, as mentioned above, he has passed away. His comrades remember him with affection.

It is also worth repeating at this point that while this is a memoir of ten young RNVR Officers they did not serve alone and could not have enjoyed any of the experiences recounted above without the full-hearted participation of every other member of the officers and crew that made up the complement of HMS *Warrior*.

For the rest, we set out brief details of their post-*Warrior* lives below.

Michael 'Mike' Anson

Because he had built up a considerable leave entitlement, Anson's National Service came to an end on the day *Warrior* returned to the UK. For the next few years he would put in a couple of weeks of sea training in minesweepers every summer, until pressure of paid-for work put a stop to this. He received a letter then from the Ministry of Defence in October 1965 accepting his resignation from the *permanent* Royal Naval Reserve. It stated that he now reverted to Temporary Status in the rank of Lieutenant without a training commitment.

After the Navy it was back to academic work – which was a big effort after a very different life at sea. He was offered a place at Edinburgh University and after four years, in 1962, achieved an Honours 2.1 in Chemistry (just like Mrs Thatcher!) In the months before he went up to Edinburgh, he worked in the Photographic Research Department of May & Baker Ltd in Dagenham. Whilst working there, he was able to prove that one of their proprietary chemicals had the wrong formula, which was quite a triumph – and, for the first and only time in his career, he went on strike – because everyone else stopped work and there was no option but to do the same.

Whilst at Edinburgh, he met Claire. They married in 1963 and set up home in London where he was recruited by legendary David Ogilvy to work in his multi-national advertising agency Mather & Crowther. M&C subsequently bought a technical agency and there he worked with a number of famous brands – Mazda Lamps, Go to Work on an Egg, Air India, ICT, Tetley Tea and others – for which he was paid the magnificent sum of £750 p.a. He ended up controlling the advertising of a large American company – Dow Chemical – in fourteen different European countries. Quite a feat for someone who only spoke English! This entailed considerable travel and it was not unusual for him to have to visit ten countries over a fourteen-day period.

As their family grew, the London house seemed to shrink and so, in 1969, the Ansons swapped their three bedrooms in London for *fifteen* in a spacious Cotswold ex-rectory and he moved his job to a technical agency in Cheltenham. He worked there for several years and then made a complete career change, joining an investment broker called Towry Law (TL) – whose business involved helping people with their investments and financial planning. After about three years, with three others, each with a slightly different specialisation, he broke away from TL and they formed their own company. The new company, Chesham Hill Ltd, was initially part of the ABACO Group, based in London. One of their best-selling products was The Family Bond – a totally tax-free savings plan underwritten by a Friendly Society called Family Assurance. They promoted the Family Bond through the post by sending out massively large mail shots to as many as 300,000 people at a time. In this way they built up a client base of some 18,000 names.

In addition to the mailings, the ordinary investment side of the business was also going well, but throughout the industry at that time there was no means of advising clients which unit trusts might perform better than the others. This all changed after Anson met Chris Poll who had started a company called Micropal. This company collected the performance data from all the available unit trusts and sold it on in computerised form. Anson made the discovery that relative performance graphs could be produced and that *past* relative performance was, in fact, a very good predictor of *future* relative performance. At last there was a way of analysing existing unit trust portfolios and advising on the best unit trusts for future investment. The company made very handsome profits and the bonuses that came his way went towards Windrush Hill, a seven-bed house that Claire and he were building out of a ruined stone barn, set in one hundred acres of grassland in an idyllic part of Gloucestershire. When he reached sixty, Anson decided to sell the company to The Falcon Group PLC and he took early retirement.

He and Claire have continued to run their small farm where they try to survive the winters at 1,000 feet above sea level in the Cotswolds! Their three daughters have graduated from Oxford, Cambridge and Edinburgh, having grown up at Windrush Hill. They are now married to three super chaps and have given their parents eight grandchildren between them. As grandparents, the Ansons feel well-blessed. Anson's interest in investment planning continues and, among other things, he has been able to put his village church onto a firm financial footing with a healthy annual income. Claire and he have had connections with India for many years where they actively support a very worthwhile home for orphaned and abandoned girls.

Rupert Cooper

When he left *Warrior*, Cooper's National Service was almost over but he volunteered to attend the Navigators' Course at HMS *Dryad* for his last few weeks. It proved very useful with his passion for sailing. Then it was back to civilian life and he joined Unigate as a management trainee. To maintain his Navy connections, he joined HMS *Flying Fox*, the RNVR ship in Bristol.

Then, somewhat to his surprise, he was security vetted and attached to Naval Intelligence which led to small boat clandestine operations at Fort Gilkicker, Portsmouth. Unigate very helpfully released him to take part in several training operations where he was sometimes partnered by Gillespie Robertson. He continued his membership of the RNR for a number of years and was eventually 'retired' with the rank of Lieutenant Commander.

In civilian life he took a two-year course in Technical Dairying and worked his way up through the ranks in Unigate to the point where, in 1965, he was sent to be the CEO of Unigate Ireland where he lived for the next ten years. From there he became Managing Director of Unigate Foods, UK and Ireland, and CEO of Cow & Gate Foods; based in Wiltshire and employing 12,000 people.

The next step was quite a transition since, in 1978 he left Unigate and formed his own dairy company in Scotland with only 120 employees. He had bought a redundant whisky distillery in Campbeltown in Argyll and built up a business buying all the milk from the local farmers and making cheese and selling bottled milk. He also bought a sheep farm in the west of Scotland. Ten years later, however, he sold the cheese company to the local Farmers' Co-operative and decided to take some time off.

Over the next three years, in a 60-foot ketch he bought with three friends, he sailed round the world in three separate stages going via the Atlantic and Panama to the Marquesas Islands, Tahiti, Tonga, New Zealand and Australia, returning via Mauritius, South Africa and Brazil.

In 1989 he became the founder chairman and a shareholder in a medical company that pioneered magnetic resonance imaging. The company ran the MRI facilities at NHS hospitals, fifteen in total throughout the UK, employing over 200 people. That business was sold to Australian interests in 1998, but Cooper remained on the board in Australia for a few years.

He had enjoyed his earlier circumnavigation so much that in 1999 he bought a 93-foot ketch and did it all again but this time adding East Africa, Indonesia and Madagascar to the itinerary.

From 2001 to 2009, he was chairman of an agricultural company and from 2009 to the present day he has been the founder and chairman of a specialist internet search company which has contracts with many large companies and organisations.

His son and daughter have made him a grandfather six times over; three boys and three girls.

Richard Dennis

Following the *Warrior* operation, Dennis was posted to HMS *Murray* where he served as a Deck Officer until January 1958.

HMS *Murray* was a T-34 frigate based in Portland and attached to the 2nd Training Squadron. Every day it took classes of students who were training in anti-submarine warfare at HMS *Osprey* for practical training at sea using sonar depth sounding equipment to track submarines under water. At the end of National Service he was attached to HMS *Mersey* in Salthouse Dock, Liverpool, for the minimum national service requirement of three years in the RNR. He attended weekly training classes, annual inspections and undertook an annual two-week training with the RN. As a volunteer RNR Officer he benefited from training weekends at sea based on Portland and Portsmouth in Mersey Division's coastal minesweeper. He left the RNR in 1964 to live in Italy having attained the rank of Lieutenant RNR.

In 1958, in parallel with his RNR commitments, he was articled to a Liverpool-based firm of Chartered Accountants with whom he spent five years training. He passed his final exams in 1963 and became an Associate member of the Institute of Chartered Accountants in England and Wales (ICAEW). During his career, he specialised in Financial Management, Financial Control and Audit. In 1970, he became a Fellow of the Institute and, in 2013, he was made an honorary Life Member of ICAEW.

In 1963, he moved to the Rover Motor Co, Solihull, UK, where he was a trainee in cost and management accounting in industry. This was followed in 1964 by a year's trainee course with Pirelli S.p.a in Milan, Italy, which covered management, finance and administration related to the electrical industry. There followed ten years from late 1965 as a director of an electrical equipment manufacturers in the UK private sector covering company administration.

He went to Brussels in 1975 where he took up the post as Financial Controller – Europe of a US financial leasing company. For his work he travelled throughout Western Europe and visited the Head Office in New York.

In 1978, as a financial management consultant he was engaged by international aid organisations including the World Bank and UK's ODA and worked in North and West Africa, Madagascar and the Indian Ocean region. Their projects covered building and construction, food processing, tropical agriculture and environment.

From 1992 until 2010, he was an independent consultant engaged by the European Commission on short- and long-term assignments which took him to work and live in Central and Eastern Europe. He assisted in the restructuring of their economies to facilitate their entry into the EU, in such countries as Poland, Slovakia, Hungary, Bulgaria and Romania.

Since 2010, he lives and works in Malta as a qualified TEFL English teacher to a wide variety of international business students.

Ian Maitland Hume

On leaving HMS *Warrior*, Hume was posted to HMS *Diligence*, the minesweeper base at Hythe, on Southampton Water. He was First Lieutenant of HMS *Walkerton* and acquired a good knowledge of minesweeping in the Solent. For the last two months of his National Service the ship was based in Portsmouth. He served as an active member of the RNR from 1958 to 1977, retiring in the rank of Lieutenant Commander. During this time he took courses at HMS *Dryad*, HMS *Mercury* and HMS *Excellent* and spent a useful amount of sea time in minesweepers and latterly in Darings, as a relief watch-keeper for officers away on courses; this included two visits to Gibraltar. He recalls being First Lieutenant of a minesweeper visiting Guernsey and greeting Vice Admiral Sir Geoffrey Robson, CINCSASA at the time of *Warrior*'s South American visits, as he came on board the ship as Lieutenant Governor. His last duties in the RNR were ashore as part of a team controlling UK minesweeping efforts.

He spent the next three years with international commodity brokers C. Czarnikow, in the City and under their auspices went to study at Munich University and then work in Düsseldorf, to improve his German. He was familiar with Berlin at the time; the Wall was built in 1961. On his return to London he worked for Mining and Metallurgical Agency Ltd, iron ore brokers, before venturing out as a consultant in the import/export field. Later this work focused on tourist development schemes in Europe with a year living abroad, working on holiday village projects in Greece, before returning to London as consultant to a UK tour operator.

In 1971 he and his wife moved to Gloucestershire and, since his work at the time was largely in France, he launched a small wine importing business. He sold this business in 1984. He continued his consultancy work until 1993 when he moved to Scotland. In addition to the innovative Cotswold wine business, he and his wife joined the Historic Houses Association, as well as Wolsey Lodge, welcoming guests from America. In Gloucestershire he was an elected member of a large rural authority for twenty years and served as chairman and leader for three years. He served as a magistrate in the county and was also chairman of the Gloucestershire Rural Housing Association and the Gloucestershire Historic Churches Trust, as well as being a churchwarden.

A new life started in Scotland when, in 1993, he joined the University of Edinburgh as a mature student, gaining a double first in Scottish History and Ethnology, followed by a PhD in the School of Scottish Studies there. He has lectured throughout the UK with NADFAS and in USA and Canada on many Scottish historical, cultural and contemporary topics. He currently guides and talks to groups visiting Scotland from the USA. He is a Fellow of the Society of Antiquaries of Scotland. Before returning recently to Edinburgh he and his wife were in the Borders for eighteen years, where he served as president of the Berwickshire Naturalists Club for Antiquities, chairman and then president of the Berwickshire Civic Society, convenor and now vice-president of the Clan Home Association and past chairman and trustee of the Hume Castle Preservation Trust.

His elder daughter lives in Warwickshire, with four children; his son lives in Edinburgh, with three children and his younger daughter lives in Genoa, with two children.

John Hutchinson

After *Warrior*, Hutchinson studied Navigation at HMS *Dryad* and then, in January 1958 he joined HMS *Russell*, a frigate on fishery protection duties in the North Atlantic – a complete contrast with an aircraft carrier in the South Pacific – unable to do any star sights on these dark and turbulent seas but enjoying wonderfully fresh cod at the Wardroom dining table. In March, he was made up to Sub-Lieutenant, three months accelerated promotion. In April he was transferred to HMS *St Vincent* to be second-in-command school naval cadet courses for a month before being moved on to HMS *Diligence*, at Hythe opposite Southampton, where his routine duties involved checking up on the minesweepers in mothballs that were kept there in reserve. In May 1958 he was discharged from National Service.

From October 1958, he read Modern History at Brasenose College, Oxford. Somehow he was able to combine this with travel to Salzburg in 1959 and hitch-hiking with Robertson through Northern Europe all the way to Russia in 1960, to Berlin in 1961 with Reed and Robertson to witness the building of the Wall and then down to Italy to take up a teaching post at the English School in Rome. He came back to England in 1962 to take an appointment at Wolverhampton Grammar School where he was Head of History and in charge of Cricket. At this time Jeremy Riches became his solicitor for the rest of their working lives.

After nine years there, he resigned from that post, married Anthea and they set off to travel in Latin America, taking a cargo boat from Le Havre to Buenos Aires; it was half the size of *Warrior* but it too was beset by storms in the Bay of Biscay and suffered engine failure which left them becalmed for two days in the tropics. From Buenos Aires they travelled by public transport, air, road and rail; and in Brazil on the Saõ Francisco by riverboat. In Patagonia and elsewhere they hitch-hiked. While he was in favour of occasional respite in a decent hotel, Anthea was made of sterner stuff. They visited old *Warrior* haunts in the Straits of Magellan, Rio de Janeiro, Santiago, Lima and Kingston in Jamaica, as well as many new places from Ushuaia to the Iguacu Falls and through most countries all the way up to Mexico, returning home by Icelandic Airways from the Bahamas after seven months. He had lost two stone in weight from an already fairly spare frame!

Back once more in England, he studied at the Institute of Education in London and then taught at Dulwich College. He and his wife then went out to join the UWCSEA in Singapore. There he was Deputy Head for three years, becoming Head in 1978. They had a marvellous time professionally, introducing the International Baccalaureate and supporting a jungle study centre, travelling widely again from Peking to Bali. Anthea taught at Singapore University and the Polytechnic, as well as part-time at the College. They returned to Europe in 1983 to International College Spain, recently formed on the Costa del Sol by refugees from the Iranian revolution, before resettling the school in Madrid with only forty students and twelve staff! He retired in 1997 when there were around 500 students. Today it has nearer 700 students from forty-five different nationalities; forty per cent Spanish and Latin American with substantial groups of Americans, Scandinavians, British and Dutch ranging in age from three to eighteen, studying the International Baccalaureate at all levels. He still attends the Advisory Board meetings.

They retired to Andalucía where they live in a fishing port but often go back to stay inland on the hill of their first home – which fell down, but that's another (long) story – where they have built a *casita* to enjoy the views and six acres of olive, almond, broom, bay and cypress, and landscape gardening. He can see both Africa and Gibraltar where he first visited in *Warrior*. He supports, directly or indirectly, schools, old people and folk hit by natural disaster. They play music and tennis, paint in watercolour and write short stories and essays. They travel, sticking to the surface of the earth now rather than flying, from Agadir to Zagreb and many places in between in search of architecture and music, landscapes and local colour. And often, they exchange visits with family, old friends from the Colleges and, of course, his *Warrior* colleagues.

Michael Johnston

After *Warrior*, Johnston was assigned to the Target Towing Boat Squadron based at HMS *Drake* in Devonport as First Lieutenant to Lt Nicholas Barker who was to become Captain Barker on HMS *Endeavour* at the time of the Falklands war. He enjoyed a pleasant life driving high-speed, triple-screw boats, and streaming targets for the Gunnery School, HMS *Cambridge*, at Wembury Point. While acting as 'crash boat' for the times when aerial targets were being towed, his boat was secured to a buoy in Cawsand Bay. This allowed him to exchange his 'blue liners' for live crab from the French fishing boats that came there and take the crabs to Genoni's to be cooked and dressed. His last month was spent at HMS *Diligence*, the shore base opposite Southampton where the Navy mothballed newly built minesweepers in case of emergency. Then it was back home to Scotland and a job waiting for him in his father's weaving mill. However, he started spending time taking news-film on an old Bolex camera for the four TV stations that aimed to cover the Borders. He freelanced as a television news cameraman until his father put his foot down and insisted he turn up to work at the mill. He then swam with the current of the sixties and seventies, acquiring on the way a very talented wife and four wonderful children before moving to live on the southern fringe of Edinburgh.

He flirted with politics then and, but for the offer of a well-paid job as the UK representative of a New York based fabric importer, he might well have stood in the first elections for the European Parliament. The American work allowed him time to read as he travelled, and to freelance when at home as a radio journalist for BBC Radio Scotland. In the early eighties, he joined the London headquarters in Carlton Gardens of what became The Woolmark Company which then had offices in thirty countries. The job meant being out of the UK in every calendar month and regular travel to the USA, Far East, South East Asia and Australasia as well as all round Europe. This was how he found the time to read the whole of Proust, as well as everything else, from Austen to Zola!

Leaving The Woolmark Company in the early nineties when it ran out of the money he had been helping it to spend generously, and now divorced and remarried, he tried to retire to write but, instead, became co-founder of a school of strategic management studies run from a stately home near Harrogate. He also found time to write more radio documentaries for the BBC including one about the relatively unknown romance between Lord Thomson, Secretary of State for Air in Ramsay MacDonald's cabinet and the Romanian novelist, Princess Marthe Bibesco, in which the actress Janet Suzman played the leading role.

He tried to retire for a second time but not hard enough. He was elected a local councillor and, in 1997, became the Leader of Harrogate Borough Council and later a Board Member of the new Regional Development Agency, Yorkshire Forward. Retiring for the third time in 2001 and moving to London, he embarked on his 'too long postponed career' as a novelist and a programme of study with the Open University culminating in a first class BA (Honours) in Literature. In parallel with his studies he was writing *Brideshead Regained* so as to be able to publish this *hommage* to Waugh in time for the writer's centenary in 2003. The Waugh Estate, alas, did *not* appreciate the gesture. In 2009, he was awarded an MA (with Distinction) in Modern and Contemporary Literature by Birkbeck College, University of London. His dissertation, called 'The Blue River of Truth' was on the impact of Margaret Thatcher on contemporary fiction. Finished with studies for a while, he finally completed the thirty-year long project of writing of his art forgery novel, *Rembrandt Sings*.

He was living contentedly in Barnet, when his *Warrior* colleagues suggested he ought to write and compile this memoir. 'It has truly been a labour of love.'

Laurance Reed

For the last six months of his National Service Reed served in HMS *Lynx* at the Simonstown naval base in South Africa. Earlier in the year, Britain had handed over the base to the South African government but in fulfilment of its obligations under the Simonstown Agreement the Royal Navy kept several frigates there to defend the Cape route. Britain was still influential in the country and the Queen was still the Head of State.

Before Christmas the *Lynx* took part in the CAPEX exercises with the South African Navy and then in the New Year she went up the coast to Port Elizabeth, East London, Durban and Portuguese East Africa. In April, Vice-Admiral Robson sailed home on the Castle Line to become Governor and Commander-in-Chief of Guernsey. *Lynx* followed three weeks later, calling at Ascension Island and Dakar en route for the UK.

Reed left the *Lynx* as soon as she arrived in Portsmouth and, after a few days at home, drove down to HMS *Drake* in Devonport. He was given three weeks 'demobilisation' leave and his National Service came to an end on 29 May 1958. He remained in the RNVR/RNR until 1965 when major cuts were made to the strength of the Navy including the reserve.

In 1960 he went up to Oxford to read Law. He was active there in the Oxford Union Debating Society and became the Treasurer. Immediately after graduating, he spent a couple of years on the Continent studying the workings and the institutions of the Common Market. He met many influential people and they all urged him to write a book on the subject. His offering, entitled *Europe in a Shrinking World*, was published in 1967.[6] Largely on the strength of his book, Ernest Marples, the former Cabinet Minister, invited him to join the Public Sector Research Unit in London. At about the same time he was selected to fight the parliamentary seat of Bolton East for the Conservatives. The Labour majority was over 8,000 and it was considered a long shot for the Tories. He went on to win it in the 1970 General Election with a swing well above the national average.

In Parliament he took a keen interest in environmental issues and persuaded the Government to spend many millions on an environmental improvement programme in our old industrial cities. The scheme was called 'Operation Eyesore' and the North West of England received the lion's share of the money. He also persuaded his constituents to support the case for joining the Common Market but both he and they 'voted for a European Community of nations and peoples and not for a European super-state dominated by one country, which is largely the case in the Eurozone today.'

During his life he has written a number of books and tracts on issues and matters that have interested him. He has also travelled the globe and been lucky enough to see most of the world's natural wonders, but, to his regret, not (so far) Antarctica or the Galapagos.

Jeremy Riches

After Christmas leave Riches left the Navy and, on the 15 January 1958, set off for Wolverhampton in order to start his five years as an articled clerk with a firm of solicitors which he was the latest, and as it turned out, the last family member to join. He arrived in one of the thick yellow pea soup fogs, which plagued Britain's industrial areas in those days, a sharp contrast to his time at sea! He qualified in 1963 and in 1970 set up a branch office of the firm in Bridgnorth, Shropshire, where he specialised in agricultural law, probate and Inheritance Tax Planning. After forty-five years in practice he retired in 2003 as senior partner of the seven-partner firm.

As a solicitor one often acquires various outside appointments, one of the most interesting in his case being legal adviser to The Lichfield Diocesan Board of Education responsible for advising on legal matters affecting over 200 church schools in the diocese. Practicing in a market town he became involved in local rural activities and he served on the committee of one of the largest one day agricultural shows in the country for twenty-seven years and latterly as sponsorship officer – 'a poisoned chalice if ever there was one.' In Wolverhampton he is currently a trustee of a medical research charity connected to the main Wolverhampton hospital. After retirement he has helped out with The Prince's Trust, acting as a mentor for youngsters starting up in business, bringing reward and frustration in equal measure.

Remaining with the same firm during the whole of his professional career has allowed him and Sue (whom he married in 1967) to remain in the same house in the village of Pattingham in Staffordshire for (so far) forty-six years. This in turn has enabled them to enjoy and contribute to the life of the village. He has been chairman of the Parish Council, a governor of two local state schools, taken part in the Village Drama Group (more fun for the participants than the spectators) sung in local choirs, taken on various roles in their flourishing church and altogether had a lot of enjoyment. They have three children, and at the moment four grandchildren – there could be more!

For a while, he was involved in politics, becoming chairman of The Wrekin Constituency Conservative Association and even toyed with the idea of becoming a parliamentary candidate 'but luckily, unlike Laurance, I saw the light in time!' He finds the greatest benefit of quitting office is not having to attend the Party Conference.

On the sporting front he was a Master of a pack of beagles for twenty-five years, ran the London Marathon in 1982 and, having beautiful unspoilt country along the Welsh Borders within easy reach, Sue and he try, with varying degrees of success, to keep fit by walking the hills and cycling. However, one of the benefits of living where they do is that not only do they have beautiful country on their doorstep but a large industrial area to the east, so they can enjoy visits to the theatre and concerts – particularly to the splendid Symphony Hall in Birmingham. His interests, apart from hunting, have included meteorology and gardening. They have a large garden where he grows most of the vegetables they eat and where for a number of years they kept a variety of chickens. One of the joys of living in the same house for so many years is that he now looks out of the window and knows that *every* tree that can be seen they have planted – and there are many.

They celebrated his retirement in 2003 by cycling across France from Cherbourg to Aigues Mortes on the Mediterranean – almost 900 miles in eighteen days. They have since then taken to travelling far and wide and some three years ago visited Chile walking in the Torres del Paine national park (but not any of his RN stops), and Argentina, where they found Buenos Aires to be in a depressed state compared to 1957. On this trip they also spent a week in the Falklands looking at wild life in the outer islands and taking a war tour of the hills around Stanley. The Falklands in mid-summer are unrecognisable from the place he visited in mid-winter – quite beautiful and they want to return. Their Mandarin-speaking son took them to Tibet in 1998. They travelled hard class on a Chinese train, and the whole trip was more an experience than a holiday! They have paid New Zealand two visits; the second time when their son married a New Zealand girl – it's a long way from home, but a beautiful place.

Riches remained in the Royal Naval Volunteer Supplementary Reserve for two years after leaving, doing evening training and attending a fortnight's course at the Royal Naval Barracks in Chatham. During this time he was promoted to Sub-Lieutenant. So, since leaving the Navy his life has been possibly unexciting to some, 'but very varied in scope and full of interest and much fun.'

'Dizzy' Gillespie Robertson

After Grapple and a short navigation course at HMS *Dryad*, Robertson completed his full-time National Service in a destroyer, HMS *Brocklesby*, testing new anti-submarine detection devices off Gibraltar. He proudly recalls scoring the winning try for the ship's seven-a-side rugby team when they won the Portland United Services annual tournament.

Shortly after full-time service, he was 'approached by a man in a raincoat in a pub.' For the next three years he took occasional weekends away from his civilian career to do part-time RNR service in the Special Branch. (He says he had decided against university, feeling that it was time for him to earn a proper living.) 'List 14' work consisted primarily of landing 'secret agents' from small boats at dead of night on 'heavily-guarded and armed foreign shores' (in actual fact the Isle of Wight.) It involved mainly rubber dinghies launched from submarines, but also included lessons on how to penetrate barbed wire and shoot or garrotte 'the enemy.' Robertson's old *Warrior* shipmate Cooper was in the same 'hush-hush' group. List 14 was eventually closed on economy grounds, and Robertson finally left the Navy as Lieutenant RNR.

Chartering of tramp ships on the Baltic Exchange, to carry bulk cargoes to mining companies' customers, was his first civilian job. In 1962 he moved to a small sales agency representing overseas mining interests in European markets, and travelled widely selling raw materials to the hundreds of steel companies then still in existence in the region. Ian Hume from *Warrior* briefly worked for the same company.

More than a decade later the agency was swallowed up by one of its principals, US-headquartered Utah International, whose European sales agency for its Australian metallurgical coal Robertson had been instrumental in acquiring. He was by then married, with two children, having met German-Latvian Sigrid, now his wife of more than fifty years, while visiting San Francisco where she was working for a Japanese trading company. Utah International was subsequently bought by Australia's Broken Hill (BHP.)

The old 'Utah' mines, especially Australian coal and iron ore and Chilean copper, are still the jewels in the crown of BHP Billiton, now the world's biggest mining company. Robertson's career had grown with the various acquisitions, involving lengthy spells living in both USA and Australia. He eventually set up and ran BHP's entire global minerals marketing organisation, in fields ranging from basic industrial raw materials through to gold and silver and even gem diamonds.

After spending a life in aeroplanes and moving home with his ever-supportive spouse more than thirty times, Robertson finally returned to the UK, and in 1995 took early retirement as BHP's senior man in Europe, Russia, Africa and the Middle East. Since then he has lived mainly in London, and devoted himself to family (an NHS speech therapist daughter, an independent film producer son, five grandchildren including a London Bobby and a Berlin restaurateur, and a 'grand-dog';) to a select few charitable causes; and to fighting what he considers to be climate change alarmism. Among old Warriors, Ian Hume's son is his godson; John Hutchinson's father was his daughter's godfather; and Rupert Cooper's first wife is his son's godmother; and he travels the opera circuit most years with John Hutchinson, with whom he had hitch-hiked from London to Moscow and back at the end of the 1950s. He chairs a fund which promotes an outreach programme preparing and supporting intellectually outstanding state school pupils for entry to his old school, Eton, as King's Scholars; and he is an active Council member and Vice Chairman of the Clan Donnachaidh Society, Clan Donnachaidh being recognised by many historians as Scotland's oldest and one of her noblest Clans.

---

1 ADM1/27019

2 Lorna Arnold, *Britain and the H-Bomb*, (Basingstoke: Palgrave Macmillan, 2001) p.222

3 Arnold dismisses and disproves any suggestion that any attempt was made to bluff the USA. pp.222–4.

4 Donald McIntyre, 'The Development of Britain's Megaton Warheads'; unpublished MA Dissertation, University of Chester, 2006, p.52

5 Some of the information in this part of the chapter is paraphrased or quoted from Dombey & Grove, *'Britain's Thermonuclear Bluff'*, London Review of Books, 15 October 1992, with the authors' permission.

6 *Europe in a Shrinking World: a technological perspective*, London, Oldbourne, 1967

Acknowledgements

This memoir is the story of all of the National Service members of the HMS *Warrior* 1957 Gunroom. The words of each one of us make up a not insignificant proportion of the text.

Many other people and many sources were consulted in writing and compiling this memoir. My particular thanks are due to Thomas Harmsworth Publishing for permission to quote from Air Vice Marshal Wilfred Oulton's own account of Operation Grapple, *Christmas Island Cracker*. Penguin Random House gave permission for the quotation from Richard Vinen's book *National Service: A Generation in Uniform 1945–1963* (Allen Lane, 2014). Other sources are cited in the text of which Captain R A Begg's unpublished memoir *One Man's Ditty Bag* deserves special mention. And what a man! Professor Norman Dombey and Naval historian Eric Grove helped considerably to get my mind round the technicalities of nuclear weaponry, both fission and fusion.

Warm thanks are due to the Rowsell family for their permission to use the many photographs taken by the late Lieutenant Peter Rowsell RN. Kari Young on Pitcairn provided the picture of Parkin Christian. Other photographs, drawings and paintings are by members of the Gunroom. It was from their Journals, diaries, letters home and subsequent recollections and research that it has been possible to compile such a comprehensive account of ten months in 1957 that shaped all of our lives subsequently. I am in their debt for all their helpfulness. However, if there are any errors and omissions in the text, they are my sole responsibility.

All of us National Service RNVR officer members of HMS *Warrior*'s 1957 Gunroom, probably the last Gunroom at sea, are extremely grateful to HRH The Duke of Edinburgh, the Lord High Admiral, for contributing his Foreword to this book.

Michael Johnston